Learning Elastic Stack

A beginner's guide to distributed search, analytics, and
visualization using Elasticsearch, Logstash, and Kibana

Pranav Shukla

Sharath Kumar M N

BIRMINGHAM - MUMBAI

Learning Elastic Stack 6.0

First published: December 2017

Production reference: 1201217

Published by Packt Publishing Ltd.
Livery Place
35 Livery Street
Birmingham
B3 2PB, UK.
ISBN 978-1-78728-186-8

www.packtpub.com

Credits

Authors
Pranav Shukla
Sharath Kumar M N

Reviewer
Marcelo Ochoa

Commissioning Editor
Amey Varangaonkar

Acquisition Editor
Varsha Shetty

Content Development Editor
Cheryl Dsa

Technical Editor
Sagar Sawant

Copy Editors
Safis Editing
Vikrant Phadkay

Project Coordinator
Nidhi Joshi

Proofreader
Safis Editing

Indexer
Aishwarya Gangawane

Graphics
Tania Dutta

Production Coordinator
Shantanu Zagade

Disclaimer

About the Authors

Pranav Shukla is the founder and CEO of Valens DataLabs, a technologist, husband, and father of two. He is a big data architect and software craftsman who uses JVM-based languages. Pranav has diverse experience of over 14 years in architecting enterprise applications for Fortune 500 companies and start-ups. His core expertise lies in building JVM-based, scalable, reactive, and data-driven applications using Java/Scala, the Hadoop ecosystem, Apache Spark, and NoSQL databases. He is a big data engineering, analytics, and machine learning enthusiast.

Pranav founded Valens DataLabs with a vision to help companies leverage data to their competitive advantage. Valens DataLabs specializes in developing next-generation, cloud-based, reactive, and data-intensive applications using big data and web technologies. The company believes in agile practices, lean principles, test-driven and behavior-driven development, continuous integration, and continuous delivery for sustainable software systems.

In his free time, he enjoys reading books, playing musical instruments, singing, listening to music, and watching cricket. You can reach him via email at pranav.shukla@valensdatalabs.com and follow him on Twitter at @pranavshukla81.

I would like to thank my wife Kruti Shukla for her unconditional love and support, our sons Sauhadra and Pratishth, my parents Dr Sharad Shukla and Varsha Shukla. I would like to thank my brother Vishal Shukla for playing an inspirational role in my career and also for inspiring me to write this book. I would like to thank Parth Mistry, Gopal Ghanghar, and Krishna Meet for their valuable feedback for the book. I am grateful to many who have contributed in shaping my career through fruitful interactions, particularly I would like to thank Umesh Kakkad, Eddie Moojen, Wart Fransen, Praveen Sameneni, Vinod Patel, Gopal Shah, and Sachin Bakshi.

Sharath Kumar M N has done his masters in Computer Science at The University of Texas, Dallas, USA. He has been in the IT industry for more than ten years now and is the Elasticsearch Solutions Architect at Oracle. He is an Elastic Stack advocate, and being an avid speaker he has also given several tech talks in conferences such as the Oracle Code Event. Sharath is a certified trainer—**Elastic Certified Instructor**—one of the few technology experts in the world who has been certified by Elastic Inc to deliver their official *from the creators of Elastic* training. He is also a data science and machine learning enthusiast.

In his free time, he enjoys trekking, listening to music, playing with his lovely pets Guddu and Milo and the geek in him loves exploring his Python skills for stock market analysis. You can reach him via email at mnsk07@gmail.com.

I would like to thank my parents, Geetha and Nanjaiah, sister Dr Shilpa M N, brother-in-law Dr Sridhar and my friends - without their support I wouldn't have been able to finish my part of this book in time. I would also like to thank Packt Publishing team(specially Cheryl, Samuel, Varsha, Sagar) for providing a great opportunity for me to take part in this exciting journey.

About the Reviewer

Marcelo Ochoa works at the systems laboratory of Facultad de Ciencias Exactas, Universidad Nacional del Centro de la Provincia de Buenos Aires, Argentina. He is the CTO at www.scotas.com, a company that specializes in near-real-time search solutions using Apache Solr and Oracle. He divides his time between university jobs and external projects related to Oracle and big data technologies. He has worked on several Oracle-related projects, such as the translation of Oracle manuals and multimedia CBTs. His background is in database, network, web, and Java technologies. In the XML world, Marcelo is known as the developer of DB Generator for the Apache Cocoon project. He has worked on the open source projects DBPrism and DBPrism CMS, Lucene-Oracle integration using the Oracle JVM Directory implementation, and the Restlet.org project, where he worked on the Oracle XDB Restlet Adapter, an alternative to writing native REST web services inside a database-resident JVM.

Since 2006, he has been part of an Oracle ACE program and has recently linked to a Docker Mentor program.

Marcelo has coauthored *Oracle Database Programming Using Java and Web Services* by Digital Press and *Professional XML Databases* by Wrox Press. He has been a technical reviewer on several Packt books, such as *Mastering Elastic Stack, Mastering Elasticsearch 5.x - Third Edition, Elasticsearch 5.x Cookbook - Third Edition*, and so on.

www.PacktPub.com

For support files and downloads related to your book, please visit `www.PacktPub.com`. Did you know that Packt offers eBook versions of every book published, with PDF and ePub files available?

You can upgrade to the eBook version at `www.PacktPub.com` and as a print book customer, you are entitled to a discount on the eBook copy. Get in touch with us at `service@packtpub.com` for more details. At `www.PacktPub.com`, you can also read a collection of free technical articles, sign up for a range of free newsletters and receive exclusive discounts and offers on Packt books and eBooks.

`https://www.packtpub.com/mapt`

Get the most in-demand software skills with Mapt. Mapt gives you full access to all Packt books and video courses, as well as industry-leading tools to help you plan your personal development and advance your career.

Why subscribe?

- Fully searchable across every book published by Packt
- Copy and paste, print, and bookmark content
- On demand and accessible via a web browser

Customer Feedback

Thanks for purchasing this Packt book. At Packt, quality is at the heart of our editorial process. To help us improve, please leave us an honest review on this book's Amazon page at https://www.amazon.in/dp/1787281868.

If you'd like to join our team of regular reviewers, you can email us at customerreviews@packtpub.com. We award our regular reviewers with free eBooks and videos in exchange for their valuable feedback. Help us be relentless in improving our products!

Table of Contents

Preface

Elastic Stack is a powerful combination of tools for the distributed search, analytics, logging, and visualization of data from medium to massive data sets. The newly released Elastic Stack 6.0 brings new features and capabilities that empower users to find unique, actionable insights through these techniques. This book will give you a fundamental understanding of what the stack is all about, and how to use it efficiently to build powerful real-time data processing applications.
After a quick overview of the newly introduced features in Elastic Stack 6.0, you'll learn how to set up the stack by installing the tools, and see their basic configurations. Then the book shows you how to use Elasticsearch for distributed searching and analytics, along with Logstash for logging, and Kibana for data visualization. It also demonstrates the creation of custom plugins using Kibana and Beats. You'll find out about Elastic X-Pack, a useful extension for effective security and monitoring. We also provide useful tips on how to use the Elastic Cloud and deploy Elastic Stack in production environments.

What this book covers

Chapter 1, *Introducing Elastic Stack*, motivates the reader by introducing the core components of Elastic Stack, importance of distributed, scalable search and analytics that Elastic Stack offers with use cases of ElasticSearch. The chapter gives a brief introduction to all core components, shows where do they fit in the overall stack, and details the purpose of each component. It concludes with instructions for downloading and installing ElasticSearch and Kibana to get started.

Chapter 2, *Getting Started with ElasticSearch*, introduces the core concepts involved in ElasticSearch, which forms the backbone of the Elastic Stack. Concepts such as indexes, types, nodes, and clusters are introduced. The reader is introduced to the REST API for performing essential operations, datatypes, and mappings.

Chapter 3, *Searching What Is Relevant*, focuses on the search use-case for ElasticSearch. It introduces the concepts of text analysis, tokenizers, analyzers, and the need for analysis and relevance-based searching. The chapter uses and example use-case to cover the relevance based search topics.

Chapter 4, *Analytics with ElasticSearch*, covers various types of aggregations with examples to gain fundamental understanding. It starts off with very simple to complex aggregations to get powerful insights from terabytes of data. The chapter also covers reasons for using different types of aggregations.

Chapter 5, *Analyzing Log Data*, lays the foundation for the motivation behind logstash, the architecture of logstash, and installing and configuring logstash to set up basic data pipelines. Elastic 5 introduced Ingest Node, which can be used instead of a dedicated Logstash setup. We will also cover building pipelines using Elastic Ingest Nodes.

Chapter 6, *Building Data Pipelines with Logstash*, builds on the fundamental knowledge of Logstash by transformations and aggregation related filters. It covers how a rich set of filters brings Logstash closer to the other real-time and near-real-time stream processing frameworks with zero coding. It introduces the Beats platform, and the FileBeat component, which is used to transport log files from the edge machines.

Chapter 7, *Visualizing Data with Kibana*, covers how to effectively use Kibana to build beautiful dashboards for effective storytelling about your data. It uses a sample dataset and provides step-by-step guidance on creating visualizations in a few clicks.

Chapter 8, *Elastic X-Pack*, since we have covered ElasticSearch and the core components that help us build data pipelines and visualize data, it's now time to add the extensions needed for specific use cases. This chapter shows you how to install and configure X-Pack components in Elastic Stack and teaches you to secure, monitor, and use alerting extensions.

Chapter 9, *Building a Sensor Data Analytics Application*, puts together a complete application for sensor data analytics with the concepts learned so far. It shows you how to model your data in ElasticSearch, how to build the data-pipeline to ingest the data and how to visualize it using Kibana. The chapter also demonstrates how to effectively use X-Pack components to secure and monitor your pipeline, and get alerts when certain conditions are met.

Chapter 10, *Running Elastic Stack in Production*, covers recommendations on how to deploy Elastic Stack to production. It provides recommendations for taking your application to production and guidelines on typical configurations that need to be looked at for different use cases. It also covers deploying into cloud-based hosted providers such as Elastic Cloud.

Chapter 11, *Monitoring Server Infrastructure*, shows how we can use Elastic Stack to set up a real-time monitoring solution for your servers, applications that are built completely using Elastic Stack. It introduces another component of the Beats platform, MetricBeat, which is used to monitor servers/applications.

What you need for this book

This book will guide you through the installation of all the tools that you need to follow the examples and download the following files with the version:

- Elasticsearch 6.0
- Kibana 6.0

Who this book is for

This book is for data professionals who want to get amazing insights and business metrics from their data sources. If you want to get a fundamental understanding of Elastic Stack for the distributed, real-time processing of data, this book will help you. A fundamental knowledge of JSON would be useful, but is not mandatory. No previous experience with Elastic Stack is required.

Conventions

In this book, you will find a number of text styles that distinguish between different kinds of information. Here are some examples of these styles and an explanation of their meaning. Code words in text, database table names, folder names, filenames, file extensions, pathnames, dummy URLs, user input, and Twitter handles are shown as follows: "The next lines of code read the link and assign it to the `BeautifulSoup` function." A block of code is set as follows:

```
#import packages into the project
from bs4 import BeautifulSoup
from urllib.request import urlopen
import pandas as pd
```

When we wish to draw your attention to a particular part of a code block, the relevant lines or items are set in bold:

```
[default] exten => s,1,Dial(Zap/1|30)
exten => s,2,Voicemail(u100)
exten => s,102,Voicemail(b100)
exten => i,1,Voicemail(s0)
```

Any command-line input or output is written as follows:

```
C:\Python34\Scripts> pip install –upgrade pip
C:\Python34\Scripts> pip install pandas
```

New terms and **important words** are shown in bold. Words that you see on the screen, for example, in menus or dialog boxes, appear in the text like this: "In order to download new modules, we will go to **Files | Settings | Project Name | Project Interpreter**."

Warnings or important notes appear like this.

Tips and tricks appear like this.

Reader feedback

Feedback from our readers is always welcome. Let us know what you think about this book-what you liked or disliked. Reader feedback is important for us as it helps us develop titles that you will really get the most out of. To send us general feedback, simply email feedback@packtpub.com, and mention the book's title in the subject of your message. If there is a topic that you have expertise in and you are interested in either writing or contributing to a book, see our author guide at www.packtpub.com/authors.

Customer support

Now that you are the proud owner of a Packt book, we have a number of things to help you to get the most from your purchase.

Downloading the example code

You can download the example code files for this book from your account at `http://www.packtpub.com`. If you purchased this book elsewhere, you can visit `http://www.packtpub.com/support` and register to have the files emailed directly to you. You can download the code files by following these steps:

1. Log in or register to our website using your email address and password.
2. Hover the mouse pointer on the **SUPPORT** tab at the top.
3. Click on **Code Downloads & Errata**.
4. Enter the name of the book in the **Search** box.
5. Select the book for which you're looking to download the code files.
6. Choose from the drop-down menu where you purchased this book from.
7. Click on **Code Download**.

Once the file is downloaded, please make sure that you unzip or extract the folder using the latest version of:

- WinRAR / 7-Zip for Windows
- Zipeg / iZip / UnRarX for Mac
- 7-Zip / PeaZip for Linux

The code bundle for the book is also hosted on GitHub at `https://github.com/PacktPublishing/Learning-Elastic-Stack-6`. We also have other code bundles from our rich catalog of books and videos available at `https://github.com/PacktPublishing/`. Check them out!

Downloading the color images of this book

We also provide you with a PDF file that has color images of the screenshots/diagrams used in this book. The color images will help you better understand the changes in the output. You can download this file from `https://www.packtpub.com/sites/default/files/downloads/LearningElasticStack6_ColorImages.pdf`.

Errata

Although we have taken every care to ensure the accuracy of our content, mistakes do happen. If you find a mistake in one of our books-maybe a mistake in the text or the code-we would be grateful if you could report this to us. By doing so, you can save other readers from frustration and help us improve subsequent versions of this book. If you find any errata, please report them by visiting http://www.packtpub.com/submit-errata, selecting your book, clicking on the **Errata Submission Form** link, and entering the details of your errata. Once your errata are verified, your submission will be accepted and the errata will be uploaded to our website or added to any list of existing errata under the Errata section of that title. To view the previously submitted errata, go to https://www.packtpub.com/books/content/support and enter the name of the book in the search field. The required information will appear under the **Errata** section.

Piracy

Piracy of copyrighted material on the internet is an ongoing problem across all media. At Packt, we take the protection of our copyright and licenses very seriously. If you come across any illegal copies of our works in any form on the internet, please provide us with the location address or website name immediately so that we can pursue a remedy. Please contact us at copyright@packtpub.com with a link to the suspected pirated material. We appreciate your help in protecting our authors and our ability to bring you valuable content.

Questions

If you have a problem with any aspect of this book, you can contact us at questions@packtpub.com, and we will do our best to address the problem.

Introducing Elastic Stack 1

We are living in an advanced stage of the information age. The emergence of the web, mobiles, social networks, blogs, and photo sharing has created a massive amount of data in recent years. These new data sources create information that cannot be handled using traditional data storage technology, typically relational databases. As an application developer or business intelligence developer, your job is to fulfill the search and analytics needs of the application.

A number of big data scale data stores have emerged in the last few years. This includes Hadoop ecosystem projects, several NoSQL databases, and search and analytics engines such as Elasticsearch. Hadoop and each NoSQL database have their own strengths and use cases.

Elastic Stack is a rich ecosystem of components serving as a full search and analytics stack. The main components of Elastic Stack are Kibana, Logstash, Beats, X-Pack, and Elasticsearch. Elasticsearch is at the heart of Elastic Stack, providing storage, search, and analytics capabilities. Kibana, which is also called a **window** into Elastic Stack, is a great visualization and user interface for Elastic Stack. Logstash and Beats help in getting the data into Elastic Stack. X-Pack provides powerful features including monitoring, alerting, and security to make your system production ready. Since Elasticsearch is at the heart of Elastic Stack, we will cover the stack inside-out, starting from the heart and moving on to the surrounding components.

In this chapter, we will cover the following topics:

- What is Elasticsearch, and why use it?
- A brief history of Elasticsearch and Apache Lucene
- Elastic Stack components
- Use cases of Elastic Stack

We will look at what Elasticsearch is and why you should consider it as your data store. Once you know the key strengths of Elasticsearch, we will look at the history of Elasticsearch and its underlying technology, Apache Lucene. We will then look at some use cases of Elastic Stack, and we will provide an overview of the Elastic Stack components.

What is Elasticsearch, and why use it?

Since you are reading this book, you probably already know what Elasticsearch is. For the sake of completeness, let us define Elasticsearch.

Elasticsearch is a realtime, distributed search and analytics engine that is horizontally scalable and capable of solving a wide variety of use cases. At the heart of Elastic Stack, it centrally stores your data so you can discover the expected and uncover the unexpected.

Elasticsearch is at the core of Elastic Stack, playing the central role of a search and analytics engine. Elasticsearch is built on a radically different technology, Apache Lucene. This fundamentally different technology in Elasticsearch sets it apart from traditional relational databases and other NoSQL solutions. Let us look at the key benefits of using Elasticsearch as your data store:

- Schemaless, document-oriented
- Searching
- Analytics
- Rich client library support and the REST API
- Easy to operate and easy to scale
- Near real time
- Lightning fast
- Fault tolerant

Let us look at each benefit one by one.

Schemaless and document-oriented

Elasticsearch does not impose a strict structure on your data; you can store any JSON documents. JSON documents are first class citizens in Elasticsearch as opposed to rows and columns in a relational database. A document is roughly equivalent to a record in a relational database table. Traditional relational databases require a schema to be defined beforehand to specify a fixed set of columns and their datatypes and sizes. Often the nature of data is very dynamic, requiring support for new or dynamic columns. The JSON documents naturally support this type of data. For example, take a look at the following document:

```
{
  "name": "John Smith",
  "address": "121 John Street, NY, 10010",
  "age": 40
}
```

This document may represent a customer's record. Here the record has the name, address, and age of the customer. Another record may look like the following one:

```
{
  "name": "John Doe",
  "age": 38,
  "email": "john.doe@company.org"
}
```

Note that the second customer doesn't have the address field, but instead has an email address. In fact, other customer documents may have completely different sets of fields. This provides a tremendous amount of flexibility in terms of what can be stored.

Searching

The core strength of Elasticsearch lies in its text processing capabilities. Elasticsearch is great at searching, especially a full-text search. Let us understand what a full-text search is.

Full-text search means searching through all the terms of all the documents available in the database. This requires the entire contents of all documents to be parsed and stored beforehand. When you hear full-text search, think of Google Search. You can enter any search term and Google looks through all of the web pages on the internet to find the best matching web pages. This is quite different from simple SQL queries run against columns of type `string` in relational databases. Normal SQL queries with a `WHERE` clause and an equals (=) or `LIKE` clause try to do an exact or wild-card match with underlying data. SQL queries can, at best, just match the search term to a sub-string within the text column.

When you want to perform a search similar to Google search on your own data, Elasticsearch is your best bet. You can index emails, text documents, PDF files, web pages, or practically any unstructured text documents and search across all your documents with search terms.

At a high level, Elasticsearch breaks up text data into terms and makes every term searchable by building Lucene indexes. You can build your own Google-like search for your application which is very fast and flexible.

In addition to supporting text data, Elasticsearch also supports other data types such as numbers, dates, geolocations, IP addresses, and many more. We will take an in-depth look at search in `Chapter 3`, *Searching-What is Relevant*.

Analytics

Apart from search, the second most important **functional** strength of Elasticsearch is analytics. Yes, what was originally known just as a full-text search engine is now used as an analytics engine in a variety of use cases. Many organizations are running analytics solutions powered by Elasticsearch in production.

Search is like zooming in and finding a needle in a haystack. Search helps zoom in on precisely what is needed in huge amounts of data. Analytics is exactly the opposite of search; it is about zooming out and taking a look at the bigger picture. For example, you may want to know how many visitors on your website are from the United States as opposed to every other country, or you may want to know how many of your websites visitors use macOS, Windows, or Linux.

Elasticsearch supports a wide variety of aggregations for analytics. Elasticsearch aggregations are quite powerful and can be applied to various datatypes. We will take a look at the analytics capabilities of Elasticsearch in Chapter 4, *Analytics with Elasticsearch*.

Rich client library support and the REST API

Elasticsearch has very rich client library support to make it accessible by many programming languages. There are client libraries available for Java, C#, Python, JavaScript, PHP, Perl, Ruby, and many more. Apart from the official client libraries, there are community driven libraries for 20 plus programming languages.

Additionally, it has a very rich **REST (Representational State Transfer)** API which works on an HTTP protocol. The REST API is very well documented and quite comprehensive, making all operations available over HTTP.

All this means that Elasticsearch is very easy to integrate in any application to fulfill your search and analytics needs.

Easy to operate and easy to scale

Elasticsearch can run on a single node and easily scale out to hundreds of nodes. It is very easy to start a single node instance of Elasticsearch; it works out of the box without any configuration changes and scales to hundreds of nodes.

Horizontal scalability is the ability to scale a system horizontally by starting up multiple instances of the same type rather than making one instance more and more powerful. **Vertical scaling** is about upgrading a single instance by adding more processing power (by increasing the number of CPUs or CPU cores), memory, or storage capacity. There is a practical limit to how much a system can be scaled vertically due to cost and other factors, such as the availability of higher end hardware.

Unlike most traditional databases which only allow vertical scaling, Elasticsearch can be scaled horizontally. It can run on tens or hundreds of commodity nodes instead of one extremely expensive server. Adding a node to an existing Elasticsearch cluster is as easy as starting up a new node in the same network, with virtually no extra configuration. The client application doesn't need to change, whether it is running against a single node or a hundred node cluster.

Near real time

Data is available for querying typically within a second after it has been indexed (saved). Not all big data storage systems are real-time capable. Elasticsearch allows you to index thousands to hundreds of thousands of documents per second and makes them available for searching almost immediately.

Lightning fast

Elasticsearch uses Apache Lucene as its underlying technology. By default, Elasticsearch indexes all the fields of your documents. This is extremely invaluable as you can query or search by any field in your records. You will never be in a situation in which you think *if only I had chosen to create an index on this field*. Elasticsearch contributors have leveraged Apache Lucene to its best advantage, and there are other optimizations which make it lightning fast.

Fault tolerant

Elasticsearch clusters can keep running even when there are hardware failures such as node failure and network failure. In the case of node failure, it replicates all the data that was on the failed node to another node in the cluster. In the case of network failure, Elasticsearch seamlessly elects master replicas to keep the cluster running. Whether it is node or network failure, you can rest assured that your data is safe.

Now that you know when and why Elasticsearch could be a great choice, let us take a high level view of the ecosystem—the Elastic Stack.

Exploring the components of Elastic Stack

The Elastic Stack components are shown in the following figure. It is not necessary to include all of them in your solution. Some components are general purpose and they can be used outside of Elastic Stack without using any of the other components.

Let us look at the purpose of each component and how they fit in the stack:

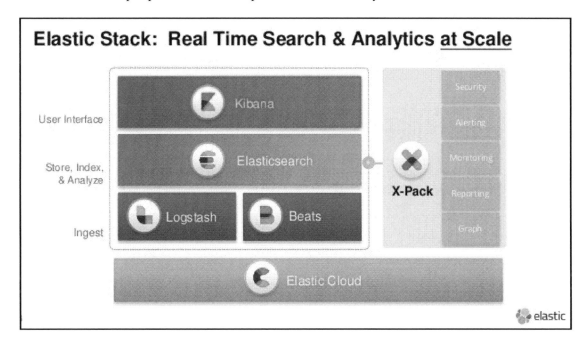

Elasticsearch

Elasticsearch is at the heart of Elastic Stack. It stores all your data and provides search and analytic capabilities in a scalable way. We have already looked at the strengths of Elasticsearch and why you would want to use it. Elasticsearch can be used without using any other components to power your application in terms of search and analytics. We will cover Elasticsearch in great detail in Chapter 2, *Getting Started with Elasticsearch*, Chapter 3, *Searching-What is Relevant*, and Chapter 4, *Analytics with Elasticsearch*.

Logstash

Logstash helps in centralizing event data such as logs, metrics, or any other data in any format. It can perform a number of transformations before sending it to a stash of your choice. It is a key component of Elastic Stack, used to centralize the collection and transformation processes in your data pipeline.

Logstash is a server side component. Its role is to centralize the collection of data from a wide number of input sources in a scalable way, and transform and send the data to an output of your choice. Typically, the output is sent to Elasticsearch, but Logstash is capable of sending it to a wide variety of outputs. Logstash has a plugin-based, extensible architecture. It supports three types of plugin: input plugins, filter plugins, and output plugins. Logstash has a collection of 200 plus supported plugins and the count is ever increasing.

Logstash is an excellent general purpose data flow engine which helps in building real-time, scalable data pipelines.

Beats

Beats is a platform of open source lightweight data shippers. Its role is complementary to Logstash. Logstash is a server-side component, whereas Beats has a role on the client side. Beats consists of a core library, `libbeat`, which provides an API for shipping data from the source, configuring the input options, and implementing logging. Beats is installed on machines that are not part of server-side components such as Elasticsearch, Logstash, or Kibana. These agents reside on non-cluster nodes which may also be called **edge nodes** sometimes.

There are many Beat components that have already been built by the Elastic team and the open source community. The Elastic team has built Beats including, Packetbeat, Filebeat, Metricbeat, Winlogbeat, Audiobeat, and Heartbeat.

Filebeat is a single-purpose Beat built to ship log files from your servers to a centralized Logstash server or Elasticsearch server. Metricbeat is a server monitoring agent that periodically collects metrics from the operating systems and services running on your servers. There are already around 40 community Beats built for specific purposes such as monitoring Elasticsearch, Cassandra, the Apache web server, JVM performance, and so on. You can build your own beat using libbeat if you don't find one that fits your needs.

We will take a deep dive into Logstash and Beats in `Chapter 5`, *Analyzing Log Data* and `Chapter 6`, *Building Data Pipelines with Logstash*.

Kibana

Kibana is the visualization tool of Elastic Stack which can help you gain powerful insights about your data in Elasticsearch. It is often called a window into Elastic Stack. It offers many visualizations including histograms, maps, line charts, time series, and more. You can build visualizations with just a few clicks and interactively explore the data. It lets you build beautiful dashboards by combining different visualizations, sharing with others, and exporting high quality reports.

Kibana also has management and development tools. You can manage settings and configure X-Pack security features for the Elastic Stack. Kibana also has development tools which enable developers to build and test REST API requests.

We will explore Kibana in `Chapter 7`, *Visualizing Data with Kibana*.

X-Pack

X-Pack adds essential features to make Elastic Stack production ready. It adds security, monitoring, alerting, reporting, and graph capabilities to Elastic Stack.

Security

The security plugin within X-Pack adds authentication and authorization capabilities to Elasticsearch and Kibana so that only authorized people have access to the data, and they see only what they are allowed to see. The security plugin works across components seamlessly, securing access to Elasticsearch and Kibana.

The security extension also lets you configure fields and document level security with the licensed version.

Monitoring

You can monitor your Elastic Stack components so that there is no downtime. The monitoring component in X-Pack lets you monitor your Elasticsearch clusters and Kibana.

You can monitor clusters, nodes, and index level metrics. The monitoring plugin maintains a history of performance so that you can compare the current metrics with the past metrics. It also has a capacity planning feature.

Reporting

The reporting plugin within X-Pack allows for generating printable, high-quality reports from Kibana visualizations. The reports can be scheduled to run periodically or on a per event basis.

Alerting

X-Pack has sophisticated alerting capabilities that can alert you in multiple possible ways when certain conditions are met. It gives tremendous flexibility in terms of when, how, and who to alert.

You may be interested in detecting security breaches, such as when someone has five login failures within an hour from different locations, or when your product is trending on social media. You can use the full power of Elasticsearch queries to check when complex conditions are met.

Alerting provides a wide variety of options in terms of how alerts are sent. It can send alerts via email, Slack, Hipchat, and PagerDuty.

Graph

Graph lets you explore relationships in your data. The data in Elasticsearch is generally perceived as a flat list of entities without connections to other entities. This relationship opens up the possibility of new use cases. Graph can surface relationships among entities which share common properties such as people, places, products, or preferences.

Graph consists of Graph API and a UI within Kibana to let you explore this relationship. Under the hood, it leverages distributed querying, indexing at scale, and the relevance capabilities of Elasticsearch.

We will look at the some of X-Pack components in Chapter 8, *Elastic X-Pack*.

Elastic Cloud

Elastic Cloud is the cloud-based, hosted, and managed setup of Elastic Stack components. The service is provided by the company Elastic (`https://www.elastic.co/`). Elastic is the company behind the development of Elasticsearch and other Elastic Stack components. All Elastic Stack components are open source except X-Pack (and Elastic Cloud). The company Elastic provides services for Elastic Stack components including training, development, support, and cloud hosting.

Apart from Elastic Cloud, there are other hosted solutions available for Elasticsearch including one from **Amazon Web Services** (**AWS**). The advantage of Elastic Cloud is that it is developed and maintained by the original creators of Elasticsearch and other Elastic Stack components.

Use cases of Elastic Stack

Elastic Stack components have a variety of practical use cases, and new use cases are emerging as more plugins are added to existing components. As mentioned earlier, you may use a subset of the components for your use case. The following example use cases are by no means exhaustive, but are some of the most common ones:

- Log and security analytics
- Product search
- Metrics analytics
- Web search and website search

Let us look at each use case.

Log and security analytics

The Elasticsearch, Logstash, and Kibana trio was very popular as an ELK stack previously. The presence of Elasticsearch, Logstash, and Kibana (also known as **ELK**) makes Elastic Stack an excellent stack for aggregating and analyzing logs in a central place.

The application support teams face a great challenge administering and managing large numbers of applications deployed across tens or hundreds of servers. The application infrastructure could have the following components:

- Web servers
- Application servers
- Database servers
- Message brokers

Typically, enterprise applications have all or most of the types of servers which were explained earlier, and there are multiple instances of each server. In the event of an error or production issue, the support team has to log in to individual servers and look at the errors. It is quite inefficient to log in to individual servers and look at the raw log files. Elastic Stack provides a complete tool set to collect, centralize, analyze, visualize, alert, and report the errors as they occur. Here is how each component can be used to solve this problem:

- The Beats framework, Filebeat in particular, can run as a lightweight agent to collect and forward the logs.
- Logstash can centralize the events received from Beats, and parse and transform each log entry before sending it to the Elasticsearch cluster.
- Elasticsearch indexes the logs. It enables both search and analytics on the parsed logs.
- Kibana then lets you create visualizations based on errors, warnings, and other information logs. It lets you create dashboards where you can centrally monitor events as they occur, in real time.
- With X-Pack, you can secure the solution, configure alerts, get reports, and analyze relationships in the data.

As you can see, you can get a complete log aggregation and monitoring solution using Elastic Stack.

A security analytics solution would be very similar to this; the logs and events being fed into the system would pertain to firewalls, switches, and other key network elements.

Product search

Product search involves searching for the most relevant product from thousands or tens of thousands of products and presenting the most relevant products at the top of the list before the other less relevant products. You can directly relate this problem to e-commerce websites which sell huge numbers of products sold by many vendors or resellers.

Elasticsearch's full-text and relevance search capabilities can find the best matching results. Presenting the best matches on the first page has great value as it increases the chances of the customer actually buying the product. Imagine a customer searching for the iPhone 7, and the results on the first page showing different cases, chargers, and accessories for previous iPhone versions. The text analysis capabilities backed by Lucene, and innovations added by Elasticsearch, ensure that you get iPhone 7 chargers and cases after the best match.

This problem, however, is not limited to e-commerce websites. Any application that needs to find the most relevant item from millions or billions of items can use Elasticsearch to solve this problem.

Metrics analytics

Elastic Stack has excellent analytics capabilities thanks to the rich aggregations API in Elasticsearch. This makes it a perfect tool for analyzing data with lots of metrics. Metric data consists of numeric values as opposed to unstructured text such as documents and web pages. Some examples are data generated by sensors, IoT devices, metrics generated by mobile devices, servers, virtual machines, network routers, switches, and so on. The list is endless.

Metric data is typically also of the time series nature, that is, values or measures are recorded over the period of time. The metrics that are recorded are usually related to some entity. For example, a temperature reading (which is a metric) is recorded for a particular sensor device with a certain identifier. The type, name of the building, department, floor, and so on are the dimensions associated with the metric. The dimensions may also include the location of the sensor device, that is, the longitude and latitude.

Elasticsearch and Kibana allow for the slicing and dicing of metric data along different dimensions to provide deep insight about your data. Elasticsearch is very powerful at handling time-series and geo-spatial data, which means you can plot your metrics on line charts and area charts aggregating millions of metrics. You can also do geo-spatial analysis on a map.

We will build a metrics analytics application using Elastic Stack in `Chapter 9`, *Building a Sensor Data Analytics Application*.

Web search and website search

Elasticsearch can serve as a search engine for your website and perform a Google-like search across the entire contents of your site. GitHub, Wikipedia, and many other platforms power their searches using Elasticsearch.

Elasticsearch can be leveraged to build content aggregation platforms. *What is a content aggregator or a content aggregation platform?* Content aggregators scrape/crawl multiple websites, index the web pages, and provide a search functionality on the underlying content. This is a powerful way to build domain specific aggregated platforms.

Apache Nutch, an open source, large scale web crawler, was created by *Doug Cutting*, the original creator of Apache Lucene. Apache Nutch crawls the web, parses the HTML pages, stores them, and also builds indexes to make the content searchable. Apache Nutch supports indexing into Elasticsearch or Apache Solr for its search engine.

As it is evident, Elasticsearch and Elastic Stack have many practical use cases. Elastic Stack is a platform with a complete set of tools to build end-to-end search and analytics solutions. It is a very approachable platform for developers, architects, business intelligence analysts, and system administrators. It is possible to put together an Elastic Stack solution with almost zero coding and with only configuration. At the same time, Elasticsearch is very customizable, that is, developers and programmers can build powerful applications using its rich programming language support and the REST API.

Downloading and installing

Now that we have enough motivation and reasons to learn about Elasticsearch and Elastic Stack, let us start by downloading and installing the key components. Firstly, we will download and install Elasticsearch and Kibana. We will install the other components as we need them on the course of our journey. We also need Kibana because, apart from visualizations, it also has a UI for developer tools and for interacting with Elasticsearch.

Starting from Elastic Stack 5.x, all Elastic Stack components are now released together; they share the same version, and are tested for compatibility with each other. This is true for Elastic Stack 6.x components as well.

At the time of this writing, the current released version of Elastic Stack is 6.0.0. We will use this version for all components.

Installing Elasticsearch

Elasticsearch can be downloaded as a ZIP, TAR, DEB, or RPM package. If you are on Ubuntu, Red Hat, or CentOS Linux, it can be directly installed using `apt` or `yum`.

We will use the ZIP format as it is the least intrusive and the easiest for development purposes.

1. Go to `https://www.elastic.co/downloads/elasticsearch` and download the ZIP distribution. You can also download an older version if you are looking for an exact version.
2. Extract the file and change your directory to the top level extracted folder. Run `bin/elasticsearch` or `bin/elasticsearch.bat`.
3. Run `curl http://localhost:9200` or open the URL in your favorite browser.

You should see an output like this:

```
$ curl http://localhost:9200?pretty
{
  "name" : "bhbP6GV",
  "cluster_name" : "elasticsearch",
  "cluster_uuid" : "QQhvZ7YGTjORn5HcSsQf_Q",
  "version" : {
    "number" : "6.0.0",
    "build_hash" : "8f0685b",
    "build_date" : "2017-11-10T18:41:22.859Z",
    "build_snapshot" : false,
    "lucene_version" : "7.0.1",
    "minimum_wire_compatibility_version" : "5.6.0",
    "minimum_index_compatibility_version" : "5.0.0"
  },
  "tagline" : "You Know, for Search"
}
$
```

Congratulations! You have just set up a single node Elasticsearch cluster.

Installing Kibana

Kibana is also available in a variety of packaging formats such as ZIP, TAR.GZ, RMP, and DEB for 32-bit and 64-bit architecture machines:

1. Go to `https://www.elastic.co/downloads/kibana` and download the ZIP or TAR.GZ distribution for the platform that you are on.
2. Extract the file and change your directory to the top level extracted folder. Run `bin/kibana` or `bin/kibana.bat`.
3. Open the URL `http://localhost:5601` in your favorite browser.

Congratulations! You have a working setup of Elasticsearch and Kibana.

Summary

In this chapter, we started off by understanding the motivations of alternate search and analytics technologies other than relational databases and NoSQL stores. We looked at the strengths of Elasticsearch, which is at the heart of Elastic Stack. We then looked at the rest of the components of Elastic Stack and how they fit into the ecosystem. We also looked at real-world use cases of Elastic Stack. We have successfully downloaded and installed Elasticsearch and Kibana to begin the journey of learning about Elastic Stack.

In the next chapter, we will understand the core concepts of Elasticsearch. We will learn about indexes, types, shards, data types, mappings, and other fundamentals. We will also interact with Elasticsearch by using **CRUD (Create, Read, Update, and Delete)** operations, and learn the basics of search.

2
Getting Started with Elasticsearch

In the first chapter we looked at the reasons for learning about and using Elastic Stack, and the use cases of Elastic Stack.

In this chapter, we will start our journey of learning about Elastic Stack, starting at the core of Elastic Stack—Elasticsearch. Elasticsearch is the search and analytics engine behind Elastic Stack. We will learn the core concepts of Elasticsearch while doing some hands-on practice; we will learn about querying, filtering, and searching.

We will cover the following topics in this chapter:

- Using the Kibana Console UI
- Core concepts
- **CRUD (Create, Read, Update, Delete)** operations
- Creating indexes and taking control of mapping
- REST API overview

Using the Kibana Console UI

Before we start writing our first queries to interact with Elasticsearch, we should familiarize ourselves with a very important tool: Kibana Console. This is important because Elasticsearch has a very rich REST API, allowing you to do all possible operations with Elasticsearch. Kibana Console has an editor which is very capable and aware of the REST API. It allows for auto-completion, and for the formatting of queries as you write them.

What is a REST API? **REST** stands for **Representational State Transfer**. It is an architectural style to make systems inter-operate and interact with each other. REST has evolved along with the HTTP protocol, and almost all REST-based systems use HTTP as their protocol. HTTP supports different methods including GET, POST, PUT, DELETE, HEAD, and so on, which are used for different semantics. For example, GET is used for getting or searching for something. POST is used for creating a new resource, PUT may be used for creating or updating an existing resource, and DELETE may be used for deleting a resource permanently.

In Chapter 1, *Introducing Elastic Stack*, we successfully installed Kibana and launched the UI at http://localhost:5601. As previously said, Kibana is the window into Elastic Stack. It not only provides insight into the data through visualizations, but it also has developer tools like the **Console**. The following diagram shows the Console UI:

Fig 2.1 Kibana Console

After launching Kibana, you need to click on the **Dev Tools** link from the left-hand side navigation pane. The Console is divided into two parts, the editor pane and the results pane. You can type the REST API command and press the green triangle-like icon, which sends the query to the Elasticsearch instance (or cluster).

Here, we have simply sent the query GET /. This is equivalent to the curl command that we sent to Elasticsearch for testing the setup, curl http://localhost:9200. As you can see, the length of the command sent via the Console is already more concise than the curl command. You don't need to type http followed by the host and port of the Elasticsearch node, that is, http://localhost:9200. But as mentioned earlier, there is much more to it than just skipping the host and port with every request. As you start typing in the Console editor, you will get an auto suggestion dropdown, as displayed in the following screenshot:

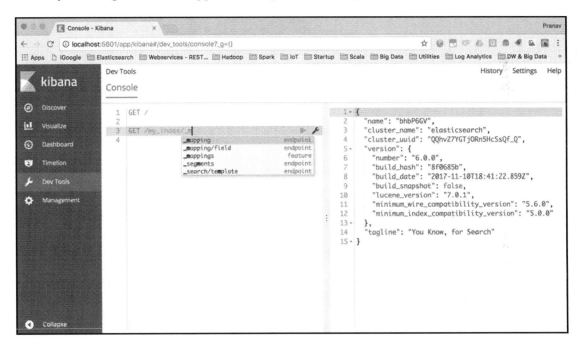

Fig 2.2 Kibana Dev Tools Console auto suggestions

Now that we have the right tool to generate and send queries to Elasticsearch, let's continue learning the core concepts.

Core concepts

Relational databases have concepts such as rows, columns, tables, and schema. Elasticsearch and other document-oriented stores are based on different abstractions. Elasticsearch is a document-oriented store. JSON documents are first class citizens in Elasticsearch. These JSON documents are organized within different types and indexes. We will look at the following core abstractions of Elasticsearch:

- Index
- Type
- Document
- Cluster
- Node
- Shards and replicas
- Mappings and types
- Inverted index

Let us start learning these with an example:

```
PUT /catalog/product/1
{
    "sku": "SP000001",
    "title": "Elasticsearch for Hadoop",
    "description": "Elasticsearch for Hadoop",
    "author": "Vishal Shukla",
    "ISBN": "1785288997",
    "price": 26.99
}
```

Copy and paste this example into the editor of your Kibana Console UI and execute it. This will index a document which represents a product in the product catalog of a system. All examples written for the Kibana Console UI can be very easily converted to `curl` commands that can be executed from the command line. The following is the curl version of the previous Kibana console UI command:

```
curl -XPUT http://localhost:9200/catalog/product/1 -d '{ "sku": "SP000001",
"title": "Elasticsearch for Hadoop", "description": "Elasticsearch for
Hadoop", "author": "Vishal Shukla", "ISBN": "1785288997", "price": 26.99}'
```

We will use this example to understand the following concepts: indexes, types, and documents.

In the previous code block, the first line is `PUT /catalog/product/1`, which is followed by a JSON document.

PUT is the `HTTP` method used to index a new document. PUT is among the other `HTTP` methods covered earlier. Here, **catalog** is the name of the index, **product** is the name of type where the document will be indexed, and **1** is the ID to be assigned to the document after it is indexed.

The following sections explain each concept in depth.

Index

Index is a container which stores and manages documents of a single **Type** in Elasticsearch. We will look at Type in the next section. Index can contain documents of a single Type as depicted in the following figure:

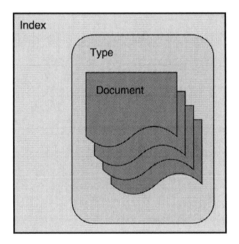

Fig 2.3 Organization of Index, Type, and Documents

Index is a logical container of a type. Some configuration parameters are defined at the Index level while other configuration parameters are defined at the Type level as we will see in the later parts of this chapter.

The concept of Index in Elasticsearch is roughly analogous to the database schema in a relational database. Going by that analogy, the **Type** in Elasticsearch is equivalent to a table and **Document** is equivalent to a record in the table. But please keep in mind that this analogy is just for ease of understanding. Unlike relational database schemas which almost always contain multiple tables, one Index can just contain one Type.

 Prior to Elasticsearch 6.0, one Index could contain multiple Types. This has been changed since 6.0 to allow only one Type within an Index. If you have an existing index with multiple types created prior to 6.0 and you are upgrading to Elasticsearch 6.0, you can still use your old index. You cannot create a new index with more than one type in Elasticsearch 6.0 and above.

Type

In our example, of a product catalog, the document that was indexed was of the product type. Each document stored in the product type represents one product. As the same index cannot have other types such as customers, orders, and order line items etc. Types help in logically grouping or organizing the same kind of documents within an index.

Typically, documents with mostly common sets of fields are grouped under one type. Elasticsearch is schemaless, allowing you to store any JSON document with any set of fields into a type. In practice, we should avoid mixing completely different entities like customers & products into a single type. It makes sense to store them in separate types within separate indexes.

Document

As mentioned earlier, JSON documents are first class citizens in Elasticsearch. Document consists of multiple fields and is the basic unit of information stored in Elasticsearch. For example, you may have a document representing a single product, a single customer, or a single order line item.

As depicted in the figure showing the relationship between index, type, and documents, documents are contained within indexes and types.

Documents contain multiple **fields**. Each field in the JSON document is of a particular **type**. In the product catalog example that we saw earlier, these fields were `sku`, `title`, `description`, `price`, and so on. Each field and its value can be seen as a key value pair in the document, where key is the field name and value is the field value. The field name is similar to a column name in a relational database. The field value can be thought of as value of the column for a given row, that is, the value of a given cell in the table.

In addition to the fields that are sent by the user in the document, Elasticsearch maintains internal meta fields. These fields are as follows:

- `_id`: This is the unique identifier of the document within the type, just like a primary key in a database table. It can be autogenerated or specified by the user.
- `_type`: This field contains the type of the document.
- `_index`: This field contains the index name of the document.

Node

Elasticsearch is a distributed system. It consists of multiple processes running across different machines in a network and communicating with the other processes. In `Chapter 1`, *Introducing Elastic Stack,* we downloaded, installed, and started Elasticsearch. It started what is called a single node of Elasticsearch or a single node Elasticsearch cluster.

An Elasticsearch node is a single server of Elasticsearch which may be part of a larger cluster of nodes. It participates in indexing, searching, and performing other operations supported by Elasticsearch. Every Elasticsearch node is assigned a unique ID and name when it is started. A node can also be assigned a static name via the `node.name` parameter in the Elasticsearch configuration file, `config/elasticsearch.yml`.

 Every Elasticsearch node or instance has a main configuration file which is located in the config subdirectory. The file is in YML format (full form—**YAML Ain't Markup Language**). This configuration file can be used to change defaults such as node name, ports, and cluster name.

At the lowest level, a node corresponds to one instance of the Elasticsearch process. It is responsible for managing its share of data.

Cluster

A cluster hosts one or more indices and is responsible for providing operations such as searching, indexing, and aggregations. A cluster is formed by one or more nodes. Every Elasticsearch node is always part of a cluster, even if it is just a single node cluster. By default, every Elasticsearch node tries to join a cluster with the name Elasticsearch. If you start multiple nodes on the same network without modifying the `cluster.name` property in `config/elasticsearch.yml`, they form a cluster automatically.

> It is advisable to modify the `cluster.name` property in the Elasticsearch config file to avoid joining another cluster in the same network. Since the default behavior of a node is to join an existing cluster within the network, your local node may try to join another node and form a cluster. This can happen in developer machines and also in other environments as long as the nodes are in the same network.

A cluster consists of multiple nodes, where each node takes responsibility for storing and managing its share of data. One cluster can host one or more indexes. An index is logical grouping of related types of documents.

Shards and replicas

Let us first understand what a shard is. One index contains documents of one or more types. Shards help in distributing an index over the cluster. Shards help in dividing the documents of a single index over multiple nodes. There is a limit to the amount of data that can be stored on a single node, and that limit is dictated by the storage, memory, and processing capacities of that node. Shards help by splitting the data of a single index over the cluster and hence allowing the storage, memory, and processing capacities of the cluster to be utilized.

The process of dividing the data among shards is called **sharding**. Sharding is inherent in Elasticsearch and is a way to scale and parallelize, as follows:

- It helps in utilizing storage across different nodes of the cluster
- It helps in utilizing the processing power of different nodes of the cluster

By default, every index is configured to have five shards in Elasticsearch. At the time of creating the index, you can specify the number of shards from which the data will be divided for your index. Once an index is created, the number of shards cannot be modified.

The following figure illustrates how five shards of one index may be distributed on a three-node cluster:

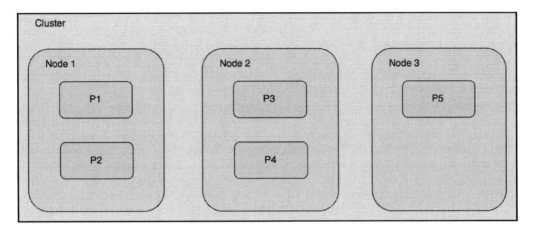

Fig 2.4 Organization of shards across the nodes of a cluster

The shards are named **P1** to **P5** in this figure. Each shard contains roughly one fifth of the total data stored in the index. When a query is made against this index, Elasticsearch takes care of going through all shards and consolidating the result.

Now, imagine that one of the nodes (**Node 1**) goes down. With Node 1, we also lose the share of data which was stored in shards **P1** and **P2**:

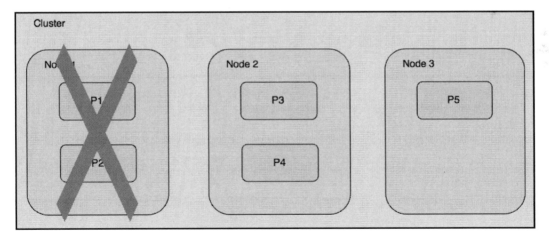

Fig 2.5 Failure of one node along with the loss of its shards

Distributed systems like Elasticsearch are expected to run in spite of hardware failure. This issue is addressed by **replica shards** or **replicas**. Each shard in an index can be configured to have zero or more replica shards. Replica shards are extra copies of the original or primary shard and provide a high availability of data.

For example, with one replica of each shard, we will have one extra copy of each replica. In the following figure, we have five primary shards with one replica of each shard:

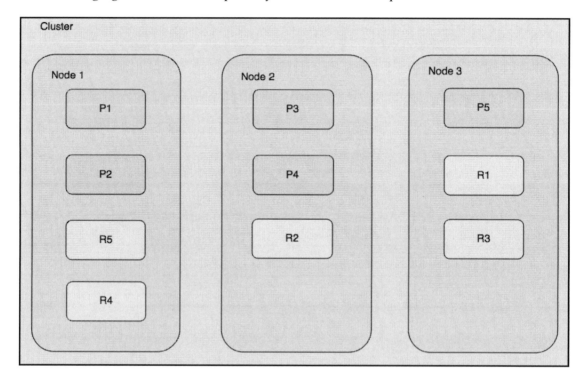

Fig 2.6 Organization of shards with replicas on cluster nodes

Primary shards are depicted in green and replica shards are in yellow. With the replicas in place, if **Node 1** goes down, we still have all shards available in **Node 2** and **Node 3**. Replica shards may be promoted to primary shards when the corresponding primary shard fails.

Apart from providing high availability and failover, replica shards also enable the querying workload to be executed over replicas. Read operations such as search, query, and aggregations can be executed on replicas as well. Elasticsearch transparently distributes the execution of queries across nodes of the cluster where the required shards or replicas are located.

To summarize, nodes get together to form a cluster. Clusters provide a physical layer of services on which multiple indexes can be created. An index may contain one or more types, with each type containing millions or billions of documents. Indexes are split into shards, which are partitions of underlying data within an index. Shards are distributed across the nodes of a cluster. Replicas are copies of primary shards and provide high availability and failover.

Mappings and data types

Elasticsearch is schema-less, meaning you can store documents with any number of fields and types of fields. In a real-world scenario, data is never completely schema-less or unstructured. There are always some sets of fields that are common across all documents in a type. In fact, types within the indexes should be created based on common fields. Typically, one type of document in an index shares some common fields.

Relational databases impose a strict structure. In a relational database, you need to define the structure of the table with column names and data types for each column at the time of creating the table. You cannot insert a record with a new column or a different data-typed column at runtime.

It is important to understand the data types supported by Elasticsearch.

Data types

Elasticsearch supports a wide variety of data types for supporting different scenarios where you want to store text data, numbers, booleans, binary objects, arrays, objects, nested types, geo-points, geo-shapes, and many other specialized datatypes such as IPv4 and IPv6 addresses.

In a document, each field has a datatype associated with it. A summary of the datatypes supported by Elasticsearch is as follows.

Core datatypes

The core datatypes supported by Elasticsearch are as follows:

- **String datatypes**:
  - `text`: The `text` datatype is useful for supporting full-text search for fields which contain a description or lengthy text values. These fields are analyzed before indexing to support full-text search.
  - `keyword`: The `keyword` type enables analytics on string fields. Fields of this type support sorting, filtering, and aggregations.
- **Numeric datatypes**:
  - `byte`, `short`, `integer`, and `long`: Signed integers with 8-bit, 16-bit, 32-bit, and 64-bit precisions respectively
  - `float` and `double`: IEEE 754 floating point numbers with single-precision 32-bit and double-precision 64-bit representations
  - `half_float`: IEEE 754 floating point number with half-precision 16-bit representation
  - `scaled_float`: Floating point number backed by a long and a fixed scaling factor
- **Date datatype**:
  - `date`: Date with an optional timestamp component capable of storing precision timestamps down to the millisecond
- **Boolean datatype**:
  - `boolean`: The Boolean datatype that is common in all programming languages
- **Binary datatype**:
  - `binary`: Allows the storing of arbitrary binary values after performing Base64 encoding
- **Range datatypes**:
  - `integer_range`, `float_range`, `long_range`, `double_range`, and `date_range`: Defines ranges of integers, floats, longs, and so on

scaled_float is a very useful datatype for storing something such as price, which always has a precision of a limited number of decimal places. Price can be stored with a scaling factor of 100, so a price of $10.98 would be internally stored as 1,098 cents and can be treated as an integer. Internally, scaled_float is much more storage efficient as integers can be compressed much better.

Complex datatypes

The complex datatypes supported by Elasticsearch are as follows:

- **Array datatype**: Arrays of the same types of instances. For example, arrays of strings, integers, and so on. Doesn't allow the mixing of datatypes in arrays.
- **Object datatype**: Allows inner objects within JSON documents.
- **Nested datatype**: Useful for supporting arrays of inner objects where each inner object needs to be independently queriable.

Other datatypes

The other datatypes supported by Elasticsearch are as follows:

- **Geo-point datatype**: Allows the storing of geo-points as longitude and latitude. The geo-point datatype enables queries such as searching across all ATMs within a distance of 2 km from a point.
- **Geo-Shape datatype**: Allows the storing of geometric shapes such as polygons, maps, and so on. Geo-Shape enables queries such as searching for all items within a shape.
- **IP datatype**: Allows the storing of IPv4 and IPv6 addresses.

Mappings

To understand mappings, let's add another product to the product catalog:

```
PUT /catalog/product/2
{
    "sku": "SP000002",
    "title": "Google Pixel Phone 32GB - 5 inch display",
    "description": "Google Pixel Phone 32GB - 5 inch display (Factory
Unlocked US Version)",
    "price": 400.00,
    "resolution": "1440 x 2560 pixels",
    "os": "Android 7.1"
```

```
}
```

Copy and paste this example into the editor of your Kibana Console UI and execute it.

As you can see, the product has many different fields, as it is of a completely different category. Yet, there are some fields that are common in all products. The common fields are the precise reason why all these documents are called **products**.

Remember, unlike relational databases, we didn't have to define the fields that would be part of each document. In fact, we didn't even have to create an index with the name catalog. When the first document about the product type was indexed in the index catalog, the following tasks were performed by Elasticsearch:

- Creating an index with the name catalog
- Defining the mappings for the type of product

Creating an index with the name catalog

The first step involves creating an index, because the index doesn't exist already. The index is created using the default number of shards. We will look at a concept called **index templates**—you can create template for any new indexes. Sometimes, an index needs to be created on the fly, just like in this case where the insertion of the first document triggers the creation of a new index. The index template kicks in and provides the matching template for the index while creating the new index. This helps in creating indexes in a controlled way, that is, with desired defaults like the number of shards and type mappings for the types within them.

An index can be created beforehand as well. Elasticsearch has a separate index API (`https://www.elastic.co/guide/en/elasticsearch/reference/current/indices.html`) which deals with index level operations. This includes create, delete, get, create mapping, and many more advanced operations.

Defining the mappings for the type of product

The second step involves defining the mappings for the type of product. This step is executed because the type catalog did not exist before the first document was indexed. Remember the analogy of type with a relational database table. The table needs to exist before any row can be inserted. When a table is created in an RDBMS, we define the fields (columns) and their datatypes in the `CREATE TABLE` statement.

When the first document is indexed within a type that doesn't yet exist, Elasticsearch tries to infer the datatypes of all the fields. This feature is called the **dynamic mapping** of types. By default, the dynamic mapping of types is enabled in Elasticsearch.

To see the mappings of the product type in the catalog index, execute the following command in the Kibana Console UI:

```
GET /catalog/_mapping/product
```

This is an example of a Get Mapping API (`https://www.elastic.co/guide/en/ elasticsearch/reference/current/indices-get-mapping.html`). You can request mappings of a specific type, all types within an index, or within multiple indexes.

The response should look like the following:

```
{
   "catalog": {
      "mappings": {
         "product": {
            "properties": {
               "ISBN": {
                  "type": "text"
                  }
               },
               "author": {
                  "type": "text"
                  }
               },
               "description": {
                  "type": "text"
                  }
               },
               "price": {
                  "type": "float"
               },
               "sku": {
                  "type": "text"
               },
               "title": {
                  "type": "text"
               }
            }
         }
      }
   }
}
```

At the top level of the JSON response, catalog is the index for which we requested mappings. The mappings child product signifies the fact that these are mappings for the product type. The actual datatype mappings for each field are under the properties element.

The actual type mappings returned will be slightly different from the ones shown in the preceding code. It has been simplified slightly. As you can see, only the price is of the `float` datatype; other fields were mapped to the text type. In reality, each `text` datatype field is mapped as follows:

```
"field_name": {
  "type": "text",
  "fields": {
    "keyword": {
      "type": "keyword",
      "ignore_above": 256
    }
  }
}
```

As you may notice, each field that was sent as a string is assigned the `text` datatype. The text datatype enables full-text search on a field. Additionally, the same field is also stored as a multi-field and it is also stored as a `keyword`. This effectively enables full-text search and analytics (sorting, aggregations, and filtering) on the same field. We will look at both search and analytics in the upcoming chapters of this book.

Inverted index

Inverted index is the core data structure of Elasticsearch and any other system supporting full-text search. Inverted index is similar to the index that you see at the end of any book. It maps the terms that appear in the documents to the documents.

For example, you may build an inverted index from the following strings:

Document ID	Document
1	It is Sunday tomorrow.
2	Sunday is the last day of the week.
3	The choice is yours.

Elasticsearch builds a data structure, which looks like the following, from the three documents indexed. The following data structure is called the **inverted index**:

Term	Frequency	Documents (Postings)
choice	1	3
day	1	2
is	3	1, 2, 3
it	1	1
last	1	2
of	1	2
sunday	2	1, 2
the	3	2, 3
tomorrow	1	1
week	1	2
yours	1	3

Notice the following things:

- Documents were broken down into terms after removing punctuation and placing them in lowercase.
- Terms are sorted alphabetically.
- The **Frequency** column captures how many times the term appears in the entire document set.
- The third column captures the documents in which the term was found. Additionally, it may also contain the exact locations (offsets within the document) where the term was found.

When searching for terms in the documents, it is blazingly fast to locate the documents in which the given term appears. If the user searches for the term *sunday*, then the looking up of *sunday* from the terms column will be really fast, because the terms are sorted in the index. Even if there were millions of terms, it is quick to look up terms when they are sorted.

Subsequently, consider a scenario in which the user searches for two words, for example *last sunday*. Inverted index can be used to individually search for the occurrence of last and sunday; document two contains both terms, so it is a better match than document one, which contains only one term.

Inverted index is the building block for performing fast searches. Similarly, it is easy to look up how many occurrences of terms are present in the index. This is a simple count aggregation. Of course, Elasticsearch uses lots of innovation on top of the bare inverted index explained here. It caters to both search and analytics.

By default, Elasticsearch builds an inverted index on all the fields in the document, pointing back to the Elasticsearch document in which the field was present.

CRUD operations

In this section we will look at how to perform basic CRUD operations, which are the most fundamental operations required by any data store. Elasticsearch has a very well designed REST API, and the CRUD operations are targeted at **documents.**

To understand how to perform CRUD operations, we will cover the following APIs. These APIs fall under the category of Document APIs that deal with documents:

- Index API
- Get API
- Update API
- Delete API

Index API

In Elasticsearch terminology, adding (or creating) a document into a type within an index of Elasticsearch is called an **indexing operation**. Essentially, it involves adding the document to the index by parsing all fields within the document and building the inverted index. This is why this operation is known as an **indexing operation**.

There are two ways we can index a document:

- Indexing a document by providing an ID
- Indexing a document without providing an ID

Indexing a document by providing an ID

We have already seen this version of the indexing operation. The user can provide the ID of the document using the PUT method.

The format of this request is PUT /<index>/<type>/<id>, with the JSON document as the body of the request:

```
PUT /catalog/product/1
{
    "sku": "SP000001",
    "title": "Elasticsearch for Hadoop",
    "description": "Elasticsearch for Hadoop",
    "author": "Vishal Shukla",
    "ISBN": "1785288997",
    "price": 26.99
}
```

Indexing a document without providing an ID

If you don't want to control the ID generation for the documents, you can use the POST method.

The format of this request is POST /<index>/<type>, with the JSON document as the body of the request:

```
POST /catalog/product
{
    "sku": "SP000003",
    "title": "Mastering Elasticsearch",
    "description": "Mastering Elasticsearch",
    "author": "Bharvi Dixit",
    "price": 54.99
}
```

The ID in this case will be generated by Elasticsearch. It is a hash string, as highlighted in the response:

```
{
  "_index": "catalog",
  "_type": "product",
  "_id": "AVrASKqgaBGmnAMj1SBe",
  "_version": 1,
  "result": "created",
  "_shards": {
    "total": 2,
    "successful": 1,
    "failed": 0
  },
  "created": true
}
```

 As per pure REST conventions, POST is used for creating a new *resource* and PUT is used for updating an existing resource. Here, the usage of PUT is equivalent to saying *I know the ID that I want to assign, so use this ID while indexing this document.*

Get API

The Get API is useful for retrieving a document when you already know the ID of the document. It is essentially a get by primary key operation:

```
GET /catalog/product/AVrASKqgaBGmnAMj1SBe
```

The format of this request is GET /<index>/<type>/<id>. The response would be as expected:

```
{
  "_index": "catalog",
  "_type": "product",
  "_id": "AVrASKqgaBGmnAMj1SBe",
  "_version": 1,
  "found": true,
  "_source": {
    "sku": "SP000003",
    "title": "Mastering Elasticsearch",
    "description": "Mastering Elasticsearch",
```

```
        "author": "Bharvi Dixit",
        "price": 54.99
    }
}
```

Update API

The Update API is useful for updating the existing document by ID.

The format of an update request is POST <index>/<type>/<id>/_update with a JSON request as the body:

```
POST /catalog/product/1/_update
{
    "doc": {
        "price": "28.99"
    }
}
```

The properties specified under the "doc" element are merged into the existing document. The previous version of this document with ID 1 had price of 26.99. This update operation just updates the price and leaves the other fields of the document unchanged. This type of update means "doc" is specified and used as a partial document to merge with an existing document; there are other types of updates supported.

The response of the update request is as follows:

```
{
    "_index": "catalog",
    "_type": "product",
    "_id": "1",
    "_version": 2,
    "result": "updated",
    "_shards": {
        "total": 2,
        "successful": 1,
        "failed": 0
    }
}
```

Internally, Elasticsearch maintains the version of each document. Whenever a document is updated, the version number is incremented.

The partial update that we have seen above will work only if the document existed beforehand. If the document with the given *id* did not exist, Elasticsearch will return an error saying that document is missing. Let us understand how do we do an `upsert` operation using the Update API. The term upsert loosely means update or insert, i.e. update the document if it exists otherwise insert new document.

The parameter `doc_as_upsert` checks if the document with the given *id* already exists and merges the provided `doc` with the existing document. If the document with the given *id* doesn't exist, it inserts a new document with the given document contents.

The following example uses `doc_as_upsert` to merge into the document with *id* 3 or insert a new document if it doesn't exist.

```
POST /catalog/product/3/_update
{
  "doc": {
    "author": "Albert Paro",
    "title": "Elasticsearch 5.0 Cookbook",
    "description": "Elasticsearch 5.0 Cookbook Third Edition",
    "price": "54.99"
  },
  "doc_as_upsert": true
}
```

We can update the value of a field based on the existing value of that field or another field in the document. The following update uses an inline script to increase the price by two for a specific product:

```
POST /catalog/product/AVrASKqgaBGmnAMj1SBe/_update
{
  "script": {
    "inline": "ctx._source.price += params.increment",
    "lang": "painless",
    "params": {
      "increment": 2
    }
  }
}
```

Scripting support allows for the reading of the existing value, incrementing the value by a variable, and storing it back in a single operation. The inline script used here is Elasticsearch's own painless scripting language. The syntax for incrementing an existing variable is similar to most other programming languages.

Delete API

The Delete API lets you delete a document by ID:

```
DELETE /catalog/product/AVrASKqgaBGmnAMj1SBe
```

The response of the delete operations is as follows:

```
{
  "found": true,
  "_index": "catalog",
  "_type": "product",
  "_id": "AVrASKqgaBGmnAMj1SBe",
  "_version": 4,
  "result": "deleted",
  "_shards": {
    "total": 2,
    "successful": 1,
    "failed": 0
  }
}
```

This is how basic CRUD operations are performed with Elasticsearch. Please bear in mind that Elasticsearch maintains data in a completely different data structure, that is, an inverted index, using the capabilities of Apache Lucene. A relational database builds and maintains B-trees, which are more suitable for typical CRUD operations.

Creating indexes and taking control of mapping

In the previous section, we learnt how to perform CRUD operations with Elasticsearch. In the process, we saw how indexing the first document to an index which doesn't yet exist results in the creation of the new index and the mapping of the type.

Usually, you wouldn't want to let things happen automatically, as you would want to control how indices are created and also how mapping is created. We will see how you can take control of this process in this section and look at the following:

- Creating an index
- Create a mapping
- Updating a mapping

Creating an index

You can create an index and specify the number of shards and replicas to create:

```
PUT /catalog
{
  "settings": {
    "index": {
      "number_of_shards": 5,
      "number_of_replicas": 2
    }
  }
}
```

It is possible to specify a mapping for a type at the time of index creation. The following command will create an index called catalog with five shards and two replicas. Additionally, it also defines a type called my_type with two fields, one of the text type and another of the keyword type:

```
PUT /catalog
{
  "settings": {
    "index": {
      "number_of_shards": 5,
      "number_of_replicas": 2
    }
  },
  "mappings": {
    "my_type": {
      "properties": {
        "f1": {
          "type": "text"
        },
        "f2": {
          "type": "keyword"
        }
      }
```

```
      }
    }
  }
}
```

Creating type mapping in an existing index

A type can be added within an index after the index is created. The mappings for the type can be specified as follows:

```
PUT /catalog/_mapping/category
{
  "properties": {
    "name": {
      "type": "text"
    }
  }
}
```

This command creates a type called **category**, with one field of the text type in the existing index catalog. Let us add a couple of documents after creating the new type:

```
POST /catalog/category
{
  "name": "books"
}
POST /catalog/category
{
  "name": "phones"
}
```

After a few documents are indexed, you realize that you need to add fields for storing the description of the category. Elasticsearch will assign a type automatically based on the value that you insert for the new field. It takes into consideration only the first value that it sees to guess the type of that field:

```
POST /catalog/category
{
  "name": "music",
  "description": "On-demand streaming music"
}
```

When the new category is indexed with fields, the field is assigned a datatype based on its value in the initial document. Let us look at the mapping after this document is indexed:

```
{
  "catalog": {
    "mappings": {
      "category": {
        "properties": {
          "description": {
            "type": "text",
            "fields": {
              "keyword": {
                "type": "keyword",
                "ignore_above": 256
              }
            }
          },
          "name": {
            "type": "text"
          }
        }
      }
    }
  }
}
```

The field description has been assigned the `text` datatype, with a field with the name `keyword`, which is of the `keyword` type. What this means is that logically there are two fields, `description` and `description.keyword`. The `description` field is analyzed at the time of indexing, whereas the `description.keyword` field is not analyzed and is stored as is without any analysis. By default, fields that are indexed with double quotes for the first time are stored as both text and keyword types.

If you want to take control of the type, you should define the mapping for the field before the first document containing that field is indexed. A field's type cannot be changed after one or more documents are indexed within that field. Let us see how to update the mapping to add a field with the desired type.

Updating a mapping

Mapping for new fields can be added after a type has been created. Mapping can be updated for a type with the PUT mapping API. Let us add a code field, which is of the keyword type, only with no analysis:

```
PUT /catalog/_mapping/category
{
  "properties": {
    "code": {
      "type": "keyword"
    }
  }
}
```

This mapping is merged into the existing mappings of the category type. The mapping looks like the following after it is merged:

```
{
  "catalog": {
    "mappings": {
      "category": {
        "properties": {
          "code": {
            "type": "keyword"
          },
          "description": {
            "type": "text",
            "fields": {
              "keyword": {
                "type": "keyword",
                "ignore_above": 256
              }
            }
          },
          "name": {
            "type": "text"
          }
        }
      }
    }
  }
}
```

Any subsequent documents that are indexed with the `code` field are assigned the right datatype:

```
POST /catalog/category
{
  "name": "sports",
  "code": "C004",
  "description": "Sports equipment"
}
```

This is how we can take control of the index creation and type mapping process, and add fields after the type is created.

REST API overview

We just looked at how to perform basic CRUD operations. Elasticsearch supports a wide variety of operation types. Some operations deal with documents, that is, creating, reading, updating, deleting, and so on. Some operations provide search and aggregations, while other operations are for providing cluster related operations, such as monitoring health. Broadly, the APIs that deal with Elasticsearch are categorized into the following types of APIs:

- Document APIs
- Search APIs
- Aggregations APIs
- Indices APIs
- Cluster APIs
- cat APIs

The Elasticsearch reference documentation has documented these APIs very nicely. In this book, we will not go into the APIs down to the last detail. We will conceptually understand, with examples, how the APIs can be leveraged to get the best out of Elasticsearch and other components of Elastic Stack.

We will look at the search and aggregation APIs in Chapter 3, *Searching-What is Relevant* and Chapter 4, *Analytics with Elasticsearch* respectively.

In the following section we will cover the Common API conventions applicable for all REST APIs.

Common API conventions

All Elasticsearch REST APIs share some common features. They can be used across almost all APIs. We will cover the following features:

- Formatting the JSON response
- Dealing with multiple indices

Let us look at each item one-by-one.

Formatting the JSON response

By default, the response of all the requests is not formatted. It returns an unformatted JSON string in a single line:

```
curl -XGET http://localhost:9200/catalog/product/1
```

The response is not formatted:

```
{"_index":"catalog","_type":"product","_id":"1","_version":3,"found":true,"
_source":{
 "sku": "SP000001",
 "title": "Elasticsearch for Hadoop",
 "description": "Elasticsearch for Hadoop",
 "author": "Vishal Shukla",
 "ISBN": "1785288997",
 "price": 26.99
}}
```

Passing `pretty=true` formats the response:

```
curl -XGET http://localhost:9200/catalog/product/1?pretty=true
{
 "_index" : "catalog",
 "_type" : "product",
 "_id" : "1",
 "_version" : 3,
 "found" : true,
 "_source" : {
 "sku" : "SP000001",
 "title" : "Elasticsearch for Hadoop",
```

```
"description" : "Elasticsearch for Hadoop",
"author" : "Vishal Shukla",
"ISBN" : "1785288997",
"price" : 26.99
}
}
```

When you are using Kibana Console UI, all responses are formatted by default.

Dealing with multiple indices

Operations such as search and aggregations can run against multiple indices in the same query. It is possible to specify which indexes should be searched by using different URLs in the get request. Let us understand how the URLs can be used to search in different indexes and the types within them. We will cover the following scenarios when dealing with multiple indices within a cluster:

- Searching all documents in all indices
- Searching all documents in one index
- Searching all documents of one type in an index
- Searching all documents in multiple indices
- Searching all documents of a particular type in all indices

The following query matches all documents. The documents actually returned by the query will be limited to 10 in this case. The default `size` of the result is 10, unless it is specified in the query:

```
GET /_search
```

This will return all documents from all indices of the cluster. The response looks similar to the following, and it is truncated to remove the unnecessary repetition of documents:

```
{
  "took": 3,
  "timed_out": false,
  "_shards": {
    "total": 16,
    "successful": 16,
    </span>"failed": 0
  },
  "hits": {
    "total": 4,
    "max_score": 1,
    "hits": [
```

```
{
  "_index": ".kibana",
  "_type": "doc",
  "_id": "config:6.0.0",
  "_score": 1,
  "_source": {
    "type": "config",
    "config": {
      "buildNum": 16070
    }
  }
},
...
...
]
  }
}
```

Clearly, this is not a very useful operation. But let's use it to understand the search response:

- `took`: The number of milliseconds taken by the cluster to return the result.
- `timed_out: false`: this means that the operation completed successfully without timing out.
- `_shards`: Shows the summary of how many shards across the entire cluster were searched for successfully, or failed.
- `hits`: Contains the actual documents matched. It contains **total** which signifies the total documents that matched the search criteria across all indices. The `max_score` displays the score of the best matching document from the search hits. The `hits` child of this element contains the actual document list.

> The hits list contained within an array doesn't contain all matched documents. It would be wasteful to return everything that matched the search criteria, as there could be millions or billions of such matched documents. Elasticsearch truncates the hits by `size`, which can be optionally specified as a request parameter using GET `/_search?size=100`. The default value for the `size` is 10, hence the search hits array will contain up to 10 records by default.

Searching all documents in one index

The following will search for all documents, but only within the catalog index:

```
GET /catalog/_search
```

You can also be more specific and also include the type in addition to the index name; like it is done in the following query.

```
GET /catalog/product/_search
```

Searching all documents in multiple indexes

The following will search for all documents within the catalog index and an index named `my_index`:

```
GET /catalog,my_index/_search
```

Searching all documents of a particular type in all indices

The following will search all indices in the cluster, but only documents of the product type will be searched:

```
GET /_all/product/_search
```

This feature can be quite handy when you have multiple indices; each index containing *the exact same type*. This type of query can help you query data for that type from all indices.

Summary

In this chapter, we learned about the essential Kibana Console UI and curl commands to interact with Elasticsearch with the REST API. Then we looked at the core concepts of Elasticsearch. We performed customary CRUD operations that are required as support for any data store. We took a closer look at how to create indexes, and how to create and manage mappings. We ended the chapter with an overview of the REST API in Elasticsearch, and the common conventions used in most APIs.

In the next chapter, we will take a deep dive into the search capabilities of Elasticsearch to understand the maximum benefits of Elasticsearch as a search engine.

3
Searching-What is Relevant

One of the core strengths of Elasticsearch is its search capabilities. In the previous chapter, we gained a good understanding of Elasticsearch's core concepts, its REST API, and its basic operations. With all that knowledge at hand, we will further our journey by learning about Elastic Stack. We will cover the following topics in this chapter.

- Basics of text analysis
- Searching from structured data
- Writing compound queries
- Searching from full-text

Basics of text analysis

Analysis of text data is different to other types of data analysis such as numbers, dates, and time. The analysis of numeric and date/time datatypes can be done in a very definitive way. For example, if you are looking for all records with a price greater than or equal to 50, the result is a simple yes or no for each record. Either the record in question qualifies or doesn't qualify for inclusion in the query's result. Similarly, when querying something by date or time, the criteria for searching through the records is very clearly defined—a record either falls into the date/time range or it doesn't.

However, the analysis of text/string data can be different. Text data can be of a different nature, and it can be used for structured analysis or unstructured analysis.

Some examples of structured types of string fields are as follows: country codes, product codes, non-numeric serial numbers/identifiers, and so on. The datatype of these fields may be a string, but often you may want to do exact-match queries on these fields.

We will first cover the analysis of unstructured text, which is also known as **full-text search**.

We already understood in the previous chapter the concepts of Elasticsearch indexes, types, and mappings within the type. All fields that are of the text type are analyzed by what is known as an **analyzer**.

In the following sections, we will cover the following topics:

- Understanding Elasticsearch analyzers
- Using built-in analyzers
- Implementing auto-complete with a custom analyzer

Understanding Elasticsearch analyzers

The main task of an analyzer is to take the value of a field and break it down into terms. In `Chapter 2`, *Getting Started with Elasticsearch*, we looked at the structure of an inverted index. The job of the analyzer is take documents, and each field of the document, and extract terms from them. These terms make the index searchable, that is, it can help us find out which documents contain particular search terms.

The analyzer performs this process of breaking up input character streams into terms. This happens twice:

- At the time of indexing
- At the time of searching

The core task of the analyzer is to parse the document fields and build the actual index.

Every field of text type needs to be analyzed before the document is indexed. This process of analysis is what makes the documents searchable by any search term that is used at the time of searching.

Analyzers can be configured on a per field basis, that is, it is possible to have two fields of the type *text* within the same document, each one using different analyzers.

Elasticsearch uses analyzers to analyze the text data. An analyzer has the following components:

- **Character filters**: Zero or more
- **Tokenizer**: Exactly one
- **Token filters**: Zero or more

The following diagram depicts how these components are used to compose an analyzer:

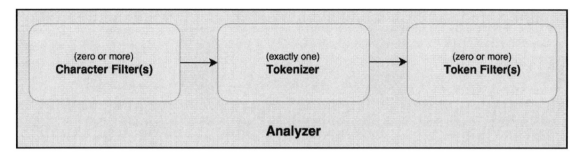

Figure 3.1 Anatomy of an analyzer

Let us understand the role of each component one by one.

Character filters

While composing an analyzer, we can configure zero or more character filters. A character filter works on a stream of characters from the input field; each character filter can add, remove, or change the characters in the input field.

Elasticsearch ships with a few built-in character filters which you can use to compose or create your own custom analyzer.

For example, one of the character filters that Elasticsearch ships with is the Mapping Char Filter. It can map a character or sequence of characters into target characters.

For example, you may want to transform emoticons into some text that represents that emoticon:

- :) should be translated to _smile_
- :(should be translated to _sad_
- :D should be translated to _laugh_

This can be achieved through the following character filter. The short name of the **Char Mapping Filter** is mapping filter:

```
"char_filter": {
  "my_char_filter": {
    "type": "mapping",
    "mappings": [
      ":) => _smile_",
      ":( => _sad_",
```

```
        ":D => _laugh_"
      ]
    }
  }
```

When this character filter is used to create an analyzer, it will have the following effect:

Good morning everyone :) will be transformed to Good morning everyone _smile_.

I am not feeling well today :(will be transformed to I am not feeling well today _sad_.

Since character filters are at the very beginning of the processing chain in an analyzer (see Figure 3.1), the tokenizer will always see the replaced characters. Character filters can be useful to replace characters with something more meaningful in certain cases, such as replacing the numeric characters from other languages with English language decimals-that is, digits from Hindi, Arabic, and other languages can be turned into zero, one, two, and so on.

You can find list of available built-in character filters here: https://www.elastic.co/guide/en/elasticsearch/reference/current/analysis-charfilters.html.

Tokenizer

An analyzer has exactly one tokenizer. The responsibility of a tokenizer is to receive a stream of characters and generate a stream of tokens. These tokens are used to build the inverted index. A token is roughly equivalent to a word. In addition to breaking down characters into words or tokens, it also produces in its output the start and end offset of each token in the input stream.

Elasticsearch ships with a number of tokenizers that can be used to compose a custom analyzer; these tokenizers are also used by Elasticsearch itself to compose its built-in analyzers.

You can find list of available built-in tokenizers here: https://www.elastic.co/guide/en/elasticsearch/reference/current/analysis-tokenizers.html.

The Standard Tokenizer is one of the most popular tokenizers as it is suitable for most languages. Let us look at what Standard Tokenizer does.

Standard Tokenizer

Loosely speaking, the Standard Tokenizer breaks down the stream of characters by separating them by white space characters and punctuation.

The following example shows how Standard Tokenizer breaks the character stream into tokens:

```
POST _analyze
{
  "tokenizer": "standard",
  "text": "Tokenizer breaks characters into tokens!"
}
```

This command produces the following output. Notice the start_offset, end_offset, and positions in the output:

```
{
  "tokens": [
    {
      "token": "Tokenizer",
      "start_offset": 0,
      "end_offset": 9,
      "type": "<ALPHANUM>",
      "position": 0
    },
    {
      "token": "breaks",
      "start_offset": 10,
      "end_offset": 16,
      "type": "<ALPHANUM>",
      "position": 1
    },
    {
      "token": "characters",
      "start_offset": 17,
      "end_offset": 27,
      "type": "<ALPHANUM>",
      "position": 2
    },
    {
      "token": "into",
      "start_offset": 28,
      "end_offset": 32,
```

```
        "type": "<ALPHANUM>",
        "position": 3
      },
      {
        "token": "tokens",
        "start_offset": 33,
        "end_offset": 39,
        "type": "<ALPHANUM>",
        "position": 4
      }
    ]
  }
```

This token stream can be further processed by the token filters of the analyzer, if any.

Token filters

There can be zero or more token filters in an analyzer. Every token filter can add, remove, or change tokens in the input token stream that it receives. Since it is possible to have multiple token filters in an analyzer, the output of each token filter is sent to the next one until all token filters are considered.

Elasticsearch comes with a number of token filters, and they can be used to compose your own custom analyzers.

Some examples of built-in token filters are:

- **Lowercase Token Filter**: Replaces all tokens in the input with their lowercase versions.
- **Stop Token Filter**: Removes stopwords, that is, words that do not add more meaning to the context. For example, in English sentences, words like *is*, *a*, *an*, and *the*, do not add extra meaning to the sentence. For many text search problems, it makes sense to remove such words as they don't add any extra meaning or context to the content.

You can find list of available built-in token filters here: https://www.elastic.co/guide/en/elasticsearch/reference/current/analysis-tokenfilters.html.

Thus far, we have understood the role of character filters, tokenizers, and token filters. This sets us up to understand how some of the built-in analyzers in Elasticsearch are composed.

Using built-in analyzers

Elasticsearch comes with a number of built-in analyzers which can be used directly. Almost all of these analyzers work without any need for additional configuration, but they provide the flexibility of configuring some parameters.

Some analyzers come packaged with Elasticsearch. Some popular analyzers are:

- **Standard Analyzer**: It is the default analyzer in Elasticsearch. If not overridden by any other field level, type level or index level analyzer, all fields are analyzed using this analyzer.
- **Language Analyzers**: Different languages have different grammatical rules. There is a difference in some languages as to how a stream of characters is tokenized into words or tokens. Additionally, each language has its own set of stopwords which can be configured while configuring language analyzers.
- **Whitespace Analyzer**: The whitespace analyzer breaks down the input into tokens wherever it finds a whitespace token such as a space, tab, new line, or carriage return.

You can find a list of available built-in analyzers here: `https://www.elastic.co/guide/en/elasticsearch/reference/current/analysis-analyzers.html`.

Standard Analyzer

The Standard Analyzer is suitable for many languages and situations. It can also be customized for the underlying language or situation. The Standard Analyzer is composed of the following components:

Tokenizer:

- **Standard Tokenizer**: A tokenizer that splits tokens on whitespace characters

Token Filters:

- **Standard Token Filter**: Standard Token Filter is used as a placeholder token filter within the Standard Analyzer. It does not change any of the input tokens but may be used in future to perform some tasks.
- **Lowercase Token Filter**: Makes all tokens in the input lowercase.
- **Stop Token Filter**: Removes the specified stopwords. The default settings has a stopword list set to _none_ which doesn't remove any stopwords by default.

Let us see how the Standard Analyzer works by default with an example:

```
PUT index_standard_analyzer
{
  "settings": {
    "analysis": {
      "analyzer": {
        "std": {
          "type": "standard"
        }
      }
    }
  },
  "mappings": {
    "my_type": {
      "properties": {
        "my_text": {
          "type": "text",
          "analyzer": "std"
        }
      }
    }
  }
}
```

Here, we created an index, `index_standard_analyzer`. There are two things to notice here:

- Under the `settings` element, we explicitly defined one analyzer with the name `std`. The type of the analyzer is `standard`. Apart from this, we did not do any additional configuration on the Standard Analyzer.
- We created one type called `my_type` in the index and explicitly set a field level analyzer on the only field, `my_text`.

Let us check how Elasticsearch will do the analysis for the `my_text` field whenever any document is indexed in this index. We can do this test using the `_analyze` API, as we saw earlier:

```
POST index_standard_analyzer/_analyze
{
  "field": "my_text",
  "text": "The Standard Analyzer works this way."
}
```

The output of this command shows the following tokens:

```
{
  "tokens": [
    {
      "token": "the",
      "start_offset": 0,
      "end_offset": 3,
      "type": "<ALPHANUM>",
      "position": 0
    },
    {
      "token": "standard",
      "start_offset": 4,
      "end_offset": 12,
      "type": "<ALPHANUM>",
      "position": 1
    },
    {
      "token": "analyzer",
      "start_offset": 13,
      "end_offset": 21,
      "type": "<ALPHANUM>",
      "position": 2
    },
    {
      "token": "works",
      "start_offset": 22,
      "end_offset": 27,
      "type": "<ALPHANUM>",
      "position": 3
    },
    {
      "token": "this",
      "start_offset": 28,
      "end_offset": 32,
      "type": "<ALPHANUM>",
      "position": 4
    },
    {
      "token": "way",
      "start_offset": 33,
      "end_offset": 36,
      "type": "<ALPHANUM>",
      "position": 5
    }
  ]
}
```

Please note that in this case, the field level analyzer for the `my_field` field was set to Standard Analyzer explicitly. Even if it wasn't set explicitly for the field, the Standard Analyzer is the default analyzer if no other analyzer is specified.

As you can see, all tokens in the output are lowercase. Even though the Standard Analyzer has a stop token filter, none of the tokens are filtered out. This is why the `_analyze` output has all words as tokens.

Let us create another index that uses English language stopwords:

```
PUT index_standard_analyzer_english_stopwords
{
  "settings": {
    "analysis": {
      "analyzer": {
        "std": {
          "type": "standard",
          "stopwords": "_english_"
        }
      }
    }
  },
  "mappings": {
    "my_type": {
      "properties": {
        "my_text": {
          "type": "text",
          "analyzer": "std"
        }
      }
    }
  }
}
```

Notice the difference here. This new index is using _english_ stopwords. You can also specify a list of stopwords directly, such as `stopwords`: (*a, an, the*).
The _english_ value includes all such English words.

When you try the _analyze API on the new index, you will see it removes the stopwords, such as the and this:

```
POST index_standard_analyzer_english_stopwords/_analyze
{
  "field": "my_text",
  "text": "The Standard Analyzer works this way."
}
```

It returns a response like the following:

```
{
  "tokens": [
    {
      "token": "standard",
      "start_offset": 4,
      "end_offset": 12,
      "type": "<ALPHANUM>",
      "position": 1
    },
    {
      "token": "analyzer",
      "start_offset": 13,
      "end_offset": 21,
      "type": "<ALPHANUM>",
      "position": 2
    },
    {
      "token": "works",
      "start_offset": 22,
      "end_offset": 27,
      "type": "<ALPHANUM>",
      "position": 3
    },
    {
      "token": "way",
      "start_offset": 33,
      "end_offset": 36,
      "type": "<ALPHANUM>",
      "position": 5
    }
  ]
}
```

English stopwords such as the and this are removed. As you can see, with little configuration, the Standard Analyzer can be used for English and many other languages.

Let us go through a practical application of creating a custom analyzer.

Implementing autocomplete with a custom analyzer

In certain situations, you may want to create your own custom analyzer by composing character filters, tokenizers, and token filters of your choice. Please remember that most of the requirements can be fulfilled by one of the built-in analyzers with some configuration. Let us create an analyzer that can help when implementing autocomplete functionality.

To support auto-complete, we cannot rely on the Standard Analyzer or one of the pre-built analyzers in Elasticsearch. The analyzer is responsible for generating the terms at indexing time. Our analyzer should be able to generate the terms that can help with auto-completion. Let us understand this through a concrete example.

If we were to use the Standard Analyzer at indexing time, the following terms would be generated for the field with the `"Learning Elastic Stack 6"` value:

```
GET /_analyze
{
   "text": "Learning Elastic Stack 6",
   "analyzer": "standard"
}
```

The response of this request would contain the terms `Learning`, `Elastic`, `Stack`, and `6`. These are the terms that Elasticsearch would create and store in the index if the Standard Analyzer was used. Now, what we want to support is that when the user starts typing a few characters, we should be able to match possible matching products. For example, if the user has typed elas, it should still recommend **Learning Elastic Stack 6** as a product. Let us compose an analyzer which can generate terms such as el, ela, elas, elast, elasti, elastic, le, lea, and so on:

```
PUT /custom_analyzer_index
{
   "settings": {
      "index": {
         "analysis": {
            "analyzer": {
               "custom_analyzer": {
                  "type": "custom",
                  "tokenizer": "standard",
                  "filter": [
                     "lowercase",
```

```
                    "custom_edge_ngram"
                ]
            }
        },
        "filter": {
          "custom_edge_ngram": {
            "type": "edge_ngram",
            "min_gram": 2,
            "max_gram": 10
          }
        }
      }
    }
  },
  "mappings": {
    "my_type": {
      "properties": {
        "product": {
          "type": "text",
          "analyzer": "custom_analyzer",
          "search_analyzer": "standard"
        }
      }
    }
  }
}
```

This index definition creates a custom analyzer that uses a Standard Tokenizer to create the tokens, and uses two token filters—a lowercase token filter and the `edge_ngram` token filter. The edge ngram token filter breaks down each token into the lengths of two characters, three characters, and four characters, up to 10 characters. One incoming token, such as elastic, will generate tokens such as el, ela, and so on, from one token. This will enable auto-completion searches.

Given that the following two products are indexed, and the user has typed Ela so far, the search should return both the products:

```
POST /custom_analyzer_index/my_type
{
   "product": "Learning Elastic Stack 6"
}

POST /custom_analyzer_index/my_type
{
   "product": "Mastering Elasticsearch"
}
```

```
GET /custom_analyzer_index/_search
{
  "query": {
    "match": {
      "product": "Ela"
    }
  }
}
```

Since the index contains the terms el, ela, and so on, the query would return both the products. This would not have been possible if the index was built using the Standard Analyzer at indexing time. We will cover the match query later in this chapter. For now, you can assume that it applies the Standard Analyzer (the analyzer configured as the `search_analyzer`) on the given search terms and then uses the output terms for performing the search. In this case, it would search for the term ela in the index. Since the index was built using a custom analyzer using an _ngram edge token filter, it would find a match for both the products.

In this section, we have learnt about analyzers. Analyzers play a vital role in the functioning of Elasticsearch. Analyzers decide which terms get stored in the index. As a result, what kind of search operations can be performed on the index after it has been built are decided by the analyzer used at index time. For example, a Standard Analyzer cannot fulfill the requirement of supporting the auto-completion feature. We have looked at the anatomy of analyzers, tokenizers, token filters, character filters, and some built-in support in Elasticsearch. We also looked at a scenario in which building a custom analyzer solves a real business problem regarding supporting the auto-complete function in your application.

Before we move onto the next section and start looking at different query types, let us set up the necessary index with the data required for the next section. We are going to use product catalog data taken from popular e-commerce site www.amazon.com. The data is downloadable from http://dbs.uni-leipzig.de/file/Amazon-GoogleProducts.zip.

Before we start with the queries, let us create the required index and import some data:

```
PUT /amazon_products
{
  "settings": {
    "number_of_shards": 1,
    "number_of_replicas": 0,
    "analysis": {
      "analyzer": {
      }
    }
  },
  "mappings": {
```

```
"products": {
  "properties": {
      "id": {
        "type": "keyword"
      },
      "title": {
        "type": "text"
      },
      "description": {
        "type": "text"
      },
      "manufacturer": {
        "type": "text",
        "fields": {
          "raw": {
            "type": "keyword"
          }
        }
      },
      "price": {
        "type": "scaled_float",
        "scaling_factor": 100
      }
    }
  }
}
```

The title and description fields are analyzed text fields on which analysis should be performed. This will enable full-text queries on these fields. The manufacturer field is of the text type, but it also has a field with the name raw. The manufacturer field is stored in two ways, as `text`, and `manufacturer.raw` is stored as `keyword`. All fields of the `keyword` type internally use the keyword analyzer. The keyword analyzer consists of just the keyword tokenizer, which is a noop tokenizer, simply returning the whole input as one token. Remember, in an analyzer, character filters and token filters are optional. Thus, by using the keyword type on the field, we are choosing a noop analyzer and hence skipping the whole analysis process on that field.

The price field is chosen to be of the `scaled_float` type. This is a new type introduced with Elastic 6.0 which internally stores floats as scaled whole numbers. For example, 13.99 will be stored as 1399 with a scaling factor of 100. This is space efficient as float or double datatypes occupy much more space.

To import the data, please follow the instructions in the book's accompanying source code repository at GitHub: `https://github.com/pranav-shukla/learningelasticstack`.

The instructions for importing data are in `chapter-03/README.md`.

After you have imported the data, verify that your data is imported with the following query:

```
GET /amazon_products/products/_search
{
  "query": {
    "match_all": {}
  }
}
```

In the next section, we will look at structured search queries.

Searching from structured data

In certain situations, we want to find out whether the given document should be included or not; that is, a simple binary answer. On the other hand, there are other types of queries which are relevance-based. Such relevance-based queries also return a score against each document to say how well that document fits the query. Most structured queries do not need relevance-based scoring, and the answer is a simple yes/no for any item to be included or excluded from the result. These structured search queries are also referred to as **term level queries**.

Let us understand the flow of a term-level query's execution:

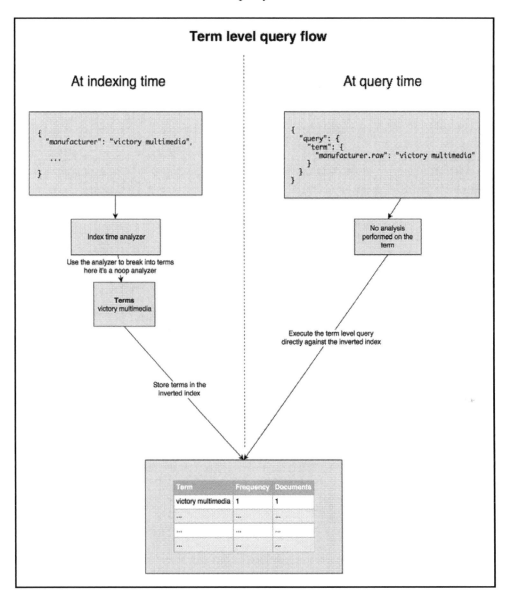

Fig-3.2 Term level query flow

As you can see, the figure is divided into two parts. The left half of the figure depicts what happens at the time of indexing, and the right half of the figure depicts what happens at query time when a term-level query is executed.

Looking at the left half of the figure, we can see what happens during indexing. Here, specifically, we are looking at how the inverted index is built and queried for the `manufacturer.raw` field. Remember, from our definition of the index, `manufacturer.raw` field is of the `keyword` type. The keyword type fields are not analyzed; the field's value is directly stored as a term in the inverted index.

At query time, when we search using a `term` query, which is a term-level query, we see the flow of execution on the right half of the figure. The `term` query, as we will see in this section later, is a term-level query which directly passes on the search term's **victor multimedia** without breaking it down using an analyzer. This is how term-level queries completely skip the analysis process at query time and directly search for the given term in the inverted index.

These term-level queries create a foundation layer on which other, high-level, full-text queries are built. We will look at high-level queries in the next section.

We will cover the following structured or term-level queries:

- Range query
- Exists query
- Term query
- Terms query

Range query

Range queries can be applied to the fields with datatypes that have natural ordering. For example, integers, longs, and dates have a natural order. There is no ambiguity in deciding whether one value is less, equal to, or greater than the other values. Because of this well-defined order of these datatypes, a range query can be applied on them.

We will look at how to apply range queries in the following ways:

- On numeric types
- With score boosting
- On dates

Let us look at the most typical range query on a numeric field.

Range query on numeric types

Suppose we are storing products with their prices in an Elasticsearch index and we want to get all products within a range. The following is the query to get products in the range of $10 to $20:

```
GET /amazon_products/products/_search
{
  "query": {
    "range": {
      "price": {
        "gte": 10,
        "lte": 20
      }
    }
  }
}
```

The response of this query looks like the following:

```
{
  "took": 1,
  "timed_out": false,
  "_shards": {
    "total": 1,
    "successful": 1,
    "failed": 0
  },
  "hits": {
    "total": 201,                                    1
    "max_score": 1,                                  2
    "hits": [
      {
        "_index": "amazon_products",
        "_type": "products",
        "_id": "AV5lK4WiaMctupbz_61a",
        "_score": 1,                                 3
        "_source": {
          "price": "19.99",                          4
          "description": "reel deal casino championship edition (win 98 me
nt 2000 xp)",
          "id": "b00070ouja",
          "title": "reel deal casino championship edition",
          "manufacturer": "phantom efx",
          "tags": []
        }
      },
```

Please take a note of the following:

- The `hits.total` field in the response shows how many search hits were found. Here, there were 201 search hits.
- The `hits.max_score` field shows the score of the best matching document to the query. Since a `range` query is a structured query without any importance or relevance, it is executed as a filter. It doesn't do scoring. All documents have a score of one.
- The `hits.hits` array lists all the actual `hits`. Elasticsearch doesn't return all 201 hits in a single pass by default. It just returns the first 10 records. If you wish to scroll through all results, you can do so easily by issuing multiple queries, as we will see later.
- The **price** field in all search hits would be within the requested range, that is, 10: `<= price <= 20`.

Range query with score boosting

By default, the `range` query assigns a score of 1 to each matching document. What if you are using a range query in conjunction with some other query and you want to assign a higher score to the resulting document if it satisfies some criteria? We will look at compound queries like the bool query, where you can combine multiple types of queries. The range query allows you to provide a boost parameter to boost its score relative to other query/queries that it is combined with:

```
GET /amazon_products/products/_search
{
  "from": 0,
  "size": 10,
  "query": {
    "range": {
      "price": {
        "gte": 10,
        "lte": 20,
        "boost": 2.2
      }
    }
  }
}
```

All documents which pass the filter will have a score of 2.2 instead of 1 in this query.

Range query on dates

The range query can also be applied to date fields since dates are also inherently ordered. You can specify the date format while querying on a date range:

```
GET /orders/order/_search
{
    "query": {
        "range" : {
            "orderDate" : {
                "gte": "01/09/2017",
                "lte": "30/09/2017",
                "format": "dd/MM/yyyy"
            }
        }
    }
}
```

The preceding query will filter all the orders that were placed in the month of September 2017.

Elasticsearch allows us to use dates with or without the time in its queries. It also supports the usage of special terms including now to denote the current time. For example, the following query queries data from the last 7 days up until now, that is, data from exactly 24 x 7 hours till now with the precision of milliseconds.

```
GET /orders/order/_search
{
    "query": {
        "range" : {
            "orderDate" : {
                "gte": "now-7d",
                "lte": "now"
            }
        }
    }
}
```

The ability to use terms such as now makes this easier to comprehend.

Elasticsearch supports many date math operations. As part of its date support, it supports the special keyword `now`. It also supports adding or subtracting time with different units of measurement. It supports single character shorthands such as `y` (year), `M` (month), `w` (week), `d` (day), `h` or `H` (hours), `m` (minutes), and `s` (seconds). For example, `now - 1y` would mean a time of exactly one year ago till this moment. It is possible to round time into different units. For example, to round the interval by day inclusive of both the start and end interval day, use `"gte": "now - 7d/d"` or `"lte": "now/d"`. Specifying `/d` rounds the time by days.

The range query runs in filter context by default. It doesn't calculate any scores and the score is always set to one for all matching documents.

Exists query

Sometimes it is useful to get only those records which have non-null and non-empty values in a certain field. For example, getting all products which have description fields defined:

```
GET /amazon_products/products/_search
{
  "query": {
    "exists": {
      "field": "description"
    }
  }
}
```

The exists query turns the query into a filter; in other words, it runs in a **Filter Context**. This is similar to the range query where the scores don't matter.

 What is a **Filter Context**? When the query is just about filtering our documents, that is, deciding whether to include the document in the result or not, it is sufficient to skip the scoring process. Elasticsearch can skip the scoring process for certain types of queries and assign a uniform score of one to each document which passes the filter criteria. This not only speeds up the query (as the scoring process is skipped), but also allows Elasticsearch to cache the results of filters. Elasticsearch caches the results of filters by maintaining arrays of zeros and ones.

Term query

How would you find all products made by a particular manufacturer? We know that the manufacturer field in our data is of the string type. The name of a manufacturer can possibly contain white spaces. What we are looking for here is an exact search. For example, when we search for **victory multimedia**, we don't want any results which have a manufacturer that contains just **victory** or just **multimedia**. You can use the term query to achieve that.

When we defined the manufacturer field, we had stored it as both a `text` and `keyword` field. When doing an exact match, we have to use the field with the `keyword` type:

```
GET /amazon_products/products/_search
{
  "query": {
    "term": {
      "manufacturer.raw": "victory multimedia"
    }
  }
}
```

The term query is a low-level query in the sense that it doesn't perform any analysis on the term. Also, it directly runs against the inverted index constructed from the mentioned term field, in this case against the `manufacturer.raw` field. By default, the term query runs in query context and hence calculates scores.

The response looks like the following (only the partial response is included):

```
{
  . . .
  "hits": {
    "total": 3,
    "max_score": 5.965414,
    "hits": [
      {
        "_index": "amazon_products",
        "_type": "products",
        "_id": "AV5rBfPNNI_2eZGciIHC",
        "_score": 5.965414,
  . . .
```

As we can see, each document is scored by default. To run the term query in Filter Context without scoring, it needs to be wrapped inside a `constant_score` filter:

```
GET /amazon_products/products/_search
{
  "query": {
    "constant_score": {
      "filter": {
        "term": {
          "manufacturer.raw": "victory multimedia"
        }
      }
    }
  }
}
```

This query will now return results with a score of one for all matching documents. We will look at the `constant_score` query later in the chapter. For now, you can imagine that it turns a scoring query into a non-scoring query. In all queries where we don't need to know how well a document fits the query, we can speed up the query by wrapping it inside `constant_score` with a `filter`. There are also other types of compound queries that can help in converting different types of queries and combining other queries; we will look at them when we examine compound queries.

Searching from full text

Full-text queries can work on unstructured text fields. These queries are **aware** of the analysis process. Full-text queries apply the analyzer on the search terms before performing the actual search operation. It finds out the right analyzer to be applied by first checking if a field-level `search_analyzer` is defined, and then by checking if a field-level analyzer is defined. If analyzers at field level are not defined, it tries the analyzer defined at the index level.

The full-text queries are thus aware of the analysis process on the underlying field and apply the right analysis process before forming the actual search queries. These analysis-aware queries are also called **high-level queries**. Let us understand how the high-level query flow works.

Here, we can see how one high-level query on the field title will be executed. Remember from our index definition earlier that the title field is of the text type. At indexing time, the value is analyzed using the analyzer for the field. In this case, it was a Standard Analyzer, and hence the inverted index contains all broken down terms such as gods, heroes, rome, and so on, as depicted in the following figure:

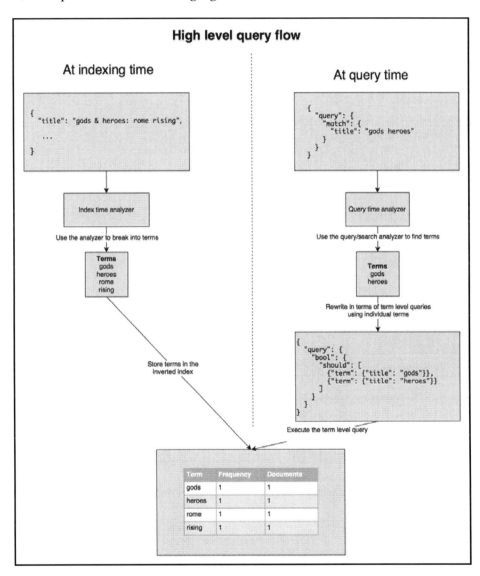

Fig-3.3 High-level query flow

At query time (see the right half of the figure), we issue a `match` query which is a high-level query. We will cover the match query in this section later on; it is one of the high-level queries. The search terms passed to the `match` query are analyzed using the Standard Analyzer. The individual terms after applying the Standard Analyzer are then used to come up with individual term-level queries.

The example here results in multiple term queries—one for each term after applying the analyzer. The original search term was **gods heroes** which results in two terms, **gods** and **heroes**, which are used as individual terms in their own term queries. The two term queries are then combined using a `bool` query, which is a compound query. We will also look at different compound queries like bool queries in the next section about compound queries.

We will cover the following full-text queries in the following sections:

- Match query
- Match phrase query
- Multi match query

Match query

A match query is the default query for most full-text search requirements. It is one of the high-level queries which is aware of the analyzer used for the underlying field. Let us understand what this means under the hood.

For example, when you use the match query on a keyword field, it knows that the underlying field is a `keyword` field and hence the search terms are not analyzed at the time of querying:

```
GET /amazon_products/products/_search
{
  "query": {
    "match": {
      "manufacturer.raw": "victory multimedia"
    }
  }
}
```

The match query in this case behaves just like a term query, which we understood in the previous section. It does not analyze the search term's **victory multimedia** as the separate terms **victory** and **multimedia**. This is because we are querying a `keyword` field, `manufacturer.raw`. In fact, in this particular case the match query gets converted into a term query, such as the following one:

```
GET /amazon_products/products/_search
{
  "query": {
    "term": {
      "manufacturer.raw": "victory multimedia"
    }
  }
}
```

The term query returns the same scores as the match query in this case, as they are both executed against a `keyword` field.

Let us see what happens if you execute a match query against a `text` field, which is the real use case of a full-text query:

```
GET /amazon_products/products/_search
{
  "query": {
    "match": {
      "manufacturer": "victory multimedia"
    }
  }
}
```

When we execute the match query, we expect it to do the following things:

- Search for the terms **victory multimedia** across all documents within the manufacturer field
- Find the best matching documents sorted by score in descending order
- If both terms appear in the same order right next to each other in a document, that document should get a higher score than other documents which have both terms but not in the same order, or not next to each other
- Include the documents which have either victory or multimedia in the result but give them a lower score

The match query with default parameters does all of these things to find the best matching documents in order, according to their scores (high to low).

By default, when only search terms are specified, this is how the `match` query behaves. It is possible to specify additional options to the `match` query. Let us look at some typical options that you would specify:

- Operator
- minimum_should_match
- Fuzziness

Operator

By default, if the search term specified results in multiple terms after applying the analyzer, we need a way to combine the results from individual terms. As we saw in the preceding example, the default behavior of the `match` query is to combine the results using the *or* operator, that is, one of the terms has to be present in the document's field.

This can be changed to use the `and` operator using the following query:

```
GET /amazon_products/products/_search
{
  "query": {
    "match": {
      "manufacturer": {
        "query": "victory multimedia",
        "operator": "and"
      }
    }
  }
}
```

In this case, both the terms victory and multimedia should be present in the document's manufacturer field.

minimum_should_match

Instead of applying the `and` operator, we can keep the or operator and specify at least how many terms should match in a given document for it to be included in the result. This allows for finer grained control:

```
GET /amazon_products/products/_search
{
  "query": {
    "match": {
      "manufacturer": {
```

```
      "query": "victory multimedia",
      "minimum_should_match": 2
    }
   }
  }
 }
```

The preceding query behaves in a similar way to the `and` operator, as there are two terms in the query and we have specified that, at the minimum, two terms should match.

With `minimum_should_match`, we can specify something similar to at least three of the terms matching in the document.

Fuzziness

With the `fuzziness` parameter, we can turn the match query into a fuzzy query. This fuzziness is based on the Levenshtein edit distance to turn one term into another by making a number of edits to the original text. The edits can be insertions, deletions, substitutions, or the transposition of characters in the original term. The `fuzziness` parameter can take one of the following values: 0, 1, 2, or AUTO.

For example, the following query has a misspelled word, **victor** instead of **victory**. Since we are using a `fuzziness` of 1, it will still be able to find all **victory multimedia** records:

```
GET /amazon_products/products/_search
{
  "query": {
    "match": {
      "manufacturer": {
        "query": "victor multimedia",
        "fuzziness": 1
      }
    }
  }
}
```

If we wanted to still allow more room for errors to be correctible, the fuzziness should be increased to 2. For example, a `fuzziness` of 2 will even match victer. Victory is two edits away from victer:

```
GET /amazon_products/products/_search
{
  "query": {
    "match": {
      "manufacturer": {
```

```
        "query": "victer multimedia",
        "fuzziness": 2
      }
    }
  }
}
```

The value AUTO means that the fuzziness numeric value of 0, 1, 2 is determined automatically based on the length of the original term. With AUTO, terms of up to two characters have fuzziness = 0 (must match exactly), terms from three to five characters have fuzziness = 1, and terms with more than five characters have fuzziness = 2.

Fuzziness comes at its own cost because Elasticsearch has to generate extra terms to match against. To control the number of terms, it supports the following additional parameters:

- max_expansions: The maximum number of terms after expanding.
- prefix_length: A number, such as zero, one, two, and so on. The edits for introducing fuzziness will not be done in the prefix characters as defined by the prefix_length parameter.

Match phrase query

When you want to match a sequence of words as opposed to separate terms in the document, the match phrase query can be useful.

For example, the following text is present as part of the description for one of the products:

```
real video saltware aquarium on your desktop!
```

What we want is all the products which have this exact sequence of words right next to each other: real video saltware aquarium. We can use the match_phrase query to achieve it. The match query will not work as it doesn't consider the sequence of terms and their proximity to each other. The match query can include all those documents that have any of the terms, even when they are out of order within the document:

```
GET /amazon_products/products/_search
{
  "query": {
    "match_phrase": {
      "description": {
        "query": "real video saltware aquarium"
      }
    }
  }
}
```

```
}
```

The response will look like the following:

```
{
  ...,
  "hits": {
    "total": 1,
    "max_score": 22.338196,
    "hits": [
      {
        "_index": "amazon_products",
        "_type": "products",
        "_id": "AV5rBfasNI_2eZGciIbg",
        "_score": 22.338196,
        "_source": {
          "price": "19.95",
          "description": "real video saltware aquarium on your
desktop!product information see real fish swimming on your desktop in full-
motion video! you'll find exotic saltwater fish such as sharks angelfish
and more! enjoy the beauty and serenity of a real aquarium at yourdeskt",
          "id": "b00004t2un",
          "title": "sales skills 2.0 ages 10+",
          "manufacturer": "victory multimedia",
          "tags": []
        }
      }
    ]
  }
}
```

The match_phrase query also supports the slop parameter which allows you to specify an integer: 0, 1, 2, 3, and so on. slop relaxes the number of words/terms that can be skipped at the time of querying.

For example, a slop value of 1 would allow one missing word in the search text but would still match the document:

```
GET /amazon_products/products/_search
{
  "query": {
    "match_phrase": {
      "description": {
        "query": "real video aquarium",
        "slop": 1
      }
    }
  }
}
```

```
}
```

The slop of 1 would allow the user to search with real video aquarium or real saltware aquarium and still match the document that contains the exact phrase real video saltware aquarium. The default value of slop is zero.

Multi match query

The multi match query is extension of the match query. The multi match query allows us to run the match query across multiple fields, and also allows many options to calculate the overall score of the documents.

The multi match query can be used with different options. We will look at the following options:

- Querying multiple fields with defaults
- Boosting one or more fields
- With types of multi match queries

Let us look at each option, one by one.

Querying multiple fields with defaults

We want to provide a product search functionality in our web application. When the end user searches for some terms, we want to query both the **title** and **description** fields. This can be done using the multi match query.

The following query will find all documents which have the terms **monitor** or **aquarium** in the title or the description fields:

```
GET /amazon_products/products/_search
{
  "query": {
    "multi_match": {
      "query": "monitor aquarium",
      "fields": ["title", "description"]
    }
  }
}
```

This query gives equal importance to both the fields. Let us look at how to boost one or more fields.

Boosting one or more fields

In an e-commerce type of web application, often the user intends to search for some item, and he/she might search for some keywords. What if we want the **title** field to be more important than the description? If one or more of the search terms appears in the **title**, it is definitely a more relevant product than the ones that have those values only in the description. It is possible to boost the score of the document if a match is found in a particular field.

Let us make the title field three times more important than the description field. This can be done by using the following syntax:

```
GET /amazon_products/products/_search
{
  "query": {
    "multi_match": {
      "query": "monitor aquarium",
      "fields": ["title^3", "description"]
    }
  }
}
```

The multi match query offers more control regarding how to combine the scores from different fields. Let us look at the options.

With types of multi match queries

In this section, we have learnt about full-text queries which are also known as high-level queries. These queries find the **best matching** documents according to the score. The high-level queries internally make use of some of the term-level queries. In the next section, we will understand how to write compound queries.

Writing compound queries

This class of queries can be used to combine one or more queries to come up with a more complex query. Some compound queries convert scoring queries into non-scoring queries, and combine multiple scoring and non-scoring queries. We will look at the following compound queries:

- Constant score query
- Bool query

Constant score query

Elasticsearch supports querying both structured data and full text. While full-text queries need scoring mechanisms to find the **best matching** documents, structured searches don't need scoring. The constant score query allows us to convert a scoring query which normally runs in query context to a non-scoring filter context. The constant score query is a very important tool in your toolbox.

For example, the term query is normally run in a query context. That means when Elasticsearch executes a term query, it not only filters the documents but also scores all of them:

```
GET /amazon_products/products/_search
{
  "query": {
    "term": {
      "manufacturer.raw": "victory multimedia"
    }
  }
}
```

Notice the highlighted part, the bold text. This part is the actual term query. By default, the query JSON element that contains the bold text defines a query context.

The response contains the score for every document. Please see the following partial response:

```
{
  ...,
  "hits": {
    "total": 3,
    "max_score": 5.966147,
    "hits": [
      {
```

```
          "_index": "amazon_products",
          "_type": "products",
          "_id": "AV5rBfasNI_2eZGciIbg",
          "_score": 5.966147,
          "_source": {
            "price": "19.95",
    ...
  }
```

Here we just intended to filter the documents, so there was no need to calculate the relevance score of each document.

The original query can be converted to run in a filter context using the following constant score query:

```
GET /amazon_products/products/_search
{
  "query": {
    "constant_score": {
      "filter": {
        "term": {
          "manufacturer.raw": "victory multimedia"
        }
      }
    }
  }
}
```

As you can see, we have wrapped the original highlighted term element and its child. It assigns a neutral score of 1 to each document by default. Please see the partial response in the following code:

```
{
  ...,
  "hits": {
    "total": 3,
    "max_score": 1,
    "hits": [
      {
        "_index": "amazon_products",
        "_type": "products",
        "_id": "AV5rBfasNI_2eZGciIbg",
        "_score": 1,
        "_source": {
          "price": "19.95",
          "description": ...
      }
    ...
```

```
}
```

It is possible to specify a `boost` parameter which will assign that score instead of the neutral score of 1:

```
GET /amazon_products/products/_search
{
  "query": {
    "constant_score": {
      "filter": {
        "term": {
          "manufacturer.raw": "victory multimedia"
        }
      },
      "boost": 1.2
    }
  }
}
```

What is the benefit of boosting the score of every document in this filter to 1.2? Well, there is no benefit if this query is used in an isolated way. When this query is combined with other queries, using a query such as the `bool` query, the boosted score becomes important. All the documents that pass this filter will have higher scores compared to other documents that are combined from other queries.

Let us look at the bool query next.

Bool query

The bool query in Elasticsearch is your Swiss Army knife. It can help you write many types of complex queries. If you are coming from an SQL background, you already know how to filter based on multiple AND and OR conditions in the WHERE clause. The bool query allows you to combine multiple scoring and non-scoring queries.

Let us first see how to implement simple AND and OR conjunctions.

A bool query has the following sections:

```
GET /amazon_products/products/_search
{
  "query": {
    "bool": {
      "must": [...],      scoring queries executed in query context
      "should": [...],    scoring queries executed in query context
      "filter": {},       non-scoring queries executed in filter context
```

```
            "must_not": [...]      non-scoring queries executed in filter context
        }
    }
}
```

The queries included in must and should clauses are executed in a query context unless the whole bool query is included inside a filter context.

The filter and `must_not` queries are always executed in the filter context. They will always return a score of zero and only contribute to filtering the documents.

Let us understand how to form a non-scoring query that just performs a structured search. We will understand how to formulate the following types of structured search queries using the Bool query:

- Combining OR conditions
- Combining AND and OR conditions
- Adding NOT conditions

Combining OR conditions

Find all products in the price range 10 to 13 OR manufactured by `valuesoft`:

```
GET /amazon_products/products/_search
{
  "query": {
    "constant_score": {
      "filter": {
        "bool": {
          "should": [
            {
              "range": {
                "price": {
                  "gte": 10,
                  "lte": 13
                }
              }
            },
            {
              "term": {
                "manufacturer.raw": {
                  "value": "valuesoft"
                }
              }
            }
```

```
            ]
          }
        }
      }
    }
  }
}
```

Since we want to OR the conditions, we have placed them under should. Since we are not interested in the scores, we have wrapped our bool query inside a constant score query.

Combining conditions AND and OR conditions

Find all products in the price range 10 to 13 AND manufactured by valuesoft or pinnacle:

```
GET /amazon_products/products/_search
{
  "query": {
    "constant_score": {
      "filter": {
        "bool": {
          "must": [
            {
              "range": {
                "price": {
                  "gte": 10,
                  "lte": 30
                }
              }
            }
          ],
          "should": [
            {
              "term": {
                "manufacturer.raw": {
                  "value": "valuesoft"
                }
              }
            },
            {
              "term": {
                "manufacturer.raw": {
                  "value": "pinnacle"
                }
              }
            }
```

```
            ]
          }
        }
      }
    }
  }
```

Please notice that all conditions that need to be ORed together are placed inside `should`. The conditions that need to be ANDed together, can be placed inside the `must` element. Although it is also possible to put all the conditions to be ANDed in the `filter` element as well.

Adding NOT conditions

It is possible to add NOT conditions, that is, specifically filtering out certain clauses using the `must_not` clause in the `bool` filter.

For example, find all products in the price range 10 to 20, but they must not be manufactured by `encore`. The following query will do just that:

```
GET /amazon_products/products/_search
{
  "query": {
    "constant_score": {
      "filter": {
        "bool": {
          "must": [
            {
              "range": {
                "price": {
                  "gte": 10,
                  "lte": 20
                }
              }
            }
          ],
          "must_not": [
            {
              "term": {
                "manufacturer.raw": "encore"
              }
            }
          ]
        }
      }
    }
  }
}
```

```
        }
    }
```

The `bool` query with the `must_not` element is useful to `negate` any query. For negating or applying a `NOT` filter to the query, it should be wrapped inside the bool with `must_not`, as follows.

```
GET /amazon_products/products/_search
{
  "query": {
    "bool": {
      "must_not": {
        .... original query to be negated ...
      }
    }
  }
}
```

Notice that we do not need to wrap the query into a constant score query when we are only using `must_not` to negate a query. The `must_not` query is always executed in a filter context.

This concludes our understanding of the different types of compound queries. There are more compound queries supported by Elasticsearch. They include the following:

- Dis Max query
- Function Score query
- Boosting query
- Indices query

Covering all these queries is beyond the scope of this book. Having learnt the other compound queries in depth, you are now well equipped to try the other queries which aren't covered here. Please refer to the Elasticsearch reference documentation to learn about their usage.

Summary

In this chapter, we took a deep dive into the search capabilities of Elasticsearch. We understood the role of analyzers and the anatomy of an analyzer. We have seen how to use some of the built-in analyzers that come with Elasticsearch, and we have also seen how to create custom analyzers. Along with a solid background regarding analyzers, we learnt about two main types of queries—term-level queries and full-text queries. We also understood how to compose different queries into more complex queries using one of the compound queries.

This chapter provided you with sound knowledge to get a foothold for querying Elasticsearch data. There are many more types of queries supported by Elasticsearch, but we have covered most essential ones. This should help you get started and help you understand other types of queries from the Elasticsearch reference documentation.

In Chapter 4, *Analytics with Elasticsearch,* we will learn about the analytics capabilities of Elasticsearch. With that chapter under your belt, we will conclude by learning the core component of Elastic Stack and Elasticsearch, and we will be well equipped to understand the other components of Elastic Stack.

4
Analytics with Elasticsearch

On our journey of learning about Elastic Stack 6.0, we have gained a strong understanding of Elasticsearch. We have learned about the strong foundations of Elasticsearch in the previous two chapters, and gained an in-depth understanding of its search use cases.

The underlying technology Apache Lucene was originally developed for text search use cases. Due to innovations in Apache Lucene and additional innovations in Elasticsearch, it has also emerged as a very powerful analytics engine. In this chapter, we will understand how Elasticsearch can serve as your analytics engine. We will look at the following:

- The basics of aggregations
- Preparing data for analysis
- Metric aggregations
- Bucket aggregations
- Pipeline aggregations

We will learn all of this by using a real-world dataset. Let us start by understanding the basics of aggregations.

The basics of aggregations

In contrast to search, analytics deals with the bigger picture. Searching addresses the need for zooming in to a few records; analytics addresses the need for zooming out and slicing the data in different ways. While learning about searching, we used the API of the following form:

```
POST /<index_name>/<type_name>/_search
{
  "query":
  {
    ... type of query ...
  }
```

}

All aggregation queries take a common form. Let us understand the structure.

The aggregations or `aggs` element allows us to aggregate data. All aggregation requests take the following form:

```
POST /<index_name>/<type_name>/_search
{
   "aggs": {
      ... type of aggregation ...
            },
   "query": {  ... type of query ... },          //optional query part
   "size": 0                                      //size typically set to
0
}
```

The `aggs` element should contain the actual aggregation query. The body depends on the type of aggregation that we want to do. We will cover these aggregations in this chapter.

The optional `query` element defines the context of the aggregation. The aggregation considers all of the documents in the given index and type if the `query` element is not specified (you can imagine it to be equivalent to the `match_all` query when no query is present). If we want to limit the context of the aggregation, it can be done by specifying the `query`. For example, we may not want to consider all the data for aggregation, but only certain documents which satisfy a particular condition. This query filters the documents to be fed to the actual `aggs` query.

The `size` element specifies how many of the search hits should be returned in the response. The default value of `size` is 10. If `size` is not specified, the response will contain 10 hits from the context under the query. Typically, if we are only interested in getting aggregation results, we should set the size to zero to avoid getting any results along with the aggregation result.

Broadly, there are four types of aggregations that Elasticsearch supports:

- Bucket aggregations
- Metric aggregations
- Matrix aggregations
- Pipeline aggregations

Bucket aggregations

Bucket aggregations segment the data in question (defined by the `query` context) into various buckets identified by the buckets key. Bucket aggregation evaluates each document in the context by deciding which bucket it falls into. At the end, bucket aggregation has a set of distinct buckets with their respective bucket keys and documents that fall into those buckets.

For people who come from an SQL background, a query that has GROUP BY, such as the following query, is doing this:

```
SELECT column1, count(*) FROM table1 GROUP BY column1;
```

This query divides the table by the different values of column 1 and returns a count of documents within each value of column 1. This is an example of bucket aggregation. There are many different types of bucket aggregation supported by Elasticsearch which we will go through in this chapter.

Bucket aggregations can be present on the top or outermost level in an aggregation query. Bucket aggregations can also be nested inside other bucket aggregations.

Metric aggregations

Metric aggregations work on numeric types of fields. They compute the aggregate value of a numeric field in the given context. For example, we have a table containing the results of a students examination. Each record contains marks obtained by the student. A metric aggregation can compute different aggregates of that numeric score column. Some examples are sum, average, minimum, maximum, and so on.

In SQL terms, the following query gives a rough analogy of what a metric aggregation may do:

```
SELECT avg(score) FROM results;
```

This query computes the average score in the given context. Here the context is the whole table, that is, all students. This is an example of metric aggregation.

Metric aggregation can be placed on the top or outermost level in the aggregations query. Metric aggregations can also be nested inside bucket aggregations. Metric aggregations cannot nest other types of aggregations inside of them.

Matrix aggregations

Matrix aggregations were introduced with Elasticsearch version 5.0. Matrix aggregations work on multiple fields and compute matrixes across all the documents within the query context.

Matrix aggregations can be nested inside bucket aggregations but bucket aggregations cannot be nested inside of matrix aggregations. This is still a relatively new feature. Coverage of matrix aggregations is not within the scope of this book.

Pipeline aggregations

Pipeline aggregations are higher order aggregations which can aggregate the output of other aggregations. These are useful for computing something, such as derivatives. We will look at some pipeline aggregations later in the chapter.

This was an overview about the different types of aggregations supported by Elasticsearch at a high level. Pipeline aggregations and matrix aggregations are relatively new and have fewer use cases compared to metric and bucket aggregations. We will look at metric and bucket aggregations in greater depth later in the chapter.

In the next section, we will load and prepare data to understand these aggregations throughout this chapter.

Preparing data for analysis

We will consider an example of network traffic data generated from Wi-Fi routers. Throughout this chapter, we will analyze the data from this example. It is important to understand what the records in the underlying system look like and what they represent. We will cover the following topics while we prepare and load the data into the local Elasticsearch instance:

- Understanding the structure of data
- Loading the data using Logstash

Understanding the structure of data

The following diagram depicts the design of the system, to help you gain a better understanding of the problem and the structure of data collected:

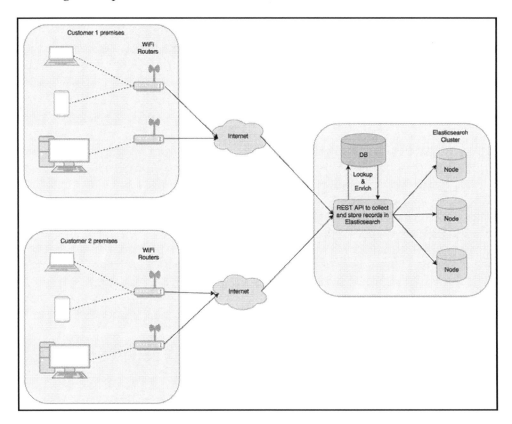

Fig 4.1 Network traffic and bandwidth usage data for Wi-Fi traffic and storage in Elasticsearch

The data is collected by the system with the following objectives:

- In the left half of the figure, there are multiple squares representing one customer's premises, with the Wi-Fi routers deployed on that site, along with all devices connected to those Wi-Fi routers. The connected devices include laptops, mobile devices, desktop computers, and so on. Each device has a unique MAC address and a user associated with that device.

- The right half of the figure represents the centralized system which collects and stores data from multiple customers into a centralized Elasticsearch cluster. Our focus will be on how to design this centralized Elasticsearch cluster and the index to gain meaningful insight.

- The routers at each customer site collect additional metrics for each connected device, such as data downloaded, data uploaded, and URLs or domain names accessed by the client in a specific time interval. The Wi-Fi routers collect such metrics and send them periodically to the centralized API server for long-term storage and analysis.

- When the data is sent by the Wi-Fi routers, it contains fewer fields, mainly the metrics captured by the Wi-Fi routers and the MAC address of the end-device for which those metrics are collected. The API server looks up and enriches the records with more information useful for analytics before storing it into Elasticsearch. The MAC address is looked up to find out the associated user to whom the device is assigned. It also looks up additional dimensions such as **department** of the user.

What are metrics and dimensions? Metric is a common term used in the analytics world to represent a numeric measure. A common example of a metric is the amount of data downloaded or uploaded in a given time period. The term **dimension** is usually used to refer to extra/auxiliary information, usually of the string datatype. In the current example, we use a MAC address to look up auxiliary information related to that MAC address, namely the username of the user to whom the device is assigned in the system. Additionally, the name of the department to which the user belongs is also another dimension.

Finally, the enriched records are stored in Elasticsearch in a flat data structure. One record looks like the following one:

```
"_source": {
  "customer": "Google"          // Customer to which the WiFi router and
device belongs to
  "accessPointId": "AP-59484",  // Identifier of the WiFi router or Access
Point
  "time": 1506148631061,        // Time of the record in milliseconds since
Epoch Jan 1, 1970
  "mac": "c6:ec:7d:c6:3d:8d",   // MAC address of the client device

  "username": "Pedro Harrison", // Name of the user to whom the device is
assigned
  "department": "Operations",   // Department of the user to which the
device belongs to
```

```
    "application": "CNBC",         // Application name or domain name for
which traffic is reported
    "category": "News",            // Category of the application

    "networkId": "Internal",       // SSID of the network
    "band": "5 GHz", // Band 5 GHz or 2.4 GHz

    "location": "23.102789,72.595381", // latitude & longitude separated by
comma

    "uploadTotal": 1340,        // Bytes uploaded since the last report
    "downloadTotal": 2129,      // Bytes downloaded since the last report
    "usage": 3469,              // Total bytes downloaded and uploaded in
current period

    "uploadCurrent": 22.33,     // Upload speed in bytes/sec in current period
    "downloadCurrent": 35.48,   // Download speed in bytes/sec in current
period
    "bandwidth": 57.82,         // Total speed in bytes/sec (Upload speed +
download speed)

    "signalStrength": -25,      // Signal strength between WiFi router and
device
    ...
}
```

One record contains various metrics for the given end-client device at the given time.

Please note that all the data included in this example is synthentic. Although the names of customers, users, and MAC addresses look realistic, the data was generated using a simulator. The data doesn't belong to any real customers.

Now that we know what our data represents and what each record represents, let's load the data in our local instance.

Loading the data using Logstash

To import the data, please follow the instructions in the book's accompanying source code repository on GitHub: `https://github.com/pranav-shukla/learningelasticstack`.

Please clone or download the repository from GitHub. The instructions for importing data are at the following path within the project: `chapter-04/README.md`.

After you have imported the data, verify that your data is imported with the following query:

```
GET /bigginsight/usageReport/_search
{
  "query": {
    "match_all": {}
          },
  "size": 1
}
```

You should see a response like the following one:

```
{
  ...
  "hits":
    {
    "total": 242835,
    "max_score": 1,
    "hits": [
          {
        "_index": "bigginsight",
        "_type": "usageReport",
        "_id": "AV7Sy4FofN33RKOLlVHO",
        "_score": 1,
        "_source": {
          "inactiveMs": 1316,
          "bandwidth": 51.03333333333333,
          "signalStrength": -58,
          "accessPointId": "AP-1D7F0",
          "usage": 3062,
          "downloadCurrent": 39.93333333333333,
          "uploadCurrent": 11.1,
          "mac": "d2:a1:74:28:c0:5a",
          "tags": [],
          "@timestamp": "2017-09-30T12:38:25.867Z",
          "application": "Dropbox",
          "downloadTotal": 2396,
          "@version": "1",
          "networkId": "Guest",
          "location": "23.102900,72.595611",
          "time": 1506164775655,
          "band": "2.4 GHz",
          "department": "HR",
          "category": "File Sharing",
          "uploadTotal": 666,
          "username": "Cheryl Stokes",
          "customer": "Microsoft"
```

```
            }
          }
        ]
      }
    }
  }
```

Now that we have the data that we want, we can get started with learning about different types of aggregations. We will learn different types of aggregations on the data that we just loaded. You can find all the queries used in this chapter in the accompanying source code at the GitHub repository, at the location `chapter-04/queries.txt`. The queries can be run directly in Kibana Dev Tools, as we have seen earlier.

Metric aggregations

Metric aggregations work with numeric data, computing one or more aggregate metrics within the given context. The context could be a query, filter, or no query to include the whole index/type. Metric aggregations can also be nested inside other bucket aggregations. In this case, these metrics will be computed for each bucket in the bucket aggregations.

We will start with simple metric aggregations without nesting them inside bucket aggregations. When we learn about bucket aggregations later in the chapter, we will also learn how to use metric aggregations inside bucket aggregations.

We will learn about the following metric aggregations:

- Sum, average, min, and max aggregations
- Stats and extended stats aggregations
- Cardinality aggregation

Let us learn about them one by one.

Sum, average, min, and max aggregations

Finding the sum of a field, the minimum value for a field, the maximum value for a field, or an average, are very common operations. For the people who are familiar with SQL, the query to find the sum would look like the following:

```
SELECT sum(downloadTotal) FROM usageReport;
```

The preceding query will calculate the sum of the `downloadTotal` field across all records in the table. This requires going through all records of the table or all records in the given context and adding the values of the given fields.

In Elasticsearch, a similar query can be written using the sum aggregation. Let us understand the sum aggregation first.

Sum aggregation

Here is how to write a simple sum aggregation:

```
GET bigginsight/_search
{
 "aggregations": {                          1
    "download_sum": {                       2
      "sum": {                              3
        "field": "downloadTotal"            4
      }
    }
  },
  "size": 0                                 5
}
```

- The **aggs** or **aggregations** element at the top level should wrap any aggregation.
- Give a name to the aggregation; here we are doing the sum aggregation on the downloadTotal field and hence the name we chose is `download_sum`. You can name it anything. This field will be useful while looking up this particular aggregation's result in the response.
- We are doing a sum aggregation, hence the `sum` element.
- We want to do term aggregation on the `downloadTotal` field.
- Specify `size = 0` to prevent raw search results from being returned. We just want aggregation results and not the search results in this case. Since we haven't specified any top level `query` elements, it matches all documents. We do not want any raw documents (or search hits) in the result.

The response should look like the following:

```
{
  "took": 92,
  ...
  "hits": {
    "total": 242836,                       1
    "max_score": 0,
```

```
    "hits": []
  },
  "aggregations": {                          2
    "download_sum": {                        3
      "value": 2197438700                    4
    }
  }
}
```

Let us understand the key aspects of the response. The key parts are numbered 1, 2, 3, and so on, and are explained in the following points:

- The `hits.total` element shows the number of documents that were considered or were in the context of the query. If there was no additional query or filter specified, it will include all documents in the type or index.
- Just like the request, this response is wrapped inside aggregations to indicate as such.
- The response of the aggregation requested by us was named `download_sum`, hence we get our response from the sum aggregation inside an element with the same name.
- The actual value after applying the sum aggregation.

The average, min, and max aggregations are very similar. Let's look at them briefly.

Average aggregation

The average aggregation finds an average across all documents in the querying context:

```
GET bigginsight/_search
{
  "aggregations": {
    "download_average": {                    1
      "avg": {                               2
        "field": "downloadTotal"
      }
    }
  },
  "size": 0
}
```

The only notable differences from the sum aggregation are as follows:

- We chose a different name, `download_average`, to make it apparent that the aggregation is trying to compute the average.
- The type of aggregation that we are doing is `avg` instead of the `sum` aggregation that we were doing earlier.

The response structure is identical but the value field will now represent the average of the requested field.

The min and max aggregations are the exactly same.

Min aggregation

Here is how we will find the minimum value of the `downloadTotal` field in the entire index/type:

```
GET bigginsight/_search
{
  "aggregations": {
    "download_min": {
      "min": {
        "field": "downloadTotal"
      }
    }
  },
  "size": 0
}
```

Let's finally look at max aggregation also.

Max aggregation

Here is how we will find the maximum value of the `downloadTotal` field in the entire index/type:

```
GET bigginsight/_search
{
  "aggregations": {
    "download_max": {
      "max": {
        "field": "downloadTotal"
      }
    }
```

```
    },
    "size": 0
  }
```

These aggregations were really simple. Now let's look at some more advanced yet simple stats and extended stats aggregations.

Stats and extended stats aggregations

These aggregations compute some common statistics in a single request without having to issue multiple requests. This saves resources on the Elasticsearch side as well because the statistics are computed in a single pass rather than being requested multiple times. The client code also becomes simpler if you are interested in more than one of these statistics. Let's look at the stats aggregation first.

Stats aggregation

The stats aggregation computes the sum, average, min, max, and count of documents in a single pass:

```
GET bigginsight/_search
{
  "aggregations": {
    "download_stats": {
      "stats": {
        "field": "downloadTotal"
      }
    }
  },
  "size": 0
}
```

The structure of the stats request is the same as the other metric aggregations we have seen so far, so nothing special is going on here.

The response should look like the following:

```
{
  "took": 4,
  ...,
  "hits": {
    "total": 242836,
    "max_score": 0,
    "hits": []
```

```
    },
    "aggregations": {
      "download_stats": {
        "count": 242835,
        "min": 0,
        "max": 241213,
        "avg": 9049.102065188297,
        "sum": 2197438700
      }
    }
  }
```

As you can see, the response with the download_stats element contains count, min, max, average, and sum; everything is included in the same response. This is very handy as it reduces the overhead of multiple requests and also simplifies the client code.

Let us look at the extended stats aggregation.

Extended stats Aggregation

The extended stats aggregation returns a few more statistics in addition to the ones returned by the stats aggregation:

```
GET bigginsight/_search
{
  "aggregations": {
    "download_estats": {
      "extended_stats": {
        "field": "downloadTotal"
      }
    }
  },
  "size": 0
}
```

The response looks like the following:

```
{
  "took": 15,
  "timed_out": false,
  ...,
  "hits": {
    "total": 242836,
    "max_score": 0,
    "hits": []
  },
  "aggregations": {
    "download_estats": {
      "count": 242835,
      "min": 0,
      "max": 241213,
      "avg": 9049.102065188297,
      "sum": 2197438700,
      "sum_of_squares": 133545882701698,
      "variance": 468058704.9782911,
      "std_deviation": 21634.664429528162,
      "std_deviation_bounds": {
        "upper": 52318.43092424462,
        "lower": -34220.22679386803
      }
    }
  }
}
```

It also returns the sum of squares, variance, standard deviation, and standard deviation bounds.

Cardinality aggregation

Finding the count of unique elements can be done with the cardinality aggregation. It is similar to finding the result of a query such as the following:

```
select count(*) from (select distinct username from usageReport) u;
```

Finding the cardinality or the number of unique values for a specific field is a very common requirement. If you have click-stream from the different visitors on your website, you may want to find out how many unique visitors you got in a given day, week, or month.

Let us understand how we find out the count of unique users for which we have network traffic data:

```
GET bigginsight/_search
{
  "aggregations": {
     "unique_visitors": {
        "cardinality": {
           "field": "username"
        }
     }
  },
  "size": 0
}
```

The cardinality aggregation response is just like the other metric aggregations:

```
{
  "took": 110,
  ...,
  "hits": {
    "total": 242836,
    "max_score": 0,
    "hits": []
  },
  "aggregations": {
    "unique_visitors": {
       "value": 79
    }
  }
}
```

Now that we have understood the simplest forms of aggregations, we can look at some of the bucket aggregations.

Bucket aggregations

Bucket aggregations are useful to analyze how the whole relates to its parts to gain better insight. They help in segmenting the data into smaller parts. Each type of bucket aggregation slices the data into different segments or buckets. Bucket aggregations are the most common type of aggregation used in any analysis process.

We will cover the following topics, keeping the network traffic data example at the center:

- Bucketing on string data
- Bucketing on numeric data
- Aggregating filtered data
- Nesting aggregations
- Bucketing on custom conditions
- Bucketing on date/time data
- Bucketing on geo-spatial data

Bucketing on string data

Sometimes, we may need to bucket the data or segment the data based on a field that has a string datatype, typically `keyword` typed fields in Elasticsearch. This is very common. Some examples of scenarios in which you may want to segment the data by a string typed field are:

- Segmenting the network traffic data per department
- Segmenting the network traffic data per user
- Segmenting the network traffic data per application or per category

The most common way to bucket or segment your string typed data is by using terms aggregation. Let us take a look at terms aggregation.

Terms aggregation

Terms aggregation is probably the most widely used aggregation. It is useful for segmenting or grouping the data by a given field's distinct values. Suppose that in the network traffic data example which we have loaded, we have the following question:

Which are the top categories, that is, categories that are surfed the most by users?

We are interested in the most surfed categories, not in terms of bandwidth used but just in terms of counts (record counts). In a relational database, we could write a query like the following one:

```
SELECT category, count(*) FROM usageReport GROUP BY category ORDER BY
count(*) DESC;
```

The Elasticsearch aggregation query, which would do a similar job, can be written as follows:

```
GET /bigginsight/usageReport/_search
{
  "aggs": {                              1
    "byCategory": {                      2
      "terms": {                         3
        "field": "category"             4
      }
    }
  },
  "size": 0                              5
}
```

Let us understand the terms of the aggregation query here. Notice the numbers that refer to different parts of the query:

- The `aggs` or `aggregations` element at the top level should wrap any aggregation.
- Give a name to the aggregation. Here we are doing term aggregation by the category field and hence the name we chose is `byCategory`.
- We are doing a term aggregation, hence the element `terms`.
- We want to do a term aggregation on the `category` field.
- Specify `size = 0` to prevent raw search results from being returned. We just want aggregation results and not the search results in this case. Since we haven't specified any top level `query` element, it matches all documents. We do not want any raw documents (or search hits) in the result.

The response looks like the following:

```
{
  "took": 11,
  "timed_out": false,
  "_shards": {
    "total": 5,
    "successful": 5,
    "failed": 0
  },
  "hits": {
    "total": 242835,                     1
    "max_score": 0,
    "hits": []                           2
  },
  "aggregations": {                      3
```

```
      "byCategory": {                                    4
        "doc_count_error_upper_bound": 0,                5
        "sum_other_doc_count": 0,                        6
        "buckets": [                                     8
          {
            "key": "Chat",                               9
            "doc_count": 52277                          10
          },
          {
            "key": "File Sharing",
            "doc_count": 46912
          },
          {
            "key": "Other HTTP",
            "doc_count": 38535
          },
          {
            "key": "News",
            "doc_count": 25784
          },
          {
            "key": "Email",
            "doc_count": 21003
          },
          {
            "key": "Gaming",
            "doc_count": 19578
          },
          {
            "key": "Jobs",
            "doc_count": 19429
          },
          {
            "key": "Blogging",
            "doc_count": 19317
          }
        ]
      }
    }
  }
```

Please notice the following in the response, and notice the numbers annotated in the response:

- The `total` element under `hits` (we will refer to this as hits.total navigating the path from the top JSON element) is `242835`. This is the number of total documents considered in this aggregation.
- The `hits.hits` array is empty. This is because we specified `"size": 0` so as not include any search hits here. What we were interested in were the aggregations and not search results.
- The `aggregations` element at the top level in the JSON response contains all the aggregation results.
- The name of the aggregation is `byCategory`. This is the name that was given by us to this term aggregation. This name helps us relate the response to the request, as the request can be generated for several aggregations at once.
- `doc_count_error_upper_bound` is the measure of error while doing this aggregation. Data is distributed in shards; if each shard sends data for all bucket keys, this results in too much data sent across the network. Elasticsearch sends across only the top *n* buckets across the network if the aggregation was requested for top *n* items. Here *n* is the number of aggregation buckets determined by `size` parameter to the bucket aggregation. We will look at bucket aggregation's size parameter later in this chapter.
- `sum_other_doc_count` is the total count of documents that are not included in the buckets returned. By default, term aggregations return the top 10 buckets if there are more than 10 distinct buckets. The remaining documents other than these 10 buckets are summed and returned in this field. In this case, there are only eight categories and hence this field is set to zero.
- The list of buckets returned by the aggregation.
- The key of one of the buckets, that is, the category of `Chat`.
- The count of documents in the bucket.

As we can see, there are only eight distinct buckets in the results of the query.

Next, we want to find out the top applications in terms of the maximum number of records for each application:

```
GET /bigginsight/usageReport/_search?size=0
{
  "aggs": {
    "byApplication": {
      "terms": {
        "field": "application"
      }
    }
  }
}
```

Notice how we have added `size=0` as a request parameter in the URL itself.

This returns a response like the following one:

```
{
  ...,
  "aggregations": {
    "byApplication": {
      "doc_count_error_upper_bound": 6325,
      "sum_other_doc_count": 129002,
      "buckets": [
        {
          "key": "Skype",
          "doc_count": 26115
        },
        ...
}
```

Notice the `sum_other_doc_count` has a big value, `129002`. This is a big number relative to the total hits; as we saw in the previous query, there are around 242,000 documents in the index. The reason for this is that term aggregation returns only 10 buckets by default. In the current setting, the top 10 buckets with the highest documents are returned in descending order. The remaining documents which are not covered in the top 10 buckets are indicated in `sum_other_doc_count`. There are actually 30 different applications for which we have network traffic data. The number in `sum_other_doc_count` is the sum of the counts for the remaining 20 applications which were not included in the buckets list.

To get the top *n* buckets instead of the default 10, we can use the `size` parameter inside the term aggregation:

```
GET /bigginsight/usageReport/_search?size=0
{
  "aggs": {
    "byApplication": {
      "terms": {
        "field": "application",
        "size": 15
      }
    }
  }
}
```

Notice that this `size` (specified inside the `terms` aggregation) is different from the `size` specified at the top level. At the top level, the `size` parameter is to prevent any search hits, whereas the `size` inside the term aggregation denotes the maximum number of term buckets to be returned.

Term aggregation is very useful for generating data for pie charts or bar charts, where we may want to analyze the relative counts of string typed field in a set of documents. In Chapter 7, *Visualizing Data with Kibana*, you will learn that Kibana term aggregation is useful for generating pie and bar charts.

Next, we will look at how to do bucketing on numeric types of fields.

Bucketing on numeric data

Another common scenario is when we want to segment or slice the data into various buckets based on a numeric field. For example, we may want to slice the product data by different price ranges such as up to $10, $10 to $50, $50 to $100, and so on. You may want to segment the data by age group, employee count, and so on.

We will look at the following aggregations in this section:

- Histogram aggregation
- Range aggregation

Histogram aggregation

Histogram aggregation can slice the data into different buckets based on one numeric field. The range of each slice, also called the interval, can be specified in the input of the query.

We have records of network traffic usage data. The usage field has the number of bytes used for uploading or downloading data. Let us try to divide or slice all the data based on the usage:

```
POST /bigginsight/_search?size=0
{
  "aggs": {
    "by_usage": {
      "histogram": {
        "field": "usage",
        "interval": 1000
      }
    }
  }
}
```

The above aggregation query will slice all the data into the following buckets:

- **0 to 999**: All records that have usage >= 0 and < 1000 will fall into this bucket
- **1,000 to 1,999**: All records that have usage >= 1000 and < 2000 will fall into this bucket
- **2,000 to 2,999**: All records that have usage >= 2000 and < 3000 will fall into this bucket

And so on.

The response should look like the following (truncated for brevity):

```
{
  ...,
  "aggregations": {
    "by_usage": {
      "buckets": [
        {
          "key": 0,
          "doc_count": 30060
        },
        {
          "key": 1000,
          "doc_count": 42880
        },
```

```
      {
        "key": 2000,
        "doc_count": 42041
      },
...
}
```

This is how the histogram aggregation creates buckets of equal ranges by using the `interval` specified in the query. By default, it includes all buckets with the given interval regardless of whether there are any documents in that bucket or not. It is possible to get back only those buckets which have at least some documents. It can be done by using the `min_doc_count` parameter. If specified, the histogram aggregation only returns those buckets that have at least the specified number of documents.

Let us look at another aggregation, range aggregation, which can be used on numeric data.

Range aggregation

What if we do not want all buckets to have the same interval? It is possible to create unequal sized buckets by using range aggregation.

The following range aggregation slices the data into three buckets: up to 1 KB, 1 KB to 100 KB, and 100 KB or more. Notice that we can specify `from` and `to` in the ranges. Both `from` and `to` are optional in the range. If only `to` is specified, that bucket includes all documents up to the specified value in that bucket. The `to` value is exclusive and is not included in the current bucket's range:

```
POST /bigginsight/_search?size=0
{
  "aggs": {
    "by_usage": {
      "range": {
        "field": "usage",
        "ranges": [
          { "to": 1024 },
          { "from": 1024, "to": 102400 },
          { "from": 102400 }
        ]
      }
    }
  }
}
```

The response of this request looks like the following one:

```
{
  ...,
  "aggregations": {
    "by_usage": {
      "buckets": [
        {
          "key": "*-1024.0",
          "to": 1024,
          "doc_count": 31324
        },
        {
          "key": "1024.0-102400.0",
          "from": 1024,
          "to": 102400,
          "doc_count": 207498
        },
        {
          "key": "102400.0-*",
          "from": 102400,
          "doc_count": 4013
        }
      ]
    }
  }
}
```

It is possible to specify custom `key` labels for the range buckets as follows:

```
POST /bigginsight/_search?size=0
{
  "aggs": {
    "by_usage": {
      "range": {
        "field": "usage",
        "ranges": [
          { "key": "Upto 1 kb", "to": 1024 },
          { "key": "1 kb to 100 kb","from": 1024, "to": 102400 },
          { "key": "100 kb and more", "from": 102400 }
        ]
      }
    }
  }
}
```

The resulting buckets will have the keys set with each bucket. This is helpful for looking up the relevant bucket from the response without iterating through all buckets.

There are more aggregations available for numeric data, but covering all of the aggregations is beyond the scope of this book.

Next, we will understand a couple of important concepts related to bucket aggregation and aggregations in general.

Aggregations on filtered data

In our quest to learn different bucket aggregations, let us take a very short detour to understand how to apply aggregations on filtered data. So far, we have been applying all aggregations on all the data of the given index/type. In the real world, you will almost always need to apply some filters before applying aggregations (either metric or bucket aggregations).

Let us revisit the example that we looked at in the *Terms aggregation* section. We found out the top categories in the whole index and type. Now what we want to do is to find the top category for a specific customer, and not for all the data for all customers:

```
GET /bigginsight/usageReport/_search?size=0
{
  "query": {
    "term": {
      "customer": "Linkedin"
    }
  },
  "aggs": {
    "byCategory": {
      "terms": {
        "field": "category"
      }
    }
  }
}
```

We modified the original query, which found the top categories, with an additional query (highlighted in the query above in bold). We added a query, and inside that query, we added a term filter for a specific customer that we were interested in.

This type of query, when used with any type of aggregation, changes the context of the data on which aggregations are calculated. The query/filter decides the data on which the aggregations will be run.

Let us look at the response of this query to understand this better:

```
{
   "took": 18,
   ...,
   "hits": {
     "total": 76607,
     "max_score": 0,
     "hits": []
   },
   ...
}
```

The hits total element in the response is now much less than the earlier aggregation query, which was run on the whole index and type. We may additionally want to apply more filters to limit the query to a smaller time window.

The following query applies multiple filters and makes the scope of the aggregation more specific, for a customer and within some subset of the time interval:

```
GET /bigginsight/usageReport/_search?size=0
{
   "query": {
     "bool": {
       "must": [
         {"term": {"customer": "Linkedin"}},
         {"range": {"time": {"gte": 1506277800000, "lte": 1506294200000}}}
       ]
     }
   },
   "aggs": {
     "byCategory": {
       "terms": {
         "field": "category"
       }
     }
   }
}
```

This is how the scope of aggregation can be modified by using filters. We will continue on our detour of learning about different bucket aggregations and look at how to nest metric aggregations inside bucket aggregations.

Nesting aggregations

Bucket aggregations split the context into one or more bucket. We can restrict the context of the aggregation by specifying the query element, as we have seen in the previous section.

When a metric aggregation is nested inside a bucket aggregation, the metric aggregation is computed within each bucket. Let us understand this by taking the following question that we may want to get an answer for:

What is the total bandwidth consumed by each user or a specific customer on a given day?

We have to take the following steps:

1. First filter the overall data for the given customer and for the given day. This can be done using a global query element of the bool type.
2. Once we have the filtered data, we want to create some buckets per user.
3. Once we have one bucket for each user, we want to compute the sum metric aggregation on the total usage field (which includes upload and download).

The following query does exactly this. Please refer to the annotated numbers which correspond to the three main objectives of the the following query:

```
GET /bigginsight/usageReport/_search?size=0
{
  "query": {                                           1
    "bool": {
      "must": [
        {"term": {"customer": "Linkedin"}},
        {"range": {"time": {"gte": 1506257800000, "lte": 1506314200000}}}
      ]
    }
  },
  "aggs": {
    "by_users": {                                      2
      "terms": {
        "field": "username"
      },
      "aggs": {
        "total_usage": {                               3
          "sum": { "field": "usage" }
```

```
            }
          }
        }
      }
    }
  }
```

The thing to notice here is that the top level `by_users` aggregation, which is a terms aggregation, contains another `aggs` element with the metric aggregation `total_usage` inside it.

The response should look like the following:

```
{
  ...,
  "aggregations": {
    "by_users": {
      "doc_count_error_upper_bound": 0,
      "sum_other_doc_count": 453,
      "buckets": [
        {
          "key": "Jay May",
          "doc_count": 2170,
          "total_usage": {
            "value": 6516943
          }
        },
        {
          "key": "Guadalupe Rice",
          "doc_count": 2157,
          "total_usage": {
            "value": 6492653
          }
        },
        ...
    }
}
```

As you can see, each of the term aggregation buckets contain a `total_usage` child which has the metric aggregation value. The buckets are sorted by the number of documents in each bucket in descending order. It is possible to change the order of buckets by specifying the order parameter within the bucket aggregation.

Please see the following partial query, modified to sort the buckets in descending order of the `total_usage` metric:

```
GET /bigginsight/usageReport/_search
{
   ...,
   "aggs": {
     "by_users": {
       "terms": {
         "field": "username",
         "order": { "total_usage": "desc"}
       },
       "aggs": {
         ...
...
}
```

The highlighted order clause sorts the buckets using the `total_usage` nested aggregation in descending order.

Bucket aggregations can be nested inside other bucket aggregations. Let us understand this by getting an answer to the following question:

Who are the top two users in each department, given the total bandwidth consumed by each user? The following query will help us get that answer:

```
GET /bigginsight/usageReport/_search?size=0
{
   "query": {                                                        1
     "bool": {
       "must": [
         {"term": {"customer": "Linkedin"}},
         {"range": {"time": {"gte": 1506257800000, "lte": 1506314200000}}}
       ]
     }
   },
   "aggs": {
     "by_departments": {                                             2
       "terms": { "field": "department" },
       "aggs": {
         "by_users": {                                               3
           "terms": {
             "field": "username",
             "size": 2,
             "order": { "total_usage": "desc"}
           },
           "aggs": {
```

```
            "total_usage": {"sum": { "field": "usage" }}        4
        }
      }
     }
    }
   }
 }
```

Please see the following explanation of the annotated numbers in the query:

- Query that filters the specific customer and time range.
- The top level terms aggregation to get a bucket for each department.
- The second level terms aggregation to get the top two users (notice `size = 2`) within each bucket.
- The metric aggregation that has the sum of usage within its parent bucket. The immediate parent bucket of the `total_usage` aggregation is the `by_users` aggregation which causes the sum of usage to be calculated for each user.

This is how we can nest bucket and metric aggregations to answer complex questions, in a very fast and efficient way, about big data stored in Elasticsearch.

Bucketing on custom conditions

Sometimes what we want is more control over how the buckets are created. The aggregations that we have looked at so far dealt with a single type of field. If the given field that we want to slice data from is of the string type, we generally use term aggregation. If the field is of numeric type, we have a few choices including histogram, range aggregation, and others to slice the data into different segments.

The following aggregations allow us to create one or more buckets based on the queries/filters chosen by us:

- Filter aggregation
- Filters aggregation

Let us look at them one by one.

Filter aggregation

Why one would use filter aggregation? Filter aggregation allows us to create a single bucket using any arbitrary filter and computes the metrics within that bucket.

For example, if we wanted to create a bucket of all records for the Chat category, we could use a term filter. We want to create a bucket of all records that have category = Chat.

```
POST /bigginsight/_search?size=0
{
  "aggs": {
    "chat": {
      "filter": {
        "term": {
          "category": "Chat"
        }
      }
    }
  }
}
```

The response should look like the following:

```
{
  "took": 4,
  ...,
  "hits": {
    "total": 242836,
    "max_score": 0,
    "hits": []
  },
  "aggregations": {
    "chat": {
      "doc_count": 52277
    }
  }
}
```

As you can see, the aggregations element contains just one item corresponding to the category Chat. It has 52277 documents. This response can be seen as subset of the term aggregation response, which contained all categories apart from Chat.

Let us look at the filters aggregation next, which allows you to bucket on more than one custom filter.

Filters aggregation

With filters aggregation, you can create multiple buckets, each with its own specified filter that will cause those documents satisfying that filter to fall into the related bucket. Let's understand it with an example.

We want to create multiple buckets to understand how much of the network traffic was caused by the Chat category. At the same time, we want to understand how much of it was caused by the Skype application versus other applications in the Chat category. This can be achieved using filters aggregation as it allows us to write arbitrary filters to create buckets:

```
GET bigginsight/_search?size=0
{
  "aggs": {
    "messages": {
      "filters": {
        "filters": {
          "chat": { "match": { "category": "Chat" }},
          "skype": { "match": { "application": "Skype" }},
          "other_than_skype": {
            "bool": {
              "must": {"match": {"category": "Chat"}},
              "must_not": {"match": {"application": "Skype"}}
            }
          }
        }
      }
    }
  }
}
```

We created three filters for the three buckets that we want, as follows:

- **Bucket with chat key**: We specify the filter category = Chat. Remember that the match query that we have used is a high-level query which understands the mapping of the underlying field. Here, the underlying field category is a keyword field and hence the match query looks for the exact term Chat.
- **Bucket with Skype key**: We specify the application = Skype filter and include only Skype traffic.
- **Bucket with other_than_skype key**: Here we use a bool query to filter documents that are in the Chat category but not Skype.

As you can see, filters aggregation is very powerful when you want custom buckets using different filters. It allows you to take full control of the bucketing process. You can choose your own fields and your own conditions to create the buckets of your choice for segmenting the data in customized ways.

Next, we will understand how to slice data on a date type column to slice it into different time intervals.

Bucketing on date/time data

We have seen how to bucket (or segment or slice) your data on different types of columns/fields. The analysis of data across the time dimension is another very common requirement. We may have questions such as the following, which require the aggregation of data on the time dimension:

- How are sales volumes growing over a period of time?
- How is profit changing month to month?

In the context of the network traffic example that we are going through, the following questions can be answered through time series analysis of the data:

- How are the bandwidth requirements changing for my organization over a period of time?
- Which are the top applications, over a period of time, in terms of bandwidth usage?

Elasticsearch has a very powerful Date Histogram aggregation that can answer questions like these. Let us look at how we can get answers to questions like the previous ones.

Date Histogram aggregation

Using Date Histogram aggregation, we will see how to first create buckets on a date field. In the process, we will go through the following:

- Creating buckets across time periods
- Using a different time zone
- Computing other metrics within sliced time intervals
- Focusing on a specific day and changing intervals

Creating buckets across time

The following query will slice the data into intervals of 1 day. Just like how we were able to create buckets on different values of strings, the following query will create buckets on different values of time, grouping it by 1 day intervals.

```
GET /bigginsight/usageReport/_search?size=0        1
{
  "aggs": {
    "counts_over_time": {
      "date_histogram": {                          2
        "field": "time",
        "interval": "1d"                           3
      }
    }
  }
}
```

- We have specified `size=0` as a request parameter instead of specifying it in the request body.
- We are using the `date_histogram` aggregation.
- We want to slice the data by day; that's why we specify the interval for slicing the data as 1 d (for 1 day). Intervals can take values like 1 d (1 day), 1 h (1 hour), 4 h (4 hours), 30 m (30 minutes), and so on. This gives tremendous flexibility when specifying a dynamic criteria.

The response to the request should look like the following:

```
{
  ...,
  "aggregations": {
    "counts_over_time": {
      "buckets": [
        {
          "key_as_string": "2017-09-23T00:00:00.000Z",
          "key": 1506124800000,
          "doc_count": 62493
        },
        {
          "key_as_string": "2017-09-24T00:00:00.000Z",
          "key": 1506211200000,
          "doc_count": 5312
        },
        {
          "key_as_string": "2017-09-25T00:00:00.000Z",
          "key": 1506297600000,
          "doc_count": 175030
```

```
                }
            ]
        }
      }
    }
```

As you can see, the simulated data that we have in our index is only for a 3 day period. The returned buckets contain keys in two forms, `key` and `key_as_string`. The `key` field is milliseconds since the epoch (January 1st 1970) and `key_as_string` is the beginning of the time interval in UTC. In our case, we have chosen the interval of 1 day. The first bucket with the `2017-09-23T00:00:00.000Z` key is the bucket that has documents between September 23rd 2017 UTC and September 24th 2017 UTC.

Using a different time zone

We actually want to slice the data by IST time zone rather than slicing it according to the UTC time zone. This is possible by specifying the `time_zone` parameter. We need to separate the offset of the required time zone from the UTC time zone. In this case we need to provide `+05:30` as the offset, as IST is 5 hours and 30 minutes ahead of UTC:

```
GET /bigginsight/usageReport/_search?size=0
{
  "aggs": {
    "counts_over_time": {
      "date_histogram": {
        "field": "time",
        "interval": "1d",
        "time_zone": "+05:30"
      }
    }
  }
}
```

The response now looks like the following:

```
{
  ...,
  "aggregations": {
    "counts_over_time": {
      "buckets": [
        {
          "key_as_string": "2017-09-23T00:00:00.000+05:30",
          "key": 1506105000000,
          "doc_count": 62493
        },
        {
```

```
            "key_as_string": "2017-09-24T00:00:00.000+05:30",
            "key": 1506191400000,
            "doc_count": 0
          },
          {
            "key_as_string": "2017-09-25T00:00:00.000+05:30",
            "key": 1506277800000,
            "doc_count": 180342
          }
        ]
      }
    }
  }
```

As you can see, the key and key_as_string for all buckets have changed. The keys are now at the beginning of the day in the IST time zone. There are no documents for September 24th 2017 now, as it is a Sunday.

Computing other metrics within sliced time intervals

So far, we have just sliced the data across time by using the Date Histogram to create the buckets on the time field. This gave us document counts in each bucket. Next we will try to answer the following question:

What is the day-wise total bandwidth usage for a given customer? The following query will provide us precisely that:

```
GET /bigginsight/usageReport/_search?size=0
{
  "query": { "term": {"customer": "Linkedin"} },
  "aggs": {
    "counts_over_time": {
      "date_histogram": {
        "field": "time",
        "interval": "1d",
        "time_zone": "+05:30"
      },
      "aggs": {
        "total_bandwidth": {
          "sum": { "field": "usage" }
        }
      }
    }
  }
}
```

We added a term filter to consider only one customer's data. Within the `date_histogram` aggregation, we nested another metric aggregation, sum aggregation, to count the sum of the usage field within each bucket. This is how we will get the total data consumed each day. The following is the shortened response to the query:

```
{
  ..,
  "aggregations": {
    "counts_over_time": {
      "buckets": [
        {
          "key_as_string": "2017-09-23T00:00:00.000+05:30",
          "key": 1506105000000,
          "doc_count": 18892,
          "total_bandwidth": {
            "value": 265574303
          }
        },
        ...
      ]
    }
  }
}
```

Focusing on a specific day and changing intervals

Next, we will see how to focus on a specific day, by filtering the data for the other time periods and changing the value of the interval to a smaller value. We are trying to get an hourly breakdown of data usage on September 25th 2017.

What we are doing is also called drilling down in the data. Often, the result of the previous query is displayed as a line chart with time on the *x* axis and data used on the *y* axis. If we want to zoom in on a specific day from that line chart, the following query can be useful:

```
GET /bigginsight/usageReport/_search?size=0
{
  "query": {
    "bool": {
      "must": [
        {"term": {"customer": "Linkedin"}},
        {"range": {"time": {"gte": 1506277800000}}}
      ]
    }
  },
  "aggs": {
    "counts_over_time": {
```

```
            "date_histogram": {
              "field": "time",
              "interval": "1h",
              "time_zone": "+05:30"
            },
            "aggs": {
              "hourly_usage": {
                "sum": { "field": "usage" }
              }
            }
          }
        }
      }
    }
```

The shortened response would look like the following:

```
{
  ...,
  "aggregations": {
    "counts_over_time": {
      "buckets": [
        {
          "key_as_string": "2017-09-25T00:00:00.000+05:30",
          "key": 1506277800000,
          "doc_count": 465,
          "hourly_usage": {
            "value": 1385524
          }
        },
        {
          "key_as_string": "2017-09-25T01:00:00.000+05:30",
          "key": 1506281400000,
          "doc_count": 478,
          "hourly_usage": {
            "value": 1432123
          }
        },
        ...
    }
}
```

As you can see, now we have buckets for 1 hour intervals with data for those hours aggregated within each bucket.

The Date Histogram aggregation allows you to do many powerful time series analyses. As we have seen in the examples, aggregating from a 1 day interval to a 1 hour interval is extremely easy. You can slice your data in the required interval with demand without planning it in advance. You can do this with big data; there are hardly any other data stores which can provide this type of flexibility with big data.

Bucketing on geo-spatial data

Another powerful feature is the ability to do geo-spatial analysis on the data. If your data contains fields of the geo-point data type where the coordinates are captured, you could perform some interesting analysis which could be rendered on a map to give you better insight into the data.

We will cover two types of geo-spatial aggregations:

- Geo distance aggregation
- GeoHash grid aggregation

Geo distance aggregation

Geo distance aggregation helps in creating buckets of distances from a given geo-point. This is better understood using a diagram:

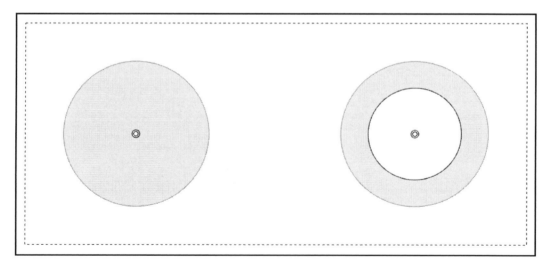

Fig 4.2 Geo distance aggregation with only to specified (left), and both to and from specified (right)

The shaded area in blue represents the area included in the geo distance aggregation.

The following aggregation will form a bucket with all the documents within the given distance from the given geo-point. This corresponds to the first (left) circle in Fig 4.2. The shaded area is from the center up to the given radius, forming a circle:

```
GET bigginsight/usageReport/_search?size=0
{
  "aggs": {
    "within_radius": {
      "geo_distance": {
        "field": "location",
        "origin": {"lat": 23.102869,"lon": 72.595692},
        "ranges": [{"to": 5}]
      }
    }
  }
}
```

As you can see, the ranges parameter is similar to the range aggregation that we saw earlier. It includes all the points up to 5 meters away from the given origin specified. This is helpful in aggregations such as getting the counts of things that are within 2 kilometers from a given location, and is often used on many websites. This is a good way to find all businesses within a given distance from your location (such as all coffee shops or hospitals within 2 km).

The default unit of distance is meters, but you can specify the unit parameter as km or mi and others to switch to different units.

Now let's look at what happens if you specify both from and to in the geo distance aggregation. This will correspond to the right circle in Fig 4.2:

```
GET bigginsight/usageReport/_search?size=0
{
  "aggs": {
    "within_radius": {
      "geo_distance": {
        "field": "location",
        "origin": {"lat": 23.102869,"lon": 72.595692},
        "ranges": [{"from": 5, "to": 10}]
      }
    }
  }
}
```

Here, we are bucketing the points which are at least 5 meters away but less than 10 meters away from the given point. Similarly, it is possible to form a bucket of a point which is at least *x* units away from the given origin by specifying only the `from` parameter.

Let us look at GeoHash grid aggregation.

GeoHash grid aggregation

GeoHash grid aggregation uses the GeoHash mechanism to divide the map into smaller units. You can read about GeoHash at `https://en.wikipedia.org/wiki/Geohash`. The GeoHash system divides the world map into a grid of rectangular regions of different precisions. Lower values of precision represent larger geographical areas and higher values represent smaller, more precise geographical areas:

```
GET bigginsight/usageReport/_search?size=0
{
  "aggs": {
    "geo_hash": {
      "geohash_grid": {
        "field": "location",
        "precision": 7
      }
    }
  }
}
```

The data that we have in our network traffic example is spread over a very small geographical area, so we have used a precision of 7. The supported values for precision are from 1 to 12. Let us look at the response to this request:

```
{
  ...,
  "aggregations": {
    "geo_hash": {
      "buckets": [
        {
          "key": "ts5e7vy",
          "doc_count": 161893
        },
        {
          "key": "ts5e7vw",
          "doc_count": 80942
        }
      ]
    }
}
```

```
      }
   }
```

After aggregating the data onto GeoHash blocks of precision 7, all the documents fell into two GeoHash regions, with the respective document counts seen in the response. We can zoom in on this map, or request the data to be aggregated on smaller hashes by increasing the value of the precision.

When you try a precision value of 9, you will see the following response:

```
{
   ...,
   "aggregations": {
      "geo_hash": {
         "buckets": [
            {
               "key": "ts5e7vy80k",
               "doc_count": 131034
            },
            {
               "key": "ts5e7vwrdb",
               "doc_count": 60953
            },
            {
               "key": "ts5e7vy84c",
               "doc_count": 30859
            },
            {
               "key": "ts5e7vwxfn",
               "doc_count": 19989
            }
         ]
      }
   }
}
```

As you can see, the GeoHash grid aggregation can allow you to slice or aggregate the data over geographical regions of different sizes/precisions, which is quite powerful. This data can be visualized in Kibana or it can be used in your application with a library that can render the data on a map.

We have covered a wide variety of bucket aggregations that let us slice and dice data on fields of various datatypes. We have looked at how to aggregate over text data, numeric data, dates/times, and geo-spatial data. Next we will understand what pipeline aggregations are.

Pipeline aggregations

Pipeline aggregations, as their name suggests, allow you to aggregate over the result of another aggregation. They let you pipe the result of an aggregation as an input to another aggregation. Pipeline aggregations are a relatively new feature and they are still experimental. At a high level, there are two types of pipeline aggregation:

- **Parent** pipeline aggregations have the pipeline aggregation nested inside other aggregations
- **Sibling** pipeline aggregations have the pipeline aggregation as the sibling of the original aggregation from which pipelining is done

Let us understand how the pipeline aggregations work by taking one example of cumulative sum aggregation, which is a parent of pipeline aggregation.

Calculating the cumulative sum of usage over time

While understanding the Date Histogram aggregation and in the section *Focusing on a specific day and changing intervals*, we looked at the aggregation, to compute hourly bandwidth usage for one particular day. After completing that exercise, we had data for September 24th with hourly consumption between 12 am to 1 am, 1 am to 2 pm, and so on. Using cumulative sum aggregation, we could also compute the cumulative bandwidth usage at the end of every hour of the day. Let's look at the query and try to understand it:

```
GET /bigginsight/usageReport/_search?size=0
{
  "query": {
    "bool": {
      "must": [
        {"term": {"customer": "Linkedin"}},
        {"range": {"time": {"gte": 1506277800000}}}
      ]
    }
  },
  "aggs": {
    "counts_over_time": {
      "date_histogram": {
        "field": "time",
        "interval": "1h",
        "time_zone": "+05:30"
      },
```

```
"aggs": {
  "hourly_usage": {
    "sum": { "field": "usage" }
  },
  "cumulative_hourly_usage": {              1
    "cumulative_sum": {                     2
        "buckets_path": "hourly_usage"      3
    }
  }
}
}
}
}
}
```

Only the part highlighted in bold is the new addition over the query that we saw previously. What we wanted was to calculate the cumulative sum over the buckets generated by the previous aggregation. Let's understand the newly added part with annotated numbers inside:

- Gives an easy to understand name to this aggregation, places it inside the parent Date Histogram aggregation which is the bucket aggregation containing this aggregation.
- We are using the cumulative sum aggregation and hence we refer to its name, cumulative_sum, here.
- The buckets_path element refers to the metric over which we want to do the cumulative sum. In our case, we want to sum over the hourly_usage metric that was created before.

The response should look as follows. It is truncated for brevity:

```
{
  ...,
  "aggregations": {
    "counts_over_time": {
      "buckets": [
        {
          "key_as_string": "2017-09-25T00:00:00.000+05:30",
          "key": 1506277800000,
          "doc_count": 465,
          "hourly_usage": {
            "value": 1385524
          },
          "cumulative_hourly_usage": {
            "value": 1385524
          }
        },
```

```
{
  "key_as_string": "2017-09-25T01:00:00.000+05:30",
  "key": 1506281400000,
  "doc_count": 478,
  "hourly_usage": {
    "value": 1432123
  },
  "cumulative_hourly_usage":
   {
    "value": 2817647
   }
}
```

As we can see, the `cumulative_hourly_usage` contains the sum of the `hourly_usage` so far. In the first bucket, hourly usage and cumulative hourly usage are the same. In the second bucket onwards, cumulative hourly usage has the sum of all hourly buckets seen so far.

Pipeline aggregations are powerful. They can compute derivatives, moving averages, average over the other buckets (also min, max, and so on), and average over previously calculated aggregations.

Summary

In this chapter, we have learnt how to use Elasticsearch to build powerful analytics applications. We have covered how to slice and dice the data to get powerful insight. We started with metric aggregation to deal with numeric datatypes. We then covered bucket aggregation to find out how to slice the data into buckets or segments in order to drill down into specific segments.

We also understood how pipeline aggregations work. We did all of this while dealing with a real-world-like dataset of network traffic data. We have seen how flexible Elasticsearch is as an analytics engine. Without much additional data modelling and extra effort, we can analyze any field, even when the data is on a **big data** scale. This is a rare capability not offered by many data stores. As you will see in Chapter 7, *Visualizing Data with Kibana*, Kibana leverages many of the aggregations that we learnt about in this chapter.

This concludes the chapters on Elasticsearch, the core of Elastic Stack. We have a very strong foundation to learn about the rest of the ecosystem of Elastic Stack. Starting from the next chapter, we shift our focus to learning about Logstash, which primarily deals with getting data into Elasticsearch from a variety of sources.

5
Analyzing Log Data

Logs contain rich information about the state and behavior of a system or an application. Each system/application generates the logs whenever an event occurs, and the frequency, amount of information, and format of the information it logs varies from one system/application to another. With so much information at our disposal, collecting them, extracting the relevant information from them, and analyzing them in near real time can be a daunting task.

In the previous chapters, we have already explored how Elasticsearch, with its rich aggregation features, assists in analyzing huge amounts of data in near real time. Before analysis can be performed, we need a tool which can assist/ease the process of collecting logs, extracting the relevant information from them, and pushing them to Elasticsearch.

In this chapter, we will be exploring Logstash, another key component of Elastic Stack which is mainly used as an **ETL (Extract, Transform, and Load)** engine. We will also be exploring the following topics:

- Challenges of log analysis
- How Logstash addresses those challenges
- High-level architecture of Logstash
- Logstash plugins
- Ingest node, a new Elasticsearch 5.x feature; it's a lightweight solution for pre-processing and enriching documents within Elasticsearch

Log analysis challenges

Logs are defined as records of incidents or observations. Logs are generated by a wide variety of resources such as systems, applications, devices, humans, and so on. A log is typically made of two things; that is, a timestamp (time the event was generated) and data (the information related to the event):

```
Log = Timestamp + Data
```

Logs are typically used for the following:

- **Troubleshooting**: When a bug or issue is reported, the first place to look for what might have caused the issue is the logs. For example, when looking at an exception stack trace in the logs one might easily find the root cause of the issue.
- **To understand system/application behavior**: When an application/system is running, it's like a black box, and in order to investigate or understand what's happening within the system/application one has to rely on logs. For example, one might log the time taken by various code blocks within the application and can use it for understanding the bottlenecks and fine-tuning their code for better performance.
- **Auditing**: Many organizations have to adhere to some compliance procedures and are compelled to maintain the logs. For example, login activity or transaction activities carried out by a user are commonly captured and maintained in logs for a certain duration of time, for the purpose of auditing or for the analysis of malicious activity by users/hackers.
- **Predictive analytics**: With advancements in machine learning, data mining, and Artificial Intelligence, a recent trend in analytics is predictive analytics. It is a branch of advanced analytics that is used to predict unknown events that may occur in the future. The patterns that result in historical and transactional data can then be utilized to identify opportunities as well as risks for the future. Predictive analytics also lets organizations become proactive and forward thinking, anticipating outcomes and behaviors based on the results acquired and not just on some assumptions. Some examples of the use cases of predictive analytics are when suggesting movies or items for users to purchase, detecting fraud, optimizing marketing campaigns, and so on.

Based on the previous sample/typical usages of logs, we can come to the conclusion that logs are data rich and can be used in a wide variety of use cases. However, logs come with their own set of own challenges. Some of the challenges are as follows:

- **No common/consistent format**: Every system generates logs in it own format, and as an administrator or end user it would require expertise in understanding the formats of logs raised by each system/application. As the formats are different, searching across different types of logs would be difficult. For the following example, the screenshot shows the typical format of SQL server logs, Elasticsearch exceptions/logs, and NGNIX logs:

- **Logs are decentralized**: As logs are generated by a wide variety of resources such as systems, applications, devices, and so on, logs are typically spread across multiple servers. With the advent of cloud computing and disturbed computing, it is now much more challenging to search across the logs, as typical tools like SSH and grep won't be scalable in these cases. Hence there is need for centralized log management, which assists the analyst/administrators in searching for the required information easily.

- **No consistent time format**: As logs are made up of timestamps, each system/application logs the time in its own format, thus making it difficult to identify the exact time of the occurrence of the event (some formats are more machine-friendly than human-friendly). Correlating events occurs across multiple systems at the same time. Some example time formats seen in the logs are:

```
Nov 14 22:20:10
[10/Oct/2000:13:55:36 -0700]
172720538
053005 05:45:21
1508832211657
```

- **Data is unstructured**: Log data is unstructured and thus it becomes difficult to perform analysis on it directly. Before analysis can be performed on it, the data would have to transformed into the right structure so that searching or performing analysis would become easier. Most analysis tools depend on structured/semi-structured data.

In the next section, let's explore how Logstash can help us in addressing the preceding challenges and thus ease the log analysis process.

Logstash

Logstash is a popular open source data collection engine with real-time pipelining capabilities. Logstash allows us to easily build a pipeline that can help in collecting data from a wide variety of input sources, and parse, enrich, unify, and store it in a wide variety of destinations. Logstash provides a set of plugins known as input filters and output plugins which are easy to use and are pluggable in nature, thus easing the process of unifying and normalizing huge volumes and varieties of data. Logstash does the work of the ETL engine:

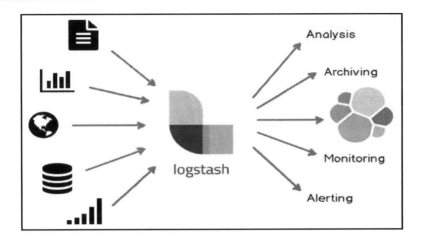

Some of the salient features of logstash are:

- **Pluggable data pipeline architecture**: Logstash contains over 200 plugins developed by Elastic and the open source community, which can be used to mix, match, and orchestrate different inputs, filters, and outputs while building pipelines for data processing.
- **Extensibility**: Logstash is written in JRuby and, as it supports pluggable pipeline architecture, one can easily build/create custom plugins to meet their custom needs.
- **Centralized data processing**: Data from disparate sources can be easily pulled using the various input plugins it provides and can be enriched and transformed and sent to different/multiple destinations.
- **Variety and volume**: Logstash handles all types of logging data, for example Apache, NGNIX logs, system logs, and window event logs, and also collects metrics from a wide range of application platforms over TCP and UDP. Logstash can transform HTTP requests to events and provides webhooks for applications like Meetup, GitHub, JIRA, and so on. It also supports consuming data from existing relational/NO-SQL databases and queues including Kafka, RabbitMQ, and so on. The Logstash data processing pipeline can be easily scaled horizontally, and since Logstash 5 it supports persistent queues, thus providing the ability to reliably process huge volumes of incoming events/data.

- **Synergy**: Logstash has a strong synergy with Elasticsearch, Beats, and Kibana, thus allowing one to build end-to-end log analysis solutions with ease.

Installation and configuration

In the following sections we will take a look at how to install and configure Logstash on your system.

Prerequisites

Java runtime is required to run Logstash. Logstash requires Java 8. Make sure `JAVA_HOME` is set as an environment variable, and to check your Java version, run the following command:

```
java -version
```

You should see the following output:

```
java version "1.8.0_65"
Java(TM) SE Runtime Environment (build 1.8.0_65-b17)
Java HotSpot(TM) 64-Bit Server VM (build 25.65-b01, mixed mode)
```

 For Java, you can use the official Oracle distribution (`http://www.oracle.com/technetwork/java/javase/downloads/index.html`), or an open source distribution such as OpenJDK (`http://openjdk.java.net/`).

Downloading and installing Logstash

Just like the other components of Elastic Stack, downloading and installing Logstash is pretty simple and straightforward. Navigate to `https://www.elastic.co/downloads/logstash#ga-release`, and depending on your operating system download the ZIP/TAR file as shown in the following screenshot:

Download Logstash

 Want to upgrade? We'll give you a hand. Migration Guide »

Version:	6.0.0
Release date:	November 14, 2017
Notes:	View detailed release notes. Not the version you're looking for? View past releases. Java 8 is required for Logstash 6.x and 5.x.
Downloads:	⬓ TAR.GZ sha ⬓ ZIP sha ⬓ DEB sha ⬓ RPM sha

 The Elastic developer community is quite vibrant, and newer releases with new features/fixes get released quite often. During your reading of this book, the latest Logstash version might have changed. Instructions in this book are based on Logstash version 6.0.0. You can click on the **past releases** link and download version 6.0.0 if you want to follow as is. The instructions/explanations in this book should hold good for any 6.x release.

Unlike Kibana, which requires major and minor version compatibility with Elasticsearch, Logstash versions starting from 5.6 are compatible with Elasticsearch 6.x. The compatibility matrix can be found at `https://www.elastic.co/support/matrix#matrix_compatibility`.

Installing on Windows

Unzip the downloaded file. Once unzipped, navigate to the newly created folder as shown in the following code snippet:

```
D:\>cd D:\packt\logstash-6.0.0
```

The Logstash installation folder with be referred to as LOGSTASH_HOME.

Installing on Linux

Unzip the `tar.gz` package and navigate to the newly created folder, shown as follows:

```
$> tar -xzf logstash-6.0.0.tar.gz
$>cd logstash/
```

Running Logstash

Logstash requires configuration to be specified while running it. Configuration can be specified directly as an argument using the -e option by specifying the configuration file (the .conf file) using the -f option/flag.

Using the terminal/command prompt, navigate to LOGSTASH_HOME/bin. Let's ensure that Logstash works fine after installation by running the following command with a simple configuration (the logstash pipeline) as a parameter:

```
D:\packt\logstash-6.0.0\bin>logstash -e 'input { stdin { } } output {
stdout {} }'
```

You should get the following logs:

```
Sending Logstash's logs to D:/packt/logstash-6.0.0/logs which is now
configured via log4j2.properties
[2017-10-30T12:42:12,046][INFO ][logstash.modules.scaffold]

Initializing module {:module_name=>"fb_apache",
:directory=>"D:/packt/logstash-6.0.0/modules/fb_apache/configuration"}
[2017-10-30T12:42:12,052][INFO ][logstash.modules.scaffold]

Initializing module {:module_name=>"netflow",
:directory=>"D:/packt/logstash-6.0.0/modules/netflow/configuration"}
 [2017-10-30T12:42:12,094][INFO ][logstash.agent ]

No persistent UUID file found. Generating new UUID
{:uuid=>"fd6c25ed-6450-40fd-912a-c83bf2aec638",
:path=>"D:/packt/logstash-6.0.0/data/uuid"}
 [2017-10-30T12:42:12,429][INFO ][logstash.pipeline ]

Starting pipeline {"id"=>"main", "pipeline.workers"=>4,
"pipeline.batch.size"=>125, "pipeline.batch.delay"=>5,
```

```
"pipeline.max_inflight"=>500}
  [2017-10-30T12:42:12,490][INFO ][logstash.pipeline ]

Pipeline main started
  The stdin plugin is now waiting for input:
  [2017-10-30T12:42:12,703][INFO ][logstash.agent ] Successfully started
Logstash API endpoint {:port=>9600}
```

Now enter any text and press **Enter**. Logstash adds a timestamp and IP address information to the input text message. Exit Logstash by issuing a CTRL-C command in the shell where Logstash is running. We just ran Logstash with some simple configurations (pipeline). In the next section, let's explore more about Logstash pipeline,.

Logstash architecture

The Logstash event processing pipeline has three stages, they are: **Inputs, Filters** and **Outputs**. A Logstash pipeline has two required elements; input, output, and, optionally, filters:

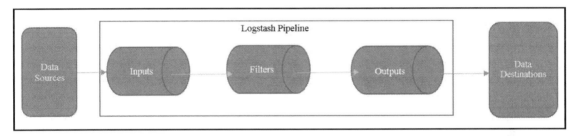

Inputs create events, **Filters** modify the input events, and **Outputs** ship them to the destination. Inputs and outputs support codecs which enable you to encode or decode the data as and when it enters or exits the pipeline without having to use a separate filter.

Logstash uses in-memory bounded queues between pipeline stages by default (**Input** to **Filter** and **Filter** to **Output**) to buffer events. If Logstash terminates unsafely, any events that are stored in memory will be lost. To prevent data loss, you can enable Logstash to persist in-flight events to the disk by making use of persistent queues.

> Persistent queues can be enabled by setting the property `queue.type: persisted` in the `logstash.yml` file found under the `LOGSTASH_HOME/config` folder. `logstash.yml` is a configuration file containing settings related to Logstash.
>
> By default, Logstash starts with a heap size of 1 GB. This can be overridden by setting the Xms and Xmx properties in the `jvm.options` file, found under the `LOGSTASH_HOME/config` folder.

The Logstash pipeline is stored in a configuration file ending with a `.conf` extension. The three sections of the configuration file are:

```
input
{
}
filter
{
}
output
{
}
```

Each of these sections contains one or more plugin configurations. A plugin can be configured by providing the name of the plugin and then its settings as a key value pair. The value is assigned to a key using the `=>` operator.

Let's use the same configuration that we used in the previous section, with some little modifications, and store it in a file:

```
#simple.conf
#A simple logstash configuration

input {
  stdin { }
}

filter {
  mutate {
    uppercase => [ "message" ]
  }
```

```
      }

  output {
    stdout {
      codec => rubydebug
      }
  }
```

Create a `conf` folder under `LOGSTASH_HOME`. Create a file called `simple.conf` under the `LOGSTASH_HOME/conf` folder.

 It's a good practice to place all the configurations in a separate directory either under `LOGSTASH_HOME` or outside of it rather than placing the files into the `LOGSTASH_HOME/bin` folder.

We may notice that this file contains two required elements, input and output, and the input section has a plugin named `stdin` which accepts default parameters. The output section has a `stdout` plugin which accepts the `rubydebug` codec. `stdin` is used for reading input from the standard input and the `stdout` plugin is used for writing the event information to standard outputs. The `rubydebug` codec will output your Logstash event data using the Ruby Awesome Print library. It also contains a filter section that has a `mutate` plugin, which converts the incoming event message to uppercase.

Let's run Logstash using this new pipeline/configuration stored in the `simple.conf` file as follows:

```
D:\packt\logstash-6.0.0\bin>logstash -f ../conf/simple.conf
```

Once Logstash has started, enter any input, say LOGSTASH IS AWESOME, and you should see the response as follows:

```
{
        "@version" => "1",
            "host" => "SHMN-IN",
     "@timestamp" => 2017-11-03T11:42:56.221Z,
        "message" => "LOGSTASH IS AWESOME\r"
}
```

As seen in the preceding code, along with the input message, Logstash automatically adds the timestamp at which the event was generated, and information such as the host and version number. The output is prettily printed due to the use of the `rubydebug` codec. The incoming event is always stored in the field named `message`.

As the configuration was specified using the file note, we used the –f flag/option when running Logstash.

Overview of Logstash plugins

Logstash has a rich collection of input, filter, codec, and output plugins. Plugins are available as self-contained packages called gems and hosted on RubyGems.org. By default, as part of the Logstash distribution many common plugins are available out of the box. One can verify the list of plugins that are part of the current installation by executing the following command:

```
D:\packt\logstash-6.0.0\bin>logstash-plugin list
```

By passing the --verbose flag to the preceding command, one can find out the version info of each plugin.

Using the -- group flag followed by either input, filter, output, or codec, one can find the list of installed input, filters, output, codecs, and plugins respectively. For example:

```
D:\packt\logstash-6.0.0\bin>logstash-plugin list --group filter
```

One can list all plugins containing a name fragment by passing the name fragment to logstash-plugin list. For example:

```
D:\packt\logstash-6.0.0\bin>logstash-plugin list 'pager'
```

In the previous example commands, D:\packt\logstash-6.0.0\bin> would refer to the LOGSTASH_HOME\bin directory on your machine.

Installing or updating plugins

If the required plugin is not bundled by default, one can install it using
the `bin\logstash-plugin install` command. For example, to install the `logstash-output-email` plugin, execute the following command:

```
D:\packt\logstash-6.0.0\bin>logstash-plugin install logstash-output-email
```

Using the `bin\logstash-plugin update` command and passing the plugin name as a
parameter to the command, one can get the latest version of the plugin:

```
D:\packt\logstash-6.0.0\bin>logstash-plugin update logstash-output-s3
```

 Executing just the `bin\logstash-plugin update` command would
update all the plugins.

Input plugins

An input plugin is used to configure a set of events to be fed to Logstash. The plugin allows
one to configure single or multiple input sources. It acts as the first section, which is
required in the Logstash configuration file. The list of available input plugins out of the box
is as follows:

```
logstash-input-beats       logstash-input-couchdb_changes  logstash-input-elasticsearch  logstash-input-ganglia
logstash-input-xmpp        logstash-input-unix             logstash-input-syslog         logstash-input-stdin
logstash-input-udp         logstash-input-twitter          logstash-input-tcp            logstash-input-sqs
logstash-input-snmptrap    logstash-input-redis            logstash-input-pipe           logstash-input-log4j
logstash-input-s3          logstash-input-rabbitmq         logstash-input-lumberjack     logstash-input-http_poller
logstash-input-exec        logstash-input-file             logstash-input-http           logstash-input-imap
logstash-input-gelf        logstash-input-jdbc             logstash-input-irc            logstash-input-generator
logstash-input-heartbeat   logstash-input-graphite
```

Details of each of these plugins and the list of other available plugins that are not part of the
default distribution can be can be found
at https://www.elastic.co/guide/en/logstash/6.0/input-plugins.html.

Output plugins

The output plugin is used to send data to a destination. Output plugins allow one to configure single or multiple output sources. It acts as the last section, which is required in the Logstash configuration file. The list of available output plugins out of the box is as follows:

```
logstash-output-cloudwatch logstash-output-nagios    logstash-output-irc    logstash-output-pagerduty
logstash-output-xmpp        logstash-output-tcp       logstash-output-stdout logstash-output-redis
logstash-output-webhdfs     logstash-output-statsd    logstash-output-sns    logstash-output-rabbitmq
logstash-output-udp         logstash-output-sqs       logstash-output-s3     logstash-output-pipe
logstash-output-csv         logstash-output-graphite  logstash-output-file   logstash-output-elasticsearch
logstash-output-http
```

Details of each of the preceding plugins and the list of other available plugins that are not part of the default distribution can be can be found at https://www.elastic.co/guide/en/logstash/6.0/output-plugins.html.

Filter plugins

A filter plugin is used to perform transformations on the data. It allows you to combine one or more plugins, and the order of the plugins defines the order in which the data is transformed. It acts as the intermediate section between input and output and its an optional section in the Logstash configuration. The list of available filter plugins out of the box is as follows:

```
logstash-filter-cidr        logstash-filter-clone      logstash-filter-grok     logstash-filter-geoip
logstash-filter-date        logstash-filter-csv        logstash-filter-throttle logstash-filter-xml
logstash-filter-fingerprint logstash-filter-dns        logstash-filter-drop     logstash-filter-dissect
logstash-filter-syslog_pri  logstash-filter-useragent  logstash-filter-split    logstash-filter-translate
logstash-filter-uuid        logstash-filter-urldecode  logstash-filter-sleep    logstash-filter-ruby
logstash-filter-mutate      logstash-filter-metrics    logstash-filter-kv       logstash-filter-json
```

Details of each of the preceding plugins and the list of other available plugins that are not part of the default distribution can be can be found at https://www.elastic.co/guide/en/logstash/6.0/filter-plugins.html.

Codec plugins

Codec plugins are used to encode or decode incoming or outgoing events from Logstash. Codecs can be used in input and output as well. Input codecs render a convenient way to decode your data before it even enters the input. Output codecs provide a convenient way to encode your data before it leaves the output. The list of available codec plugins out of the box is as follows:

```
logstash-codec-netflow    logstash-codec-cef       logstash-codec-es_bulk     logstash-codec-dots
logstash-codec-collectd   logstash-codec-multiline logstash-codec-msgpack     logstash-codec-line
logstash-codec-rubydebug  logstash-codec-json      logstash-codec-json_lines  logstash-codec-fluent
logstash-codec-plain      logstash-codec-graphite  logstash-codec-edn_lines   logstash-codec-edn
```

Details of each of the preceding plugins and the list of other available plugins that are not part of the default distribution can be can be found at `https://www.elastic.co/guide/en/logstash/6.0/codec-plugins.html`.

Exploring plugins

In these sections, let's explore some commonly used input, output, filters, and codec plugins.

Exploring Input plugins

Let us walk through some of the most commonly used input plugins in detail.

File

The file plugin is used to stream events from file(s) line by line. It works in a similar fashion to the `tail -0f` linux\unix command. For each file, it keeps track of any changes in the file, and the last location from where the file was read only sends the data since it was last read. It also automatically detects file rotation. This plugin also provides the option to read the file from the beginning of the file.

The file plugin keeps account of the current position in each file. It does so by recording the current position in a separate file named `sincedb`. This not only makes it possible but also convenient to stop and restart Logstash and have it pick up where it left off without missing the lines that were added to the file while Logstash was stopped.

The location of `sincedb` file is by default set to `<path.data>/plugins/inputs/file`, which can be overridden by providing the file path for the `sincedb_path` plugin parameter. The only required parameter for this plugin is the `path` parameter, which accepts one or more files to read from.

Let's take some example configurations to understand this plugin better:

```
#sample configuration 1
#simple1.conf

input
{ file{
    path => "/usr/local/logfiles/*"
 }
}
 output
{
 stdout {
 codec => rubydebug
 }
}
```

The preceding configuration specifies the streaming of all the new entries (that is, tailing the files) to the files found under the location `/usr/local/logfiles/`:

```
#sample configuration 2
#simple2.conf
input
{
    file{
        path => ["D:\es\app\*","D:\es\logs\*.txt"]
        start_position => "beginning"
        exclude => ["*.csv]
        discover_interval => "10s"
        type => "applogs"
    }
}

output
{
  stdout {
    codec => rubydebug
    }
}
```

The preceding configuration specifies the streaming of all the log entries/lines in the files found under the `D:\es\app\*` location, and only files of the `.txt` type. Files found under the location `D:\es\logs\*.txt`, starting from the beginning (specified by the parameter `start_position => "beginning"`), and while looking for files it excludes files of the `.csv` type (specified by the `exclude => ["*.csv]` parameter, which takes an array of values). Every line streamed would be stored in the message field by default and the preceding configuration also specified to add a new additional field type with the `applogs` value (specified by the `type => "applogs"` parameter). Adding additional fields would be helpful while transforming events in filter plugins or identifying the events in the output. The `discover_interval` parameter is used to define how often the `path` will be expanded to search for new files created inside the location specified in the `path` parameter.

Specifying the parameter/setting as `start_position => "beginning"` and `sincedb_path => "NULL"` would force the file to stream from the beginning every time Logstash is restarted.

Beats

The Beats input plugin enables Logstash to receive events from the Elastic Beats framework. Beats are a collection of lightweight daemons that collect operational data from your servers and ship to the configured outputs such as Logstash, Elasticsearch, Redis, and so on. There are several beats including Metricbeat, Filebeat, Winlogbeat, and so on. Filebeat ships log files from your servers. Metricbeat is a server monitoring agent, it periodically collects metrics from the services and operating systems running on your servers. Winlogbeat ships Windows event logs. We will be exploring the Beats framework and some of these Beats in the upcoming chapters.

By using the `beats` input plugin, we can make Logstash listen on desired ports for incoming beats connections:

```
#beats.conf

input {
  beats {
    port => 1234
  }

}
```

```
output {
  elasticsearch {
    }
  }
}
```

`port` is the only required setting for this plugin. The preceding configuration makes Logstash listen for incoming beats connections and index into Elasticsearch. When you start Logstash with the preceding configuration, you may notice Logstash starting an input listener on port 1234 in the logs as follows:

```
D:\packt\logstash-6.0.0\bin>logstash -f ../conf/beats.conf -r
Sending Logstash's logs to D:/packt/logstash-6.0.0/logs which is now
configured via log4j2.properties
[2017-11-06T15:16:46,534][INFO ][logstash.modules.scaffold] Initializing
module {:module_name=>"fb_apache",
:directory=>"D:/packt/logstash-6.0.0/modules/fb_apache/configuration"}
[2017-11-06T15:16:46,539][INFO ][logstash.modules.scaffold] Initializing
module {:module_name=>"netflow",
:directory=>"D:/packt/logstash-6.0.0/modules/netflow/configuration"}
[2017-11-06T15:16:47,905][INFO ][logstash.pipeline ] Starting pipeline
{"id"=>"main", "pipeline.workers"=>4, "pipeline.batch.size"=>125,
"pipeline.batch.delay"=>5, "pipeline.max_inflight"=>500
[2017-11-06T15:16:48,491][INFO ][logstash.inputs.beats ] Beats inputs:
Starting input listener {:address=>"0.0.0.0:1234"}
[2017-11-06T15:16:48,554][INFO ][logstash.pipeline ] Pipeline main started
[2017-11-06T15:16:48,563][INFO ][org.logstash.beats.Server] Starting server
on port: 1234
[2017-11-06T15:16:48,800][INFO ][logstash.agent ] Successfully started
Logstash API endpoint {:port=>9600}
```

Logstash starts the input listener on the address 0.0.0.0, which is the default value of the `host` parameter/setting of the plugin.

One can start multiple listeners to listen for incoming beats connections which is shown as follows:

```
#beats.conf

input {
  beats {
    host => "192.168.10.229"
    port => 1234
  }
  beats {
    host => "192.168.10.229"
    port => 5065
  }
```

```
  }

output {
  elasticsearch {
    }
  }
```

Using the −r flag during running of Logstash allows you to automatically reload the configuration whenever changes are made to it and saved. This would be useful when testing new configurations as you can modify it so that Logstash need not be started manually every time a change is made to the configuration.

JDBC

This plugin is used to import data from a database to Logstash. Each row in the results set would become an event and each column would get converted into fields in the event. Using this plugin, one can import all the data at once by running a query, or one can periodically schedule the import using a cron syntax (using the schedule parameter/setting). When using this plugin the user would need to specify the path of the JDBC drivers appropriate to the database, and the driver library can be specified using the jdbc_driver_library parameter.

The SQL query can be specified using the statement parameter or can be stored in a file; the path of the file can be specified using the statement_filepath parameter. One can use either statement or statement_filepath for specifying the query. It is good practice to store the bigger queries in a file. This plugin accepts only one SQL statement and multiple SQL statements aren't supported. If the user needs to execute multiple queries to ingest data from multiple tables/views then the user needs to define multiple JDBC inputs (that is, one JDBC input for one query) in the input section of Logstash configuration.

The results set size can be specified by using the jdbc_fetch_size parameter. The plugin will persist the sql_last_value parameter in the form of a metadata file stored in the configured last_run_metadata_path parameter. Upon query execution, this file will be updated with the current value of sql_last_value. The sql_last_value value is used to incrementally import data from the database every time the query is run based on the schedule set. Parameters to the SQL statement can be specified using the parameters setting which accepts a hash of the query parameter.

Let's see an example:

```
#jdbc.conf
input {
    jdbc {
            # path of the jdbc driver
            jdbc_driver_library => "/path/to/mysql-connector-java-5.1.36-
bin.jar"

            # The name of the driver class
            jdbc_driver_class => "com.mysql.jdbc.Driver"

            # Mysql jdbc connection string to company database
            jdbc_connection_string => "jdbc:mysql://localhost:3306/company"
            # user credentials to connect to the DB
            jdbc_user => "user"
            jdbc_password => "password"

            # when to periodically run statement, cron format (ex: every 30
minutes)
            schedule => "30 * * * *"

            # query parameters
            parameters => { "department" => "IT" }

            # sql statement
            statement => "SELECT * FROM employees WHERE department=
:department AND
            created_at >= :sql_last_value"
        }
}

output {
    elasticsearch {
        index => "company"
        document_type => "employee"
        hosts => "localhost:9200"
    }
}
```

The previous configuration is used to connect to company schema belonging to MySQLdb and is used to pull employee records from the IT department. The SQL statement is run every 30 minutes to check for new employees created since the last run. The fetched rows are sent to Elasticsearch and configured as the output.

> `sql_last_value` by default is set to Thursday, January 1st 1970 before the execution of the query, and is updated with the timestamp every time the query is run. One can force it to store a column value other than the last execution time by setting the `use_column_value` parameter to true and specifying the column name to be used using the `tracking_column` parameter.

IMAP

This plugin is used to read emails from an IMAP server. This plugin can be used to read emails, and depending on the email context, the subject of the email, or specific senders, it can be conditionally processed in Logstash and can be used to raise JIRA tickets, pagerduty events, and so on. The required configurations are host, password, and user. Depending on the settings required by the IMAP server that you want to connect to, you might need to set values for additional configurations such as port, secure, and so on. host is where you would specify your IMAP server host details, and user and password is where one needs to specify the user credentials to authenticate/connect to IMAP server:

```
#email_log.conf
input {
    imap {
      host => "imap.packt.com"
      password => "secertpassword"
      user => "user1@pact.com"
      port => 993
      check_interval => 10
      folder => "Inbox"


    }
}


output {
    stdout {
        codec => rubydebug
    }
    elasticsearch {
      index => "emails"
      document_type => "email"
```

```
            hosts => "localhost:9200"
        }
    }
```

By default, the `logstash-input-imap` plugin reads from the `INBOX` folder, and it polls the IMAP server every 300 seconds. In the preceding configuration, when using the `check_interval` parameter, the interval is overridden to every 10 seconds. Each new email would be considered an event, and as per the preceding configuration it would be sent to to the standard output and Elasticsearch.

Output plugins

In this sections, let us walk through some of the most commonly used output plugins in detail.

Elasticsearch

This plugin is used for transferring events from Logstash to Elasticsearch. This plugin is the recommended approach for pushing events/log data from Logstash to Elasticsearch. Once the data is in Elasticsearch, it can be easily visualized using Kibana. This plugin requires no mandatory parameters and it automatically tries to connect to Elasticsearch, hosted on `localhost:9200`.

The simple configuration of this plugin would be as follows:

```
#elasticsearch1.conf

input {
  stdin{
        }
  }

output {
  elasticsearch {
  }
}
```

Often Elasticsearch would be hosted on a different server, usually secured, and we might want to store the incoming data in specific indexes. Let's see an example of this:

```
#elasticsearch2.conf

input {
  stdin{
        }
```

```
    }

output {
  elasticsearch {
      index => "company"
      document_type => "employee"
      hosts => "198.162.43.30:9200"
      user => "elastic"
      password => "elasticpassword"
  }
}
```

As seen in the preceding code, incoming events would be stored in an Elasticsearch index named company (specified using the index parameter) under the employee type (specified using the document_type parameter). Elasticsearch is hosted at the 198.162.43.30:9200 address (specified using the document_type parameter), and the user credentials of Elasticsearch are elastic and elasticpassword (specified using user and password parameters).

If the index is not specified by default, the index pattern would be logstash-%(+YYYY.MM.dd) and the document_type would be set to the type event, if it existed, otherwise the document type would be assigned the value of logs/events.

One can also specify the document_type index and the document_id dynamically by using the syntax %(fieldname). In the hosts parameter, a list of hosts can be specified too. By default the protocol used would be HTTP if not specified explicitly while defining hosts.

It is recommended that you specify either the data nodes or ingest nodes in the hosts field.

CSV

This plugin is used for storing output in the CSV format. The required parameters for this plugin are the path parameter, which is used to specify the location of the output file, and the other required parameter is fields, which specifies the field names from the event that should be written to the CSV file. If a field does not exist on the event, an empty string will be written.

Let's see an example. In the following configuration, Elasticsearch is queried against the `"apachelogs"` index for all documents matching the `statuscode:200` and the `"message"`, `"@timestamp"`, and `"host"` fields are written to a `.csv` file:

```
#csv.conf

input {
 elasticsearch {
    hosts => "localhost:9200"
    index => "apachelogs"
    query => '{ "query": { "match": { "statuscode": 200 } }}'
 }
}
output {
    csv {
     fields => ["message", "@timestamp","host"]
     path => "D:\es\logs\export.csv"
     }
}
```

Kafka

This plugin is used to write events to a Kafka topic. It uses the Kafka Producer API to write messages to a topic on the broker. The only required configuration is the `topic_id`.

Let's see a basic Kafka configuration:

```
#kafka.conf

input {
  stdin{
      }
 }

output {
    kafka {
            bootstrap_servers => "localhost:9092"
            topic_id => 'logstash'
    }
}
```

The `bootstrap_servers` parameter takes the list of all server connections in the form of host1:port1, host2:port2 and the producer will only use it for getting metadata (topics, partitions, and replicas). The socket connections for sending the actual data will be established based on the broker information returned in the metadata. `topic_id` refers to the topic name where messages will published.

Note: Only Kafka version 0.10.0.x is compatible with Logstash version 2.4.x to 5.x.x and the Kafka output plugin version 5.x.x

PagerDuty

This output plugin will send notifications based on pre-configured services and escalation policies. The only required parameter for this plugin is the `service_key` to specify the Service API Key.

Let's see a simple example with basic pagerduty configuration. In the following configuration, Elasticsearch is queried against the index `"ngnixlogs"` for all documents matching the `statuscode:404`, and `pagerduty` events are raised for each document returned by Elasticsearch:

```
#kafka.conf
input {
 elasticsearch {
    hosts => "localhost:9200"
    index => "ngnixlogs"
    query => '{ "query": { "match": { "statuscode": 404} }}'
 }
}

output {
    pagerduty {
    service_key => "service_api_key"
    details => {
        "timestamp" => "%{[@timestamp]}"
        "message" => "Problem found: %{[message]}"
    }
    event_type => "trigger"
    }
}
```

Codec plugins

In the following sections we will take a look at some of the most commonly used codec plugins in detail.

JSON

This codec is useful if the data consists of `.json` documents and it is used to encode (if used in output plugins) or decode (if used in input plugins) the data in the `.json` format. If the data being sent is a JSON array at its root, multiple events will be created (that is, one per element).

The simple usage of a JSON codec plugin is as follows:

```
input{
    stdin{
    codec => "json"
    }
}
```

 If there are multiple JSON records, and those are delimited by \n, then use the `json_lines` codec.

If the "json" codec receives a payload from an input that is not valid JSON, then it will fall back to plain text and add a `tag _jsonparsefailure`.

Rubydebug

This codec will output your Logstash event data using the Ruby Awesome Print library.

The simple usage of this codec plugin is as follows:

```
output{
    stdout{
    codec => "rubydebug"
    }
}
```

Multiline

This codec is useful for merging multiple lines of data with a single event. This codec comes in very handy when dealing with stack traces or single event information that is spread across multiple lines.

The sample usage of this codec plugin is shown in the following snippet:

```
input {
  file {
    path => "/var/log/access.log"
    codec => multiline {
      pattern => "^\s "
      negate => false
      what => "previous"
    }
  }
}
```

The preceding multiline codec combines any line starting with a space with the previous line.

Filter plugins

As we will be covering different ways of transforming and enriching logs using various filter plugins in the next chapter, we won't be covering anything about filter plugins here.

Ingest node

Prior to Elasticsearch 5.0, if we wanted to pre-process documents before indexing them to Elasticsearch, then the only way was to make use of Logstash or pre-process them programmatically/manually and then index them to Elasticsearch. Elasticsearch lacked the ability to pre-process/transform the documents, and it just indexed the document as they were. However, the introduction of a feature called ingest node in Elasticsearch 5.x onwards provided a lightweight solution for pre-processing and enriching documents within Elasticsearch itself before they are indexed.

If an Elasticsearch node is implemented with the default configuration, by default it would be master, data, and ingest enabled (that is, it would act as a master node, data node, and ingest node). To disable ingest on a node, configure the following setting in the `elasticsearch.yml` file:

```
node.ingest: false
```

The ingest node can be used to pre-process documents before the actual indexing is performed on the document. This pre-processing is performed via an ingest node that intercepts bulk and index requests, it applies the transformations to the data, and then passes the documents back to the index or bulk APIs. With the release of the new ingest feature, Elasticsearch has taken out the filter part of Logstash so that we can do our processing of raw logs and enrichment within Elasticsearch.

To pre-process a document before indexing, we must define the pipeline (which contains sequences of steps known as processors for transforming an incoming document). To use a pipeline, we simply specify the `pipeline` parameter on an index or bulk request to tell the ingest node which pipeline to use:

```
POST my_index/my_type?pipeline=my_pipeline_id
{
  "key": "value"
}
```

Defining a pipeline

A pipeline defines a series of processors. Each processor transforms the document in some way. Each processor is executed in the order in which it is defined in the pipeline. A pipeline consists of two main fields: a description and a list of processors.
The `description` parameter is a non-required field which is used to store some descriptions/the usage of the pipeline; using the `processors` parameter, one can list the processors to transform the document.

The typical structure of a pipeline is shown as follows:

```
{
  "description" : "...",
  "processors" : [ ... ]
}
```

The ingest node has around 20 plus built-in processors including gsub, grok, convert, remove, rename, and so on. These can be used while building a pipeline. Along with built-in processors, ingest plugins such as ingest attachment, ingest geo-ip, and ingest user-agent are available and can be used while building a pipeline. These plugins are not available by default and can be installed just like any other Elasticsearch plugin.

Ingest APIs

The ingest node provides a set of APIs known as ingest APIs which can be used to define, simulate, remove, or find information about pipelines. The ingest API endpoint is `_ingest`.

Put pipeline API

This API is used to define a new pipeline. This API is also used to add a new pipeline or update an existing pipeline.

Let's see an example. As seen in the following code, we have defined a new pipeline named `firstpipeline` which converts the value present in the `message` field to upper case:

```
curl -X PUT http://localhost:9200/_ingest/pipeline/firstpipeline -H
'content-type: application/json'
  -d '{
  "description" : "uppercase the incoming value in the message field",
  "processors" : [
    {
      "uppercase" : {
        "field": "message"
      }
    }
  ]
}'
```

When creating a pipeline, multiple processors can be defined, and the order of the execution depends on the order in which it is defined in the definition. Let's see an example for this. As seen in the following code, we have created a new pipeline called secondpipeline that converts the uppercase value present in the "message" field and renames the "message" field to "data". It creates a new field named "label" with the value testlabel:

```
curl -X PUT   http://localhost:9200/_ingest/pipeline/secondpipeline   -H
'content-type: application/json'
-d '{
  "description" : "uppercase the incomming value in the message field",
  "processors" : [
    {
      "uppercase" : {
        "field": "message",
        "ignore_failure" : true
      }
    },
    {
      "rename": {
      "field": "message",
      "target_field": "data",
      "ignore_failure" : true
    }
    },
    {
       "set": {
      "field": "label",
      "value": "testlabel",
      "override": false
    }
    }
  ]
}'
```

Let's make use of the second pipeline to index a sample document:

```
curl -X PUT 'http://localhost:9200/myindex/mytpe/1?pipeline=secondpipeline'
H 'content-type: application/json' -d '{
  "message":"elk is awesome"
}'
```

Let's retrieve the same document and validate the transformation:

```
curl -X GET   http://localhost:9200/myindex/mytpe/1   -H 'content-type:
application/json'

Response:
{
    "_index": "myindex",
    "_type": "mytpe",
    "_id": "1",
    "_version": 1,
    "found": true,
    "_source": {
        "label": "testlabel",
        "data": "ELK IS AWESOME"
    }
}
```

> If the field used in the processor is missing, then the processor throws an exception and the document won't be indexed. In order to prevent the processor from throwing an exception, we can make use of the `"ignore_failure"` : `true` parameter.

Get Pipeline API

This API is used to retrieve the definition of an existing pipeline. Using this API, one can find the details of a single pipeline definition or find the definitions of all the pipelines.

The command to find the definition of all the pipelines is:

```
curl -X GET http://localhost:9200/_ingest/pipeline -H 'content-type:
application/json'
```

To find the definition of an existing pipeline, pass the pipeline ID to the get the pipelines .api. The following is an example of finding the definition of the pipeline named secondpipeline:

```
curl -X GET http://localhost:9200/_ingest/pipeline/secondpipeline   -H
'content-type: application/json'
```

Delete pipeline API

The delete pipeline API deletes pipelines by ID or wildcard match. Following is the example to delete the pipeline named `firstpipeline`.:

```
curl -X DELETE http://localhost:9200/_ingest/pipeline/firstpipeline  -H
'content-type: application/json'
```

Simulate pipeline API

This pipeline can be used to simulate the execution of a pipeline against the set of documents provided in the body of the request. One can either specify an existing pipeline to execute against the provided documents or supply a pipeline definition in the body of the request. To simulate the ingest pipeline, add the "`_simulate`" endpoint to the pipeline API.

The following is an example of simulating an existing pipeline:

```
curl -X POST
http://localhost:9200/_ingest/pipeline/firstpipeline/_simulate -H 'content-
type: application/json' -d '{
  "docs" : [
    { "_source": {"message":"first document"} },
    { "_source": {"message":"second document"} }
  ]
}'
```

The following is an example of a simulated request with the pipeline definition in the body of the request itself:

```
curl -X POST http://localhost:9200/_ingest/pipeline/_simulate -H 'content-
type: application/json' -d '{
  "pipeline" : {
    "processors":[
      {
        "join": {
        "field": "message",
        "separator": "-"
      }
    }]
  },
  "docs" : [
    { "_source": {"message":["first","document"]} }
  ]
}'
```

Summary

In this chapter, we laid out the foundations of Logstash. We walked you through the steps to install and configure Logstash to set up basic data pipelines, and studied Logstash's architecture.

We also learned about the ingest node that was introduced in Elastic 5.x, which can be used instead of a dedicated Logstash setup. We saw how the ingest node can be used to pre-process documents before the actual indexing takes place, and also studied its different APIs.

In the next chapter, we will show you how a rich set of filters brings Logstash closer to the other real-time and near real-time stream processing frameworks with zero coding.

6
Building Data Pipelines with Logstash

In the previous chapter, we understood the importance of Logstash in the log analysis process. We also covered its usage and its high-level architecture, and went through some commonly used plugins. One of the important processes of Logstash is converting unstructured log data into structured data, which helps in searching for relevant information easily and also assists in analysis. Apart from parsing the log data to make it structured, it would also be helpful if we could enrich the log data during this process so that we can gain further insight about our logs. Logstash comes in handy for enriching our log data, too. Also, we have seen in the previous chapter that Logstash can read from a wide range of inputs and that Logstash is a heavy process. Installing Logstash on the edge nodes of shipping logs might not always be feasible. Is there an alternative or lightweight agent that can be used to ship logs? Let's explore that in this chapter as well.

In this chapter, we will be covering the following topics:

- Parsing and enriching logs using Logstash
- The Elastic Beats platform
- Installing and configuring Filebeats for shipping logs

Parsing and enriching logs using Logstash

The analysis of structured data is easier and helps us find meaningful/deeper analysis, rather than trying to perform analysis on unstructured data. Most analysis tools depend on structured data. Kibana, which we will be making use of for analysis and visualization, can be used effectively if the data in Elasticsearch is right (the information in the log data is loaded into appropriate fields, and the data type of the fields are more appropriate than just having all the values of the log data in a single field).

Log data is typically made up of two parts:

```
logdata = timestamp + data
```

`timestamp` is the time when the event occurred and `data` is the information about the event. `data` may contain just a single piece of information or it may contain many pieces of information. For example, if we take `apache-access` logs, the data piece will contain the response code, request URL, IP address, and so on. We would need to have a mechanism for extracting this information from the data and thus converting the unstructured data/event into a structured data/event. This is where the filter section of the Logstash pipeline comes in handy. The filter section is made up of one or more filter plugins that assist in parsing and enriching the log data.

Filter plugins

A filter plugin is used to perform transformations on the data. It allows us to combine one or more plugins, and the order of the plugins defines the order in which the data is transformed. A sample filter section in Logstash pipeline would look as follows:

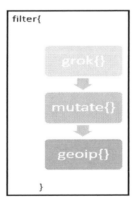

The generated event from the input plugin goes through each of the plugins defined in the filter section, during which it transforms the event based on the plugins defined. Finally, it is sent to the output plugin to send the event to the appropriate destination.

In the following sections, let's explore some common filter plugins used for transformation.

CSV filter

This filter is useful for parsing .csv files. This plugin takes the event containing CSV data, parses it, and stores it as individual fields.

Let's take some sample data and use a CSV filter to parse data out of it. Store the following data in a file named users.csv:

```
FName,LName,Age,Salary,EmailId,Gender
John,Thomas,25,50000,John.Thomas,m
Raj, Kumar,30,5000,Raj.Kumar,f
Rita,Tony,27,60000,Rita.Tony,m
```

The following code block shows the usage of the CSV filter plugin. The CSV plugin has no required parameters. It scans each row of data and uses default column names such as column1, column2, and so on to place the data. This plugin by default uses , (a comma) as a field separator. The default separator can be changed by using the separator parameter of the plugin. One can either specify the list of column names using the columns parameter, which accepts an array of column names, or by using the autodetect_column_names parameter set to true. In doing so, one can let the plugin know that it needs to detect the column names automatically:

```
#csv_file.conf
input {
    file{
        path => "D:\es\logs\users.csv"
        start_position => "beginning"
        }
}

filter {
    csv{
    autodetect_column_names => true
        }
}

output {
  stdout {
    codec => rubydebug
```

```
                  }
        }
```

Mutate filter

This filter allows one to perform general mutations on fields. One can rename, convert, strip, and modify fields in the events.

Lets enhance the `csv_file.conf` created in the previous section with the `mutate` filter and understand its usage. The following code block shows the use of the mutate filter:

```
#csv_file_mutuate.conf
input {
    file{
        path => "D:\es\logs\users.csv"
        start_position => "beginning"
        sincedb_path => "NULL"
    }

}

filter {
  csv{
    autodetect_column_names => true
  }
  mutate {
    convert => {
        "Age" => "integer"
        "Salary" => "float"
      }
    rename => { "FName" => "Firstname"
                "LName" => "Lastname" }
    gsub => [
       "EmailId", "\.", "_"
      ]
    strip => ["Firstname", "Lastname"]
    uppercase => [ "Gender" ]
  }
}

output {
  stdout {
    codec => rubydebug
    }
}
```

As seen in the preceding example, the `convert` setting within the filter helps to change the data type of a field. The valid conversion targets are integer, string, float, and Boolean.

If the conversion type is Boolean, the acceptable values are:
True: true, t, yes, y, and 1.
False: false, f, no, n, and 0.

The `rename` setting within the filter helps to rename one or more fields. The preceding example renames the `FName` field to `Firstname` and `LName` to `Lastname`.

`gsub` is used to match a regular expression against a field value and replace all matches with a replacement string. As regular expressions work only on strings, this field can only take a field containing string or an array of strings. It takes an array consisting of three elements per substitution (that is, it takes the field name, regex, and the replacement string). In the preceding example, . in the `EmailId` field is replaced with _.

Make sure to escape special characters such as \, ., +, and ? when building `regex`.

`strip` is used to strip the leading and training white spaces.

The order of the settings within the mutate filter matters. The fields are mutated in the order the settings are defined. For example, as the `FName` and `LName` fields in the incoming event were renamed to `Firstname` and `Lastname` using the `rename` setting, other settings can no longer refer to `FName` and `LName`. Rather, to refer they would have to use the newly renamed fields.

`uppercase` is used to convert the string to upper case. In the preceding example, the value in the `Gender` field is converted to upper case.

Similarly, by using various settings of the mutate filter, such as `lowercase`, `update`, `replace`, `join`, and `merge`, one can lower case a string, update an exiting field, replace the value of a field, join an array of values, or merge fields.

Grok filter

This is a powerful and often used plugin for parsing the unstructured data into structured data, thus making the data easily queryable/filterable. In simple terms, Grok is a way of matching a line against a pattern (which is based on a regular expression) and mapping specific parts of the line to dedicated fields. The general syntax of a `grok` pattern is as follows:

```
%{PATTERN:FIELDNAME}
```

`PATTERN` is the name of the pattern that will match the text. The `FIELDNAME` is the identifier for the piece of text being matched.

By default, grok'ed fields are strings. To cast either to `float` or `int` values, one can use the following format:

```
%{PATTERN:FIELDNAME:type}
```

Logstash ships with about 120 patterns by default. These patterns are reusable and extensible. One can create a custom pattern by combining existing patterns. These patterns are based on the Oniguruma regular expression library.

Patterns consist of a label and a `regex`. For example:

```
USERNAME [a-zA-Z0-9._-]+
```

Patterns can contain other patterns. For example:

```
HTTPDATE %{MONTHDAY}/%{MONTH}/%{YEAR}:%{TIME} %{INT}
```

The complete list of patterns can be found at `https://github.com/logstash-plugins/logstash-patterns-core/blob/master/patterns/grok-patterns`.

If a pattern is not available then one can use a regular expression using the following format:

```
(?<field_name>regex)
```

For example, the `regex` `(?<phone>\d\d\d-\d\d\d-\d\d\d\d)` would match telephone numbers, such as 123-123-1234, and place the parsed value into the `phone` field.

Let's look at some examples to understand `grok` better:

```
#grok1.conf

input {
    file{
        path => "D:\es\logs\msg.log"
        start_position => "beginning"
        sincedb_path => "NULL"
    }

}

filter {
  grok{
  match => {"message" => "%{TIMESTAMP_ISO8601:eventtime} %{USERNAME:userid}
%{GREEDYDATA:data}" }
  }
}

output {
  stdout {
    codec => rubydebug
    }
}
```

If the input line is of the format "`2017-10-11T21:50:10.000+00:00 tmi_19 001 this is a random message`", then the output would be as shown in the following block:

```
{
            "path" => "D:\\es\\logs\\msg.log",
      "@timestamp" => 2017-11-24T12:30:54.039Z,
            "data" => "this is a random message\r",
        "@version" => "1",
            "host" => "SHMN-IN",
       "messageId" => 1,
       "eventtime" => "2017-10-11T21:50:10.000+00:00",
         "message" => "2017-10-11T21:50:10.000+00:00 tmi_19 001 this is a
random message\r",
          "userid" => "tmi_19"
}
```

 If the pattern does not match the text, it will add a `_grokparsefailure` tag to the `tags` field.

There is a tool hosted at `http://grokdebug.herokuapp.com` which helps one to build `grok` patterns that match the log.

> X-Pack 5.5 onwards contains the Grok Debugger utility and is automatically enabled when you install X-Pack into Kibana. It is located under the **DevTools** tab in Kibana.

Date filter

This plugin is used for parsing the date from the fields. This plugin is very handy and useful when working with time series events. By default, Logstash adds a `@timestamp` field for each event, representing the time it processed the event. But the user might be interested in the actual timestamp of the generated event rather than the processed timestamp. So, using this filter, one can parse the date/timestamp from the fields and then use it as the timestamp of the event.

We can use the plugin as follows:

```
filter {
    date {
    match => [ "timestamp", "dd/MMM/YYYY:HH:mm:ss Z" ]
        }
}
```

By default, the date filter overwrites the `@timestamp` field, but this can be changed by providing an explicit target field, as shown in the following code snippet. Thus, the user can keep the event time processed by Logstash too:

```
filter {
    date {
    match => [ "timestamp", "dd/MMM/YYYY:HH:mm:ss Z" ]
    target => "event_timestamp"
        }
}
```

> By default, the timezone will be the server local time unless specified. To manually specify the timezone, use the `timezone` parameter/setting of the plugin. The valid timezone values can be found at `http://joda-time.sourceforge.net/timezones.html`.

If the time field has multiple possible time formats, then those can be specified as an array of values to the `match` parameter:

```
match => [ "eventdate", "dd/MMM/YYYY:HH:mm:ss Z", "MMM dd yyyy
HH:mm:ss","MMM d yyyy HH:mm:ss", "ISO8601" ]
```

Geoip filter

This plugin is used to enrich the log information. Given the IP address, it adds the geographical location of the IP address. It finds the geographical information by performing a lookup against the GeoLite2 City database for valid IP addresses and populates fields with results. GeoLite2 City database is a product of the Maxmind organization and is available under the CCA-ShareAlike 4.0 license. Logstash comes bundled with GeoLite2 City database, so when performing a lookup it need not perform any network call; hence the lookup is fast.

The only required parameter for this plugin is the `source`, which accepts an IP address in string format. This plugin creates a `geoip` field with geographical details such as country, postal code, region, city, and so on. A `[geoip][location]` field is created if the GeoIP lookup returns a latitude and longitude, and it is mapped to the `geo_point` type when indexing to Elasticsearch. `geop_point` fields can be used for Elasticsearch's geospatial query, facet, and filter functions, and can be used to generate Kibana's map visualization:

```
clientip => "83.149.9.216"    →    geoip{
                                       source => clientip
                                    }    →

geoip:
•{timezone: "Europe/Moscow",
•ip: "83.149.9.216",
•latitude: 55.7485,
•continent_code: "EU",
•city_name: "Moscow",
•country_name: "Russia",
•country_code2: "RU",
•country_code3: "RU",
•region_name: "Moscow",
•location:
•{lon: 37.6184,
•lat: 55.7485
•},
•postal_code: "101194",
•region_code: "MOW",
•longitude: 37.6184
}
```

Geoip filter supports both IPv4 and IPv6 lookups.

Useragent filter

This filter parses user agent strings into structured data based on BrowserScope (http://www.browserscope.org/) data. It adds information about the user agent such as family, operating system, version, device, and so on. To extract the user agent details, this filter plugin makes use of the `regexes.yaml` database that is bundled with Logstash. The only required parameter for this plugin is the `source` parameter, which accepts string containing user agent details:

```
agent: ""Mozilla/5.0 (Macintosh; Intel Mac OS X 10_9_1)
AppleWebKit/537.36 (KHTML, like Gecko) Chrome/32.0.1700.77
Safari/537.36""
```

```
useragent{
    source => agent
}
```

```
useragent:
•{patch: "1700",
•os: "Mac OS X",
•major: "32",
•minor: "0",
•build: "",
•os_minor: "9",
•os_major: "10",
•name: "Chrome",
•os_name: "Mac OS X",
•device: "Other"
    }
```

Introducing Beats

Beats are lightweight data shippers that are installed as agents on edge servers to ship operational data to Elasticsearch. Just like Elasticsearch, Logstash, Kibana, and Beats are open source products too. Depending on the use case, Beats can be configured to ship the data to Logstash for transforming the events prior to pushing the events to Elasticsearch.

The Beats framework is made up of a library called `libbeat` which provides infrastructure to simplify the process of shipping the operation data to Elasticsearch. It offers the API that all Beats can use to ship data to an output (such as Elasticsearch, Logstash, Redis, Kafka, and so on), configure the input/output options, process the events, implement logging, and more. The Libbeat library is built using the Go programming language. Go was chosen to build Beats because it's easy to learn, very resource friendly, and as it's statically compiled it's easy to deploy.

Elastic.co has built and maintained several Beats such as Filebeat, Packetbeat, Metricbeat, Heartbeat, and Winlogbeat. There are several community Beats including amazonbeat, mongobeat, httpbeat, and nginxbeat, which have been built into the Beats framework by the open source community. Some of the Beats can be extended to meet business needs, as some of them provide extension points. If a beat for one's specific use case is not available, then custom Beats can be easily built with the `libbeat` library:

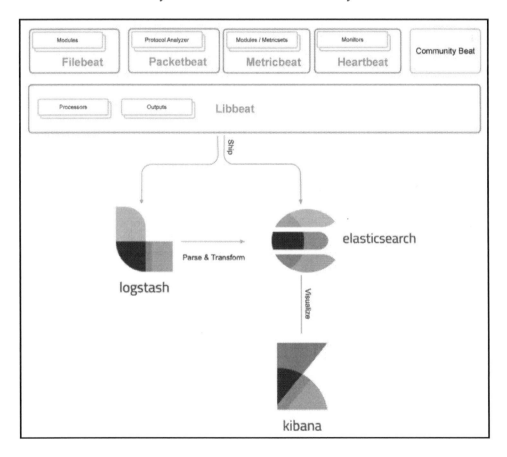

Beats by Elastic.co

Let us take a look at some of the commonly used beats by Elastic.co in the following sections.

Filebeat

Filebeat is an open source, lightweight log shipping agent that ships logs from local files. Filebeat runs as a binary and no runtime, such as JVM, is needed, hence it's very lightweight, executable, and also consumes less resources. It is installed as an agent on the edge servers from where the logs needs to be shipped. It monitors the log directories or specific log files, tails the files, and forwards them to Elasticsearch, Logstash, Redis, or Kafka. It is easily salable and provides the ability to ship logs from multiple systems to a centralized system/server, from which the logs can be parsed and processed.

Metricbeat

Metricbeat is a lightweight shipper that periodically collects metrics from the operating system and from services running on the server. It helps one to monitor servers by collecting metrics from the system, and services such as Apache, MondoDB, Redis, and so on, that are running on the server. Metricbeat can push the collected metrics directly into Elasticsearch or send them to Logstash, Redis, or Kafka. To monitor services, Metricbeat can be installed on the edge server where services are running; it provides the ability to collect metrics from a remote server as well. However, it's recommended to have it installed on the edge servers where the services are running.

Packetbeat

Packetbeat is a real-time network packet analyzer that works by capturing the network traffic between the application servers, decoding the application layer protocols (HTTP, MySQL, Redis, Memcache, and many more), correlating the requests with the responses, and recording the interesting fields for each transaction. Packetbeat sniffs the traffic between the servers, parses the application-level protocols on the fly, and converts the messages into transactions. It can help one to easily notice issues with the backend application, such as bugs or performance problems, and it makes troubleshooting them easy. Packetbeat can run on the same server, which contains application processes, or on its own servers. Packetbeat ships the collected transaction details to the configured output, such as Elasticsearch, Logstash, Redis, or Kafka.

Heartbeat

Heatbeat is a new addition to the beat ecosystem and is used to check if a service is up or not, and checks if the services are reachable. Heartbeat is a lightweight daemon that is installed on a remote server to periodically check the status of services running on the host. Heartbeat supports ICMP, TCP, and HTTP monitors for checking hosts/services.

Winlogbeat

Winlogbeat is a beat dedicated to the Windows platform. Winlogbeat is installed as a Windows service on Windows XP or later to read from one or more event log using Windows APIs. It filters the events based on user-configured criteria and then sends the event data to the configured output, such as Elasticsearch or Logstash.

Winlogbeat can capture event data such as application events, hardware events, security events, and system events.

Auditbeat

Auditbeat is a new addition to the Beats family, first implemented in Elastic Stack 6.0. Auditbeat is a lightweight shipper that is installed on servers to monitor user activity and processes and analyze the event data in the Elastic Stack without touching Linux's auditd. Auditbeat communicates directly with the Linux audit framework, collects the same data as auditd, and sends the events to Elastic Stack in real time. Auditbeat also allows one to carefully watch lists of directories for any changes. File changes are sent in real time to the configured output, and thus it can be used to identify potential security policy violations.

Community Beats

These are the beats that are developed by the open source community using the beats framework. Some of the open source beats are as follows:

Beat Name	Description
springbeat	Collects health and metrics data from Spring Boot applications running within the actuator module.
rsbeat	Ships redis slow logs to Elasticsearch.
nginxbeat	Reads the status from Nginx.
mysqlbeat	Runs any query in MySQL and send the results to Elasticsearch.

mongobeat	Monitors MongoDB instances and can be configured to send multiple document types to Elasticsearch.
gabeat	Collects data from the Google Analytics Realtime API.
apachebeat	Reads the status from Apache HTTPD server-status.
amazonbeat	Reads the data from a specified Amazon product.

The complete list of community beats can be found at `https://www.elastic.co/guide/en/beats/devguide/current/community-beats.html`.

 Elastic.co doesn't support or provide warranties for community Beats.

 The Beats Developer guide provides the necessary information to create a custom beat. The developer guide can be found at `https://www.elastic.co/guide/en/beats/devguide/current/index.html`.

Logstash versus Beats

After reading through the Logstash and Beats introduction, one might get confused as to whether Beats is a replacement for Logstash, the difference between them, or when to use one over the other. Beats are lightweight agents and consume less resources, and hence are installed on the edge servers where the operational data needs to be collected and shipped. Beats lack the powerful features of Logstash for parsing and transforming events. Logstash comes with a broad array of input, filter, and output plugins for collecting, enriching, and transforming data from a variety of sources. However, it is very resource intensive and can also be used as an independent product outside of Elastic Stack. Logstash is recommended to be installed on a dedicated server rather than edge servers, and listens for incoming events for processing. Beats and Logstash are complimentary products, and depending on the use case both of them are used or just one of them is used, as described in the *Introducing Beats* section.

Filebeat

Filebeat is an open source, lightweight log shipping agent that is installed as an agent to ship logs from local files. It monitors the log directories or specific log files, tails the files, and forwards them to Elasticsearch, Logstash, Redis, or Kafka. It is salable and provides the ability to ship logs from multiple systems to a centralized system/server, from which the logs can be parsed and processed.

Downloading and installing Filebeat

Navigate to `https://www.elastic.co/downloads/beats/filebeat` and, depending on your operating system, download the `.zip`/`.tar` file. The installation of Filebeat is simple and straightforward:

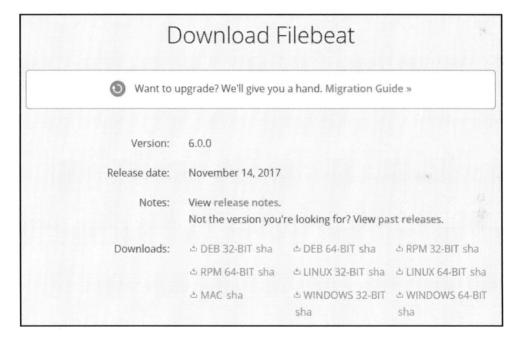

Beats version 6.0.x is compatible with Elasticsearch 5.6.x and 6.0.x, and Logstash 5.6.x and 6.0.x. The compatibility matrix can be found at `https://www.elastic.co/support/matrix#matrix_compatibility`. When you come across Elasticsearch and Logstash examples or usages with Beats in the chapter, make sure you have compatible versions of Elasticsearch and Logstash installed.

Installing on Windows

Unzip the downloaded file and navigate to the extracted location as follows:

```
D:> cd D:\packt\filebeat-6.0.0-windows-x86_64
```

To install Filebeat as a service on Windows, refer to the following steps:

1. Open Windows PowerShell as an administrator and navigate to the extracted location.
2. From the PowerShell prompt, run the following commands to install Filebeat as a Windows service:

```
PS >cd D:\packt\filebeat-6.0.0-windows-x86_64
PS D:\packt\filebeat-6.0.0-windows-
x86_64>.\install-service-filebeat.ps1
```

If script execution is disabled on your system, you need to set the execution policy for the current session to allow the script to run. For example: `PowerShell.exe -ExecutionPolicy UnRestricted -File .\install-service-filebeat.ps1`.

Installing on Linux

Unzip the `tar.gz` package and navigate to the newly created folder as follows:

```
$> tar -xzf filebeat-6.0.0-linux-x86_64.tar.gz
$> cd filebeat
```

To install using `dep` or `rpm`, execute the appropriate commands in the terminal:

```
deb:
curl -L -O
https://artifacts.elastic.co/downloads/beats/filebeat/fil
ebeat-6.0.0-amd64.deb
sudo dpkg -i filebeat-6.0.0-amd64.deb

rpm:
curl -L -O
https://artifacts.elastic.co/downloads/beats/filebeat/fil
ebeat-6.0.0-x86_64.rpm
sudo rpm -vi filebeat-6.0.0-x86_64.rpm
```

Filebeat will be installed in the `/usr/share/filebeat` directory. The configuration files will be present in `/etc/filebeat`. The `init` script will be present in `/etc/init.d/filebeat`. The `log` files will be present within the `/var/log/filebeat` directory.

Architecture

Filebeat is made up of key components called **Prospectors, Harvesters,** and **Spooler**. These components work together to tail files and send event data to the output that you specify. A Prospector is responsible for identifying the list of files to read logs from. A prospector is configured with one or many file paths, from which it identifies the files to read logs from; it starts a harvester for each file. Harvester is responsible for reading the contents of the file. The harvester reads each file, line by line, and sends the content to the output. One harvester is started for each file. The harvester is responsible for opening and closing the file, which means that the file descriptor remains open while the harvester is running. Harvester sends the read content (that is, events) to the spooler, where its aggregated and sent to the configured output.

Each instance of Filebeat can be configured with one or more prospectors. Currently, there are two types of prospectors the filebeat supports, which are of the types `log` and `stdin`. If the input type is `log`, the prospector finds all files on the drive that match the defined glob paths and starts a harvester for each file. Each prospector runs in its own Go routine. If the type is `stdin`, it reads from standard inputs.

Every time Filbebeat reads a file, the state of the last read is offset by harvester, and if the read line is sent to the output, it is maintained in a registry file which is flushed periodically to a disk. If the output (such as Elasticsearch, Logstash, Kafka, or Redis) is not reachable, Filebeat keeps track of the last lines sent and will continue reading the files as soon as the output becomes available again. While Filebeat is running, the state information is also kept in memory by each prospector. When Filebeat is restarted, data from the registry file is used to rebuild the state, and Filebeat continues each harvester at the last known position.

Filebeat will not consider a log line shipped until the output acknowledges the request and, as the state of the delivery of the lines to the configured output is maintained in the registry file, Filebeat guarantees that events will be delivered to the configured output at least once, and with no data loss.

The location of the registry would be as follows:

`data/registry` for `.tar.gz` for `.zip` archives,
`/var/lib/filebeat/registry` for DEB and RPM packages,
`C:\ProgramData\filebeat\registry` for the Windows `.zip` file, and if Filebeat is installed as a service.

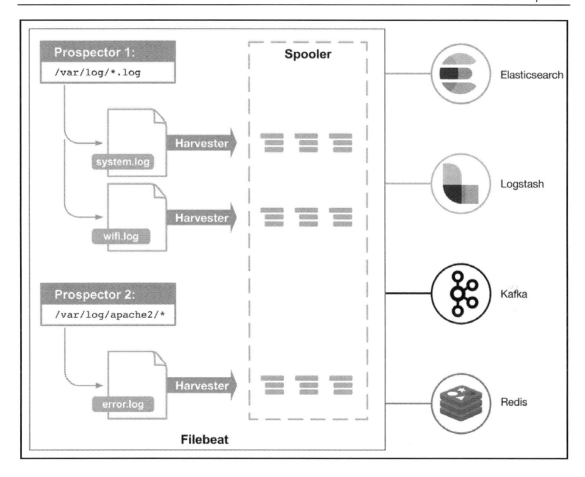

(Reference: `https://www.elastic.co/guide/en/beats/filebeat/6.0/images/filebeat.png`)

Configuring Filebeat

The configurations related to Filebeat are stored in a configuration file named `filebeat.yml`. It uses YAML syntax.

The `filebeat.yml` file contains the following sections:

- Filebeat prospectors
- Filebeat global options
- Filebeat general options

- Output configuration
- Processors configuration
- Paths configuration
- Modules configuration
- Dashboard configuration
- Logging configuration

 The `filebeat.yml` file will be present in the installation directory if `.zip` or `.tar` files are used. If `dep` or `rpm` is used for installation, then it will be present in the `/etc/filebeat` location.

Some of these sections are common for all type of Beats. Before we look into some of these sections, let's see what a simple configuration would look like. As seen in the following configuration, when Filebeat is started, it looks for files ending with the `.log` extension in the path `D:\packt\logs\`. It ships the log entries of each file to Elasticsearch, which is configured as the output, and is hosted at `localhost:9200`:

```
#filebeat.yml
#=========================== Filebeat prospectors
============================

filebeat.prospectors:
- input_type: log

  # Paths that should be crawled and fetched. Glob based paths.
  paths:
    - D:\packt\logs\*.log

#================================= Outputs
=====================================

#------------------------- Elasticsearch output ---------------------------
----
output.elasticsearch:
  # Array of hosts to connect to.
  hosts: ["localhost:9200"]
```

 Any changes made to `filebeat.yml` require a restart of Filebeat for it to pick up the changes.

It is always advisable to test the configuration after editing it. To test the configuration, use the -configtest flag:

```
D:\packt\filebeat-6.0.0-windows-x86_64>filebeat.exe -configtest
filebeat.yml
Config OK
```

 To specify flags, Filebeat needs to be started in the foreground. One can't specify command-line flags if the init.d script is used to start Filebeat on deb or rpm, or if it is run as a service on Windows.

Place some log files under D:\packt\logs\. To get Filebeat to ship the logs, execute the following command:

```
Windows:
D:\packt\filebeat-6.0.0-windows-x86_64>filebeat.exe

Linux:
[locationOfFilebeat]$ ./filebeat
```

To validate if the logs were shipped to Elasticsearch, execute the following command:

```
D:\packt>curl -X GET http://localhost:9200/filebeat*/_search?pretty
```

```
Sample Response:
{
  "took" : 1,
  "timed_out" : false,
  "_shards" : {
    "total" : 5,
    "successful" : 5,
    "failed" : 0
  },
  "hits" : {
    "total" : 6,
    "max_score" : 1.0,
    "hits" : [
      {
        "_index" : "filebeat-2017.11.23",
        "_type" : "doc",
        "_id" : "AV_niRjbPYptcfAHfGNx",
        "_score" : 1.0,
        "_source" : {
          "@timestamp" : "2017-11-23T06:20:36.577Z",
          "beat" : {
            "hostname" : "SHMN-IN",
```

```
          "name" : "SHMN-IN",
          "version" : "6.0.0"
        },
        "input_type" : "log",
        "message" : "line2",
        "offset" : 14,
        "source" : "D:\\packt\\logs\\test.log",
        "type" : "log"
      }
    },
    {
      "_index" : "filebeat-2017.11.23",
      "_type" : "doc",
      "_id" : "AV_niRjbPYptcfAHfGNy",
      "_score" : 1.0,
      "_source" : {
        "@timestamp" : "2017-11-23T06:20:36.577Z",
        "beat" : {
          "hostname" : "SHMN-IN",
          "name" : "SHMN-IN",
          "version" : "6.0.0"
        },
        "input_type" : "log",
        "message" : "line3",
        "offset" : 21,
        "source" : "D:\\packt\\logs\\test.log",
        "type" : "log"
      }
    },
  ...
  ...
  ...
```

Filebeat places the shipped logs under an index filebeat, which is a time-based index based on the `filebeat-YYYY.MM.DD` pattern. The log data would be placed in the `message` field.

To start filebeat on `deb` or `rpm` installations, execute the `sudo service filebeat start` command. If installed as a service on Windows, then use Powershell to execute the following command:
`PS C:\> Start-Service filebeat`

Filebeat prospectors

This section contains list of prospectors that Filebeat uses to locate and process log files. Each prospector item begins with a dash (–) and contains prospector-specific configuration options including one or more path to search for files to be crawled.

A sample configuration is as follows:

```
#=========================== Filebeat prospectors ================================

filebeat.prospectors:

- input_type: log
  paths:
    - /var/log/*.log
    - /var/log/messages
  # Exclude lines.
  exclude_lines: ["^DBG"]
  # Include lines.
  include_lines: ["^ERR", "^WARN"]

  tags:["java_logs"]

  fields:
    env: staging
  ### Multiline options
  multiline.pattern: '^[[:space:]]'
  multiline.negate: false
  multiline.match: after

  scan_frequency: 1s

- input_type: log
  paths:
    - /var/log/apache/httpd-*.log
  document_type: apache
```

Prospector-specific configuration options are as follows:

- `input_type`: It accepts the type as either `log` or `stdin`. The `log` type is used to read every log line from the file, and the `stdin` type is used to read from standard input. The `log` type is the default option.
- `paths`: It is used to specify one or more paths to look for files that need to be crawled. One path needs to be specified per line starting with a dash (–). It accepts Golang glob-based paths, and all the patterns Golang glob (`https://golang.org/pkg/path/filepath/#Glob`) supports are accepted by the `paths` parameter.
- `exclude_lines`: It accepts a list of regular expressions to match. It drops the lines that match any regular expression from the list. In the preceding configuration example, it drops all the lines beginning with DBG.
- `include_lines`: It accepts a list of regular expressions to match. It exports the lines that match any regular expressions from the list. In the preceding configuration example, it exports all the lines beginning with either ERR or WARN.

Regular expressions are based on RE2 (`https://godoc.org/regexp/syntax`). You can refer to this link for all the supported `regex` patterns.

- `tags`: It accepts a list of tags that will be included in the `tags` field of every event Filebeat ships. `tags` helps with the conditional filtering of events in Kibana or Logstash. In the preceding configuration example, `java_logs` is appended to the `tags` list.
- `fields`: It is used to specify option fields that need to be included in each event Filebeat ships. Like `tags`, it helps with the conditional filtering of events in Kibana or Logstash. Fields can be scalar values, arrays, dictionaries, or any nested combination of these. By default, the fields that one specifies will be grouped under a `fields` sub-dictionary in the output document. In the preceding configuration example, a new field called `env` with the `staging` value would be created under the `fields` field.

To store the custom fields as top-level fields, set the `fields_under_root` option to true.

- scan_frequency: It is used to specify the time interval after which the prospector checks for any new files under the configured paths. In the preceding configuration example, the prospector checks for new files every second. By default, the scan_frequency is set to 10 seconds.
- document_type: It is used to specify the index type if the output is Elasticsearch. The default type is log. In the preceding configuration example, Apache logs are set to the apache type so that when indexed to Elasticsearch, Apache logs can be found under the apache type. The index name would still be of the pattern filebeat-YYYY.MM.DD.
- multiline: It specifies how logs that are spread over multiple lines need to be processed. This is very beneficial for processing stack traces/exception messages.

It is made up of a pattern that specifies the regular expression pattern to match: negate, which specifies whether or not the pattern is negated, and match, which specifies how Filebeat combines matching lines with an event. The values for the negate setting are either true or false; by default it is false. The values for the match setting are either after or before. In the preceding configuration example, all the consecutive lines that begin with the space pattern are appended to the previous line that doesn't begin with a space.

> The after setting is similar to the previous Logstash multi-line setting, and before is similar to the next Logstash multi-line setting.

Filebeat global options

This section contains configuration options to control the behavior of Filebeat on a global level.

Some of the configuration options are as follows:

- registry_file: It is used to specify the location of the registry file, which is used to maintain information about files, such as the last offset read and if the read lines are acknowledge by the configured outputs or not. The default location of the registry is ${path.data}/registry:

  ```
  filebeat.registry_file: /etc/filebeat/registry
  ```

One can specify a relative path or an absolute path as a value for this setting. If a relative path is specified, it is considered relative to the `${path.data}` setting.

- `shutdown_timeout`: This setting specifies how long Filebeat waits on shutdown for the publisher to finish. If Filebeat shuts down while it's in the process of sending events, it does not wait for the output to acknowledge all events before shutting down. This setting can help Filebeat to wait a specific amount of time before shutting down, as follows:

```
filebeat.shutdown_timeout: 10s
```

Filebeat general options

This section contains configuration options and some general settings to control the behavior of Filebeat.

Some of the configuration options/settings are as follows:

- `name`: The name of the shipper that publishes the network data. By default, `hostname` is used for this field.

```
name: "dc1-host1"
```

- `tags`: The list of tags that will be included in the `tags` field of every event Filebeat ships. Tags make it easy to group servers by different logical properties and help with the filtering of events in Kibana and Logstash:

```
tags: ["staging", "web-tier","dc1"]
```

- `max_procs`: The maximum number of CPUs that can be executed simultaneously. The default is the number of logical CPUs available in the system:

```
max_procs: 2
```

Output configuration

This section is used to configure outputs where the events need to be shipped. Events can be sent to single or multiple outputs simultaneously. The allowed outputs are Elasticsearch, Logstash, Kafka, Redis, file, and console.

Some of the outputs that can be configured are as follows:

- `elasticsearch`: It is used to send the events directly to Elasticsearch.

  A sample Elasticsearch output configuration is as follows:

  ```
  output.elasticsearch:
     enabled: true
     hosts: ["localhost:9200"]
  ```

  By using the `enabled` setting, one can enable or disable the output. `hosts` accepts one or more Elasticsearch node/server. Multiple hosts can be defined for failover purposes. When multiple hosts are configured, the events are distributed to these nodes in round robin order. If Elasticsearch is secured, then the credentials can be passed using the `username` and `password` settings:

  ```
  output.elasticsearch:
     enabled: true
     hosts: ["localhost:9200"]
     username: "elasticuser"
     password: "password"
  ```

  To ship the event to the Elasticsearch ingest node pipeline so that it can be pre-processed before it is stored in Elasticsearch, the pipeline information can be provided using the `pipleline` setting:

  ```
  output.elasticsearch:
     enabled: true
     hosts: ["localhost:9200"]
     pipeline: "apache_log_pipeline"
  ```

- `logstash`: It is used to send the events to Logstash.

 To use Logstash as output, Logstash needs to be configured with the Beats input plugin to receive incoming Beats events.

A sample Logstash output configuration is as follows:

```
output.logstash:
   enabled: true
   hosts: ["localhost:5044"]
```

By using the `enabled` setting, one can enable or disable the output. `hosts` accepts one or more Logstash server. Multiple hosts can be defined for failover purposes. If the configured host is unresponsive, then the event will be sent to one of the other configured hosts. When multiple hosts are configured, the events are distributed in random order. To enable load balancing of events across the Logstash hosts, use the `loadbalance` flag, set to `true`:

```
output.logstash:
   hosts: ["localhost:5045", "localhost:5046"]
   loadbalance: true
```

- `console`: It is used to send the events to `stdout`. The events are written in JSON format. It is useful during debugging or testing.

  A sample console configuration is as follows:

```
output.console:
   enabled: true
   pretty: true
```

Filebeat modules

Filebeat modules simplify the process of collecting, parsing, and visualizing logs of common formats.

A module is made up of one or more fileset. A fileset is made up of the following:

- Filebeat prospector configurations that contain the default paths needed to look out for logs. It also provides configuration for combining multi line events when needed.
- An Elasticsearch Ingest pipeline definition to parse and enrich logs.
- Elasticsearch templates that define the field definitions so that appropriate mappings are set to the fields of the events.
- Sample Kibana dashboards, which can be used for visualizing the logs.

Filebeat modules require the Elasticsearch Ingest Node, and the version of Elasticsearch should be greater that 5.2.

The default modules that are shipped with Filebeat are:

- Apache2 module
- Auditd module
- MySQL module
- Nginx module
- Redis module
- Icinga module
- System module

The `modules.d` directory contains the default configurations for all the modules available in Filebeat. The configuration specific to a module is stored in a `.yml` file, with the name of the file being the name of the module. For example, the configuration related to the `redis` module would be stored in a `redis.yml` file.

As each module comes with the default configuration, make the appropriate changes in the module configuration file.

The basic configuration for the `redis` module would look like the following:

```
#redis.yml
- module: redis
  # Main logs
  log:
    enabled: true

    # Set custom paths for the log files. If left empty,
    # Filebeat will choose the paths depending on your OS.
    #var.paths: ["/var/log/redis/redis-server.log*"]

  # Slow logs, retrieved via the Redis API (SLOWLOG)
  slowlog:
    enabled: true

    # The Redis hosts to connect to.
    #var.hosts: ["localhost:6379"]

    # Optional, the password to use when connecting to Redis.
    #var.password:
```

To enable modules, execute the `modules enable` command, passing one or more module name:

```
Windows:
D:\packt\filebeat-6.0.0-windows-x86_64>filebeat.exe modules enable redis
mysql
```

```
Linux:
[locationOfFileBeat]$./filebeat modules enable redis mysql
```

 If a module is disabled, then in the `modules.d` directory, the configuration related to the module will be stored with a `.disabled` extension.

Similarly, to disable modules, execute the `modules disable` command, passing one or more module name to it. For example:

```
Windows:
D:\packt\filebeat-6.0.0-windows-x86_64>filebeat.exe modules disable redis
mysql
```

```
Linux:
[locationOfFileBeat]$./filebeat modules disable redis mysql
```

Once the module is enabled, to load the recommended index template for writing to Elasticsearch, and to deploy the sample dashboards for visualizing the data in Kibana, execute the `setup` command as follows:

```
Windows:
D:\packt\filebeat-6.0.0-windows-x86_64>filebeat.exe -e setup
```

```
Linux:
[locationOfFileBeat]$./filebeat -e setup
```

The `-e` flag specifies to log the output to `stdout`. Once the modules are enabled and the `setup` command is run, to load index templates and sample dashboards, start Filebeat as usual so that it can start shipping logs to Elasticsearch.

 The `setup` command has to be executed during the installation or upgrading of Filebeat, or after a new module is enabled.

Most of the modules have dependency plugins such as ingest-geoip and ingest-user-agent, which need to be installed on Elasticsearch prior to setting up the modules, else the setup will fail.

Rather than enabling the modules by passing them as command-line parameters, one can enable the modules in the configuration file `filebeat.yml` itself, and start the Filebeat as usual:

```
filebeat.modules:
- module: nginx
- module: mysql
```

Each of the modules has associated filesets which contain certain variables that can be overridden either using the configuration file or by passing it as command line parameter using the –M flag when running Filebeat.

For the configuration file, do as follows:

```
filebeat.modules:
- module: nginx
  access:
     var.paths: ["C:\ngnix\access.log*"]
```

For the command line, do as follows:

```
Windows:
D:\packt\filebeat-6.0.0-windows-x86_64>filebeat.exe –e –modules=nginx –M
"nginx.access.var.paths=[C:\ngnix\access.log*]"

Linux:
[locationOfFileBeat]$./filebeat –e –modules=nginx –M
"nginx.access.var.paths=[\var\ngnix\access.log*]"
```

Summary

In this chapter, we have covered the powerful filter section of Logstash that can be used for parsing and enriching log events. We have also covered some of the commonly used filter plugins. We also covered the Beats framework and looked at an overview of various beats including Filebeat, Heartbeat, Packetbeat, and so on, and covered Filebeat in detail.

In the next chapter, we will be covering the various features of X-Pack, a commercial offering by Elastic.co which contains features such as the security to secure Elastic stack, monitoring, alerting, graphs, reporting, and many more.

Visualizing data with Kibana

7

Kibana is an open source web-based analytics and visualization tool that lets you visualize the data stored in Elasticsearch using a variety of tables, maps, and charts. Using its simple interface, users can easily explore large volumes of data stored in Elasticsearch and perform advanced analysis of data in real time.

In this tutorial, let's explore the various components of Kibana and explore how one can use it for data analysis.

We will cover the following topics in this chapter:

- Downloading and installing Kibana
- Data discovery using Kibana
- Visualizations in Kibana
- Analysis of time-series data with Kibana
- Configuring and developing well known plugins in Kibana

Downloading and installing Kibana

Just like with other components of Elastic Stack, downloading and installing Kibana is pretty simple and straightforward.

Navigate to `https://www.elastic.co/downloads/kibana#ga-release` and, depending on your operating system, download the ZIP/TAR file as shown in the following screenshot:

 The Elastic developer community is quite vibrant, and newer releases with new features/fixes get released quite often. While you have been reading this book, the latest Kibana version might have changed. The instructions in this book are based on Kibana version 6.0.0. You can click on the **past releases** link and download version 6.0.0 if you want to follow as is, but the instructions/explanations in this book should hold good for any 6.x release.

Kibana is a visualization tool that relies on Elasticsearch for querying data that is used for generating visualizations. Hence, before proceeding further, make sure Elasticsearch is up and running.

Installing on Windows

Unzip the downloaded file. Once unzipped, navigate to the newly created folder as shown in the following code block:

```
D:\>cd D:\packt\kibana-6.0.0-windows-x86_64
```

To start Kibana, navigate to the `bin` folder, type `kibana.bat`, and press *Enter*.

Installing on Linux

Unzip the `tar.gz` package and navigate to the newly created folder, shown as follows:

```
$> tar -xzf kibana-6.0.0-darwin-x86_64.tar.gz
$> cd kibana/
```

To start Kibana, navigate to the `bin` folder, type `./kibana`, and press *Enter*.

You should get the following logs:

```
 log [04:52:06.749] [info][optimize] Optimizing and caching bundles for
kibana, stateSessionStorageRedirect, timelion and status_page. This may
take a few minutes
 log [04:55:20.118] [info][optimize] Optimization of bundles for kibana,
stateSessionStorageRedirect, timelion and status_page complete in 193.36
seconds
 log [04:55:20.241] [info][status][plugin:kibana@6.0.0] Status changed from
uninitialized to green - Ready
 log [04:55:20.402] [info][status][plugin:elasticsearch@6.0.0] Status
changed from uninitialized to yellow - Waiting for Elasticsearch
 log [04:55:20.426] [info][status][plugin:console@6.0.0] Status changed
from uninitialized to green - Ready
 log [04:55:20.454] [info][status][plugin:metrics@6.0.0] Status changed
from uninitialized to green - Ready
 log [04:55:21.987] [info][status][plugin:timelion@6.0.0] Status changed
from uninitialized to green - Ready
 log [04:55:22.001] [info][listening] Server running at
http://localhost:5601
 log [04:55:22.008] [info][status][ui settings] Status changed from
uninitialized to yellow - Elasticsearch plugin is yellow
 log [04:55:22.270] [info][status][plugin:elasticsearch@6.0.0] Status
changed from yellow to green - Kibana index ready
 log [04:55:22.273] [info][status][ui settings] Status changed from yellow
to green - Ready
```

Kibana is a web application, and unlike Elasticsearch and Logstash which run on JVM, Kibana is powered by `node.js`. During bootup, Kibana tries to connect to Elasticsearch running on `http://localhost:9200`. Kibana is started on the default port `5601`. Kibana can be accessed from a web browser using the `http://localhost:5601` URL. You can navigate to the `http://localhost:5601/status` URL to find the Kibana server status.

The status page displays information about the server's resource usage and lists the installed plugins, as shown in the following screenshot:

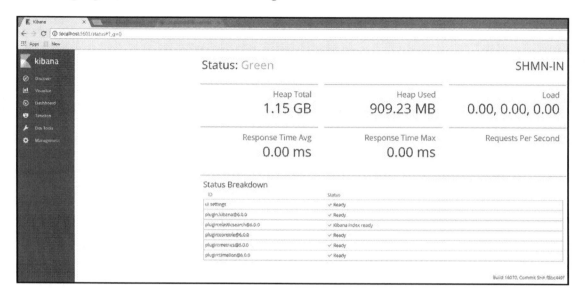

Kibana should be configured to run against an Elasticsearch node of the same version. Running different patch version releases of Kibana and Elasticsearch (for example, Kibana 6.0.0 and Elasticsearch 6.0.1) is generally supported, but not highly encouraged.

Running different major version releases of Kibana and Elasticsearch (for example, Kibana 5.x and Elasticsearch 2.x) is not supported, nor is running minor versions of Kibana that are newer than the version of Elasticsearch (for example, Kibana 6.1 and Elasticsearch 6.0).

Configuring Kibana

When Kibana was started, it started on port `5601`, and it tried to connect to Elasticsearch running on port `9200`. What if we want to change some of these settings? All the configurations of Kibana are stored in a file called `kibana.yml` which is present under the folder `config` under `$KIBANA_HOME`. When this file is opened in your favorite text editor, it contains many properties (key-value pairs) that are commented by default. What this means is that unless those are overridden, the value specified in the property is considered the default value. To uncomment the property, remove the # before the property and save the file.

The following are some of the key configuration settings that you should look for when starting out with Kibana.

`server.port`	This setting specifies the port Kibana would be serving requests. It defaults to `5601`.
`server.host`	Specifies the address to which the Kibana server will bind. IP addresses and host names are both valid values. It defaults to `localhost`.
`elasticsearch.url`	The URL of the Elasticsearch instance to use for all your queries. It defaults to `http://localhost:9200`. If your Elasticsearch is running on a different host/port, make sure you update this property.
`elasticsearch.username` `elasticsearch.password`	If Elasticsearch is secured, specify the username/password details that have access to Elasticsearch here. In the next chapter (X-pack), we will be exploring how to secure Elasticsearch.
`server.name`	A human-readable display name that identifies this Kibana instance. Defaults to hostname.
`kibana.index`	Kibana uses an index in Elasticsearch to store saved searches, visualizations, and dashboards. Kibana creates a new index if the index doesn't already exist. Defaults to `.kibana`.

The `.yml` file is space sensitive or indentation aware. Make sure all the uncommented properties have the same indentation, or else an error will be thrown upon Kibana startup and it will fail to start.

Data preparation

As Kibana is all about gaining insight from data, let's load some sample data that we will use as we follow the tutorial. One of the most common use cases is log analysis. For this tutorial, we will be loading Apache server logs into Elasticsearch using Logstash and then using it in Kibana for analysis/building visualizations.

https://github.com/elastic/elk-index-size-tests hosts a dump of Apache server logs that were collected for the site www.logstash.net for the period of May 2014 to June 2014. It contains 300,000 log events.

Navigate to https://github.com/elastic/elk-index-size-tests/blob/master/logs.gz and click the **Download** button. Unzip the logs.gz file.

Make sure you have Logstash version 5.6 and above installed. Create a config file named apache.conf in the $LOGSTASH_HOME\bin folder, as shown in the following code block:

```
input
{
  file {
        path => "D:\Learnings\data\logs\logs"
        type => "logs"
        start_position => "beginning"
        }
}

filter
{
  grok {
    match => {
      "message" => "%{COMBINEDAPACHELOG}"
            }
        }
  mutate {
    convert => { "bytes" => "integer" }
        }
  date {
    match => [ "timestamp", "dd/MMM/YYYY:HH:mm:ss Z" ]
    locale => en
    remove_field => "timestamp"
        }
  geoip {
    source => "clientip"
        }
  useragent {
    source => "agent"
    target => "useragent"
            }
}

output
{
  stdout {
    codec => dots
```

```
        }
    elasticsearch { }
}
```

Start the Logstash, shown as follows, so that it can begin processing the logs, and index it to Elasticsearch. Logstash will take a while to start and then you should see a series of dots (a dot per processed log line):

```
$LOGSTASH_HOME\bin>logstash -f apache.conf
```

Let's verify the total number of documents (log events) indexed into Elasticsearch:

```
curl -X GET http://localhost:9200/logstash-*/_count
```

In the response, you should see a count of 300,000.

Kibana UI

Open up Kibana from the browser using the `http://localhost:5601` URL. The landing page will look as follows:

User interaction

Let's understand the user interaction before diving into the core components of Kibana. A typical user interaction flow is as depicted in the following diagram:

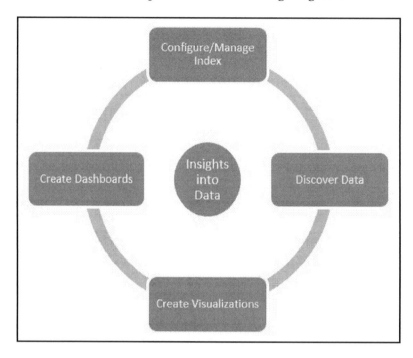

The following points will give you a clear idea of user interaction flow in Kibana:

- Prior to using Kibana for data analysis, the user would have already loaded the data in Elasticsearch.
- In order to analyze the data using Kibana, the user has to first make Kibana aware of the data stored in ES indexes. So the user would need to configure the indexes on which he wants to perform analysis.

- Once configured, the user has to find out the data structure, such as the fields present in the document and the type of fields present in the document, and explore the data. This is done so that he can decide how he can visualize this, and what type of questions he wants to pose and find answers for in terms of the data.
- After understanding the data, and having formed questions to find answers for, he would create appropriate visualizations that would help him in seeking the answers easily from huge amounts of data.
- The user then creates a dashboard from the set of visualizations created earlier, which would tell the story about the data.
- This is an iterative process and the user would juggle around the various stages to find answers to his questions. Thus in this process he might gain deeper insight about the data, and discover answers to newly formed questions which he might not even have thought of before the beginning of this process.

Now that we have an idea about how the user would use Kibana and interact with it, let's understand what Kibana is made up of. As seen in the left side of the collapsible menu/side bar, the Kibana UI consists of the following components:

- **Discover**: This page assists in exploring the data present in ES Indexes. It provides the ability to query data, filter data, and inspect the document structure.
- **Visualize**: This page assists in building visualizations. It contains a variety of visualizations such as bar charts, line charts, maps, tag clouds, and so on. The user can pick and choose the appropriate visualizations that help in analyzing the data.
- **Dashboard**: This page assists in bringing multiple visualizations onto a single page, and thus builds a story about the data.
- **Timelion**: This page assists in visualizing time-series data using a simple expression language and enables the user to combine totally independent data sources (data from disparate indexes) within a single visualization
- **Dev Tools**: This page consists of a set of plugins, each of which assists in performing different functionalities. By default this page contains only a single plugin called Console, which provides a UI to interact with the REST API of Elasticsearch.
- **Management**: This page assists in the configuring and managing of indexes. It also assists in the management (deleting, exporting, and importing) of existing visualizations, dashboards, and search queries.

Configuring the index pattern

Before you can start working with data and creating visualizations to analyze the data, Kibana requires you to configure the index pattern. Index patterns are used to identify the Elasticsearch index which will have search and analytics run against it. They are also used to configure fields. An index pattern is a string with optional wildcards that can match multiple indices. Typically, two types of index exist within Elasticsearch:

- **Time-series indexes**: If there is a correlation between the timestamp and data, the data is called **time-series data**. This data will have a timestamp field. Examples would be logs data, metrics data, and tweet data. When this data is stored in Elasticsearch, the data is stored in multiple indexes (rolling indexes) with index names appended by a timestamp, usually. For example, unixlogs-2017.10.10, tweets-2017.05, logstash-2017.08.10.
- **Regular indexes**: If the data doesn't contain any timestamp and the data has no correlation with time, then the data is called **regular data**. Typically, this data is stored in single indexes. For example, departments data and product catalog data.

On the **Configure an Index Pattern** screen, during configuration of an index pattern, if the index has a datetime field (that is, it is a time-series index), the **Time Filter field name** dropdown is visible and allows the user to select the appropriate datetime field, else the field is not visible.

As we loaded sample data in the previous section, let's configure it so that we can make use of it for the rest of the chapter's examples. In the **Index Name or Pattern** field, type `logstash-*`. For the **Time Filter field name**, select `@timestamp` and click **Create**.

You should see the following page:

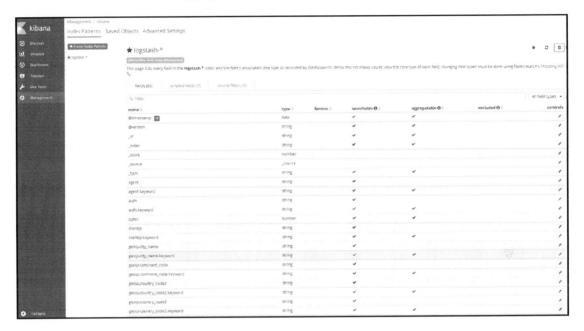

Discover

The Discover page helps you to interactively explore the data. It allows the user to interactively perform search queries, filter search results, and view document data. It also allows the user to save the search, or filter criteria so that it can be reused or used to create visualizations on top of the filtered results.

By default Discover Page displays the events of last 15 minutes. As the log events are from the period May 2014 to June 2014, set the appropriate date range in the time filter. Navigate to **Time Filter** | **Absolute Time Range** and set **From** as 2014-05-28 00:00:00.000 and >**To** to 2014-07-01 00:00:00.000. Click **Go**:

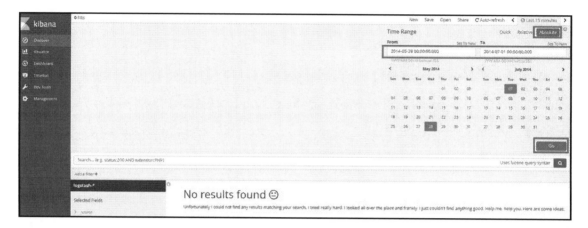

Discover page contains the sections as shown in the following image:

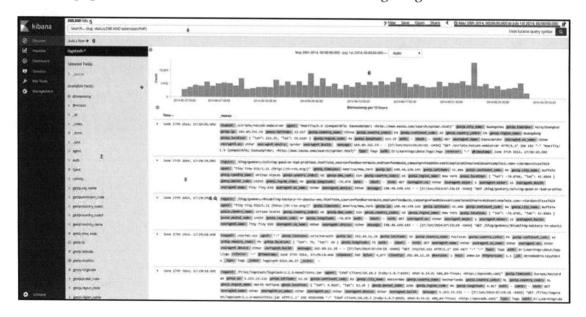

Index Pattern (**1**), Fields List (**2**), Document Table (**3**), Query Bar (**4**), Hits (**5**), Histogram (**6**), Toolbar (**7**), Time Picker (**8**), and Filters (**9**).

Let's look at each one of them:

- **Index Pattern**: All the configured Index patterns are shown here in a dropdown and the default one is selected automatically. The user can choose the appropriate index pattern for data exploration.
- **Fields List**: All the fields that are part of the document are shown in this section. Clicking on the field shows the **Quick Count**, that is, how many of the documents in the documents table contain a particular field, what the top five values are, and what percentage of documents contain each value:

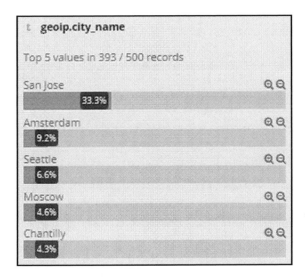

- **Document Table**: This section shows the actual document data. The table shows the 500 most recent documents that match the user entered query/filters, sorted by timestamp (if the field exists). By clicking the **Expand** button found to the left of the document's table entry, data can be visualized in table format or JSON format:

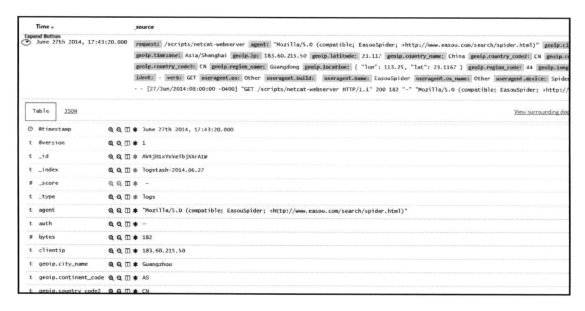

During data exploration, we are often interested in a subset of fields rather than the whole of the document. In order to add fields to the document table, either hover over the field on the fields list and click its add button, or expand the document and click the field's **Toggle column in table** button:

Added field columns replace the _source column in the Documents table. Field columns in the table can be shuffled by clicking the right or left arrows found when hovering over the column name. Similarly, when clicking the remove button, **x**, columns can be removed from the table:

Time ▾	geoip.city_name	response	request **X** «
June 27th 2014, 17:43:20.000	Guangzhou	200	Move column to the left erver
June 27th 2014, 17:42:49.000	Buffalo	200	/blog/geekery/solving-good-or-bad-problems.html? utm_source=feedburner&utm_medium=feed&utm_campaign=Fe
June 27th 2014, 17:42:49.000	Buffalo	200	/blog/geekery/disabling-battery-in-ubuntu-vms.html? utm_source=feedburner&utm_medium=feed&utm_campaign=Fe
June 27th 2014, 17:42:39.000	-	200	/style2.css
June 27th 2014, 17:42:38.000	Amsterdam	200	/files/logstash/logstash-1.1.0-monolithic.jar
June 27th 2014, 17:42:37.000	-	200	/images/jordan-80.png
June 27th 2014, 17:42:35.000	-	200	/reset.css
June 27th 2014, 17:42:30.000	-	200	/blog/tags/X11
June 27th 2014, 17:42:12.000	-	200	/images/googledotcom.png

- **Query Bar**: Using the query bar/search bar, the user can enter queries to filter the search results. Submitting a search request results in the histogram being updated (if the time field is configured for the selected index pattern), and the documents table, fields lists, and hits being updated to reflect the search results. Matching search text is highlighted in the document table. To search your data, enter your search criteria in the query bar and press **Enter**, or click the search icon.

The query bar accepts two types of queries:

- An Elasticsearch Query String Query, which is based on Lucene query syntax: https://lucene.apache.org/core/2_9_4/queryparsersyntax.html
- Full JSON-based Elasticsearch Query DSL: https://www.elastic.co/guide/en/elasticsearch/reference/5.5/query-dsl.html

Let's explore the two options in detail.

Elasticsearch query string

This provides the ability to perform various types of searches ranging from simple to complex queries that adhere to Lucene query syntax. Let's see some examples:

Free Text search: To search for text present in any of the fields, simply enter a text string in the query bar:

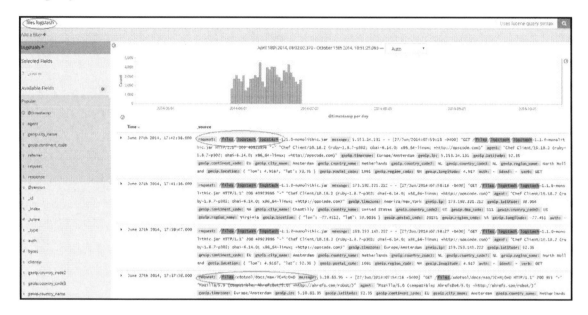

When you enter a group of words to search for, as long as the document contains any of the words or all or part of the words in any order, the document is included in search result.

If you are doing an exact phrase search, that is, the documents should contain all the words given the search criteria, and the words should be in same order, then surround the phrase with quotes. For example, **file logstash** or **files logstash**.

Field search: To search for values against a specific field use the `syntax` field: `value`:

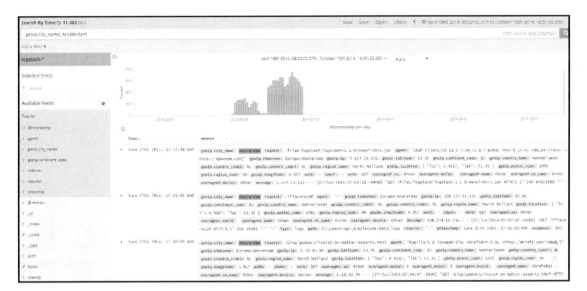

Boolean search: One can make use of Boolean operators such as AND, OR, and - (must not match) to build complex queries. Using Boolean operators, one can combine field: `value` and free text as well.

`Must Not` match.

The following is an example of a `Must Not` operator with a field:

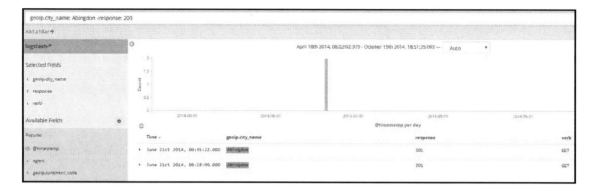

The following is an example of a `Must Not` operator with free text:

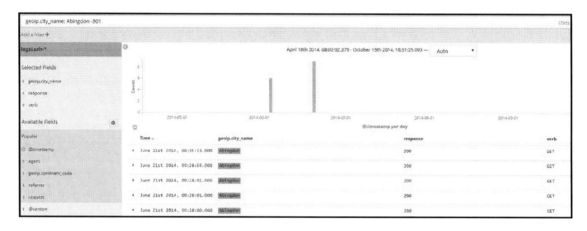

There should be no space between the – operator and the search text/field.

Grouping searches: When we want to build complex queries, often we have to group the search criteria. Grouping both by field and value is supported, as shown in the following example:

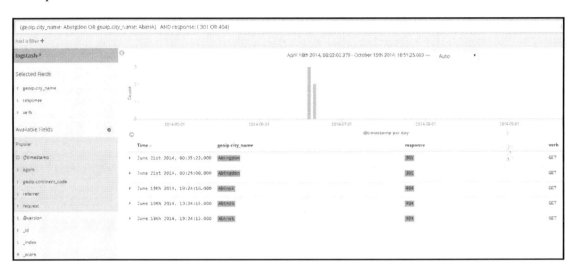

Range search: This allows you to search within a range of values. Inclusive ranges are specified with square brackets, for example [START_VALUE TO END_VALUE], and exclusive ranges with curly brackets, for example { START _VALUE   TO END_VALUE }. Ranges can be specified for dates and numeric or string fields:

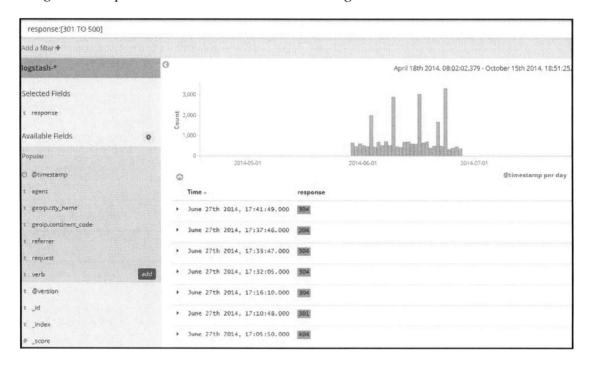

 The TO operator is case sensitive and its range values should be numeric values.

Wild card and Regex search: By using the * and ? wildcards with search text, queries can be executed. * denotes zero or more matches and ? denotes zero or one match:

Wildcard searches can be computationally expensive. It is always preferable to add a wildcard as a suffix rather than a prefix of the search text.

Like wildcards, regex queries are supported too. By using slashes (/) and square brackets ([]), regex patterns can be specified. But be cautious when using regex queries as this is very computationally expensive.

For example, search for any city starting with either **g, b**, or **a**:

Elasticsearch DSL query

By using the DSL query, queries can be performed from the query bar. The query part of the DSL query can be used to perform searches.

The following image is an example of searching for documents that have IE in the useragent.name and Washington in the geoip.region_name field:

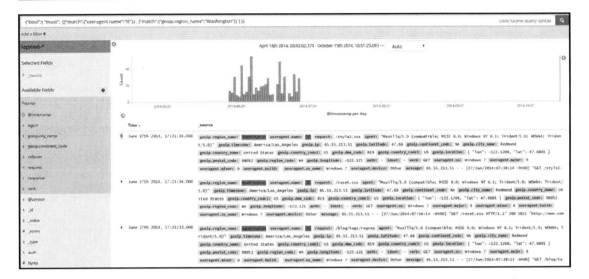

Hits: Hits represent the total number of documents that match the user inputted query/criteria.

Histogram: This section is only visible if a time field is configured for the selected index pattern. This section displays the distribution of documents over time in a histogram. By default, the best time interval for generating the histogram is automatically inferred based on the time set in the time filter. However, the histogram interval can be changed by selecting the interval from the dropdown:

During data exploration, the user can slice and dice through the histogram and filter the search results. Hovering over the histogram converts the mouse pointer to a + symbol. When left clicking, the user can draw a rectangle to inspect/filter the documents that fall in those selected intervals.

After slicing through a histogram, the time interval/period changes. To revert back, click the browser's back button.

Toolbar: User entered search queries and applied filters can be saved so that they can be reused or used to build visualizations on top of the filtered search results. The toolbar provides options for saving, reusing, and sharing the search queries. The user can refer to existing stored searches later and modify the query, and can either overwrite the existing search or save it as a new search (by checking the **Save as new search** checkbox in the **Save** window).

Create a new search based on an existing saved search:

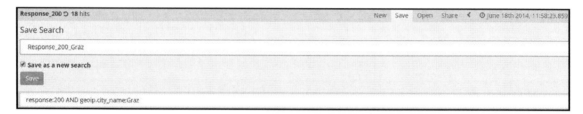

Clicking the Open button displays the **Saved Searches**:

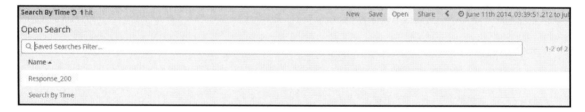

In Kibana, the state of the current page/UI is stored in the URL itself, thus allowing it to be easily shareable. Clicking the **share** button allows you to share the **Saved Search**:

Time Picker: This section is only visible if a time field is configured for the selected index pattern. The time filter restricts the search results to a specific time period, thus assisting in analyzing the data belonging to the period of interest. When the Discover page is opened, by default the time filter is set to the last 15 minutes.

Time Filter provides the following options to select the time periods. Click on **Time Filter** to access the following options:

- **Quick time filter**: This helps you to filter quickly based on some already available time ranges:

- **Relative time filter**: This helps you to filter based on the relative time with respect to the current time. Relative times can be in the past or the future. A checkbox is provided to round the time:

- **Absolute time filter**: This helps you to filter based on inputted start and end times:

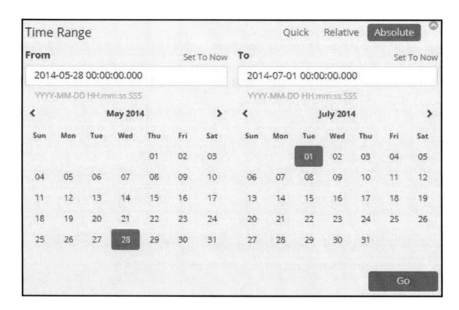

- **Auto Refresh**: During the analysis of real-time data or data that is continuously generated, a feature to automatically fetch the latest data would be very useful. Auto Refresh provides such a functionality. By default, refresh interval is turned off. The user can choose the appropriate refresh interval that assists his analysis:

Time Filter is present on the Discover, Visualize, and Dashboard pages. The time range that gets selected/set in either of these pages gets carried over to other pages, too.

Even the Timelion page has a Time Filter, however it is not affected by the time set on other pages.

Filters: By using positive filters, one can refine the the search results to display only those documents that contain a particular value in a field. One can also create negative filters that exclude documents that contain the specified field value.

One can add field filters from the Fields list or the Documents table, and even manually add a filter. In addition to creating positive and negative filters, the Documents table enables one to filter whether or not a field is present.

To add a positive or negative filter, in the **Fields List** or **Documents Table**, click on the positive icon or negative icon respectively. Similarly, to filter a search through whether or not a field is present, click on the * icon (exists filter):

One can also add filters manually by clicking the **Add a Filter** button found below the query bar. Clicking on the button will launch a popup in which filters can be specified and applied by clicking the **Save** button:

The applied filters are shown below the query bar. Negative filters are shown in red. One can add multiple filters, and the following actions can be applied on the applied filters:

- **Enable/Disable Filter**: This icon allows the enabling/disabling of the filter without removing it. Diagonal stripes indicate that a filter is disabled.
- **Pin Filter**: Pin the filter. Pinned filters persist when you switch contexts in Kibana. For example, you can pin a filter in Discover and it remains in place when you switch to the Visualize/Dashboard page.
- **Toggle Filter**: Allows you to switch from a positive filter to a negative filter and vice versa.
- **Remove Filter**: Allows you to remove the applied filter.
- **Edit Filter**: Allows you to edit the applied filter.

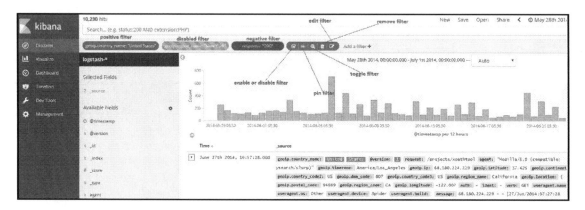

Visualize

The Visualize page helps to create visualizations in the form of graphs, tables, and charts, thus assisting in visualizing all the data that has been stored in Elasticsearch easily. By creating visualizations, the user can easily make sense of data and can obtain answers to the questions he might have formed during the data discovery process. These built visualizations can be used when building dashboards.

For our Apache access log analysis use case, he can easily find out answers to some of the typical questions raised in log analysis, such as:

- What's the traffic in different regions of the world?
- What are the top URLs requested?
- What are the top IP addresses making requests?
- How's the bandwidth usage over time?
- Is there any suspicious or malicious activity from any region/IP address?

All visualizations in Kibana are based on the aggregation queries of Elasticsearch. Aggregations provide the multi-dimensional grouping of results. For example, finding the top user agents by device and by country. Kibana provides a variety of visualizations, shown as follows:

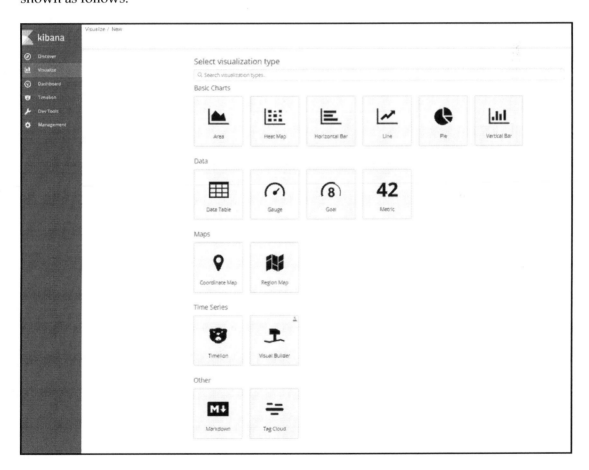

Kibana aggregations

Kibana supports two types of aggregations:

- Bucket aggregations
- Metric aggregations

As aggregation concepts are key to understanding how visualizations are built, let's get an overview of it before jumping into building visualizations.

Bucket aggregations

The grouping of documents by a common criteria is called **bucketing**. Bucketing is very similar to the GROUP BY functionality in SQL. Depending on the aggregation type, each bucket is associated with a criterion which determines whether or not a document in the current context belongs to the bucket or not. Each bucket provides the information about the total number of documents it contains.

Bucket aggregations can do the following:

- Given an employee index containing employee documents
- Find the number of employees based on their age group or location
- Given the Apache access logs index, find the number of 404 responses by country

Bucket aggregation supports sub aggregations, that is, given a bucket, all the documents present in the given bucket can be further bucketed (grouped based on criteria). For example, finding the number of 404 responses by country and also by state.

Depending on the type of bucket aggregation, some define a single bucket, some define fixed number of multiple buckets, and others dynamically create the buckets during the aggregation process.

Bucket aggregations can be combined with metric aggregations. For example, finding the average age of employees per age group.

Kibana supports the following types of bucket aggregations:

- **Histogram**: This aggregation works only on numeric fields and, given the value of the numeric field and the interval, it works by distributing them into fixed-size interval buckets. For example, histogram can be used to find the number of products per price range, with an interval of 100.

- **Date Histogram**: This is a type of histogram aggregation that works only on date fields. It works by distributing them into fixed-size date interval buckets. It supports date/time oriented intervals such as 2 hours, days, weeks, and so on. Kibana provides various intervals including auto, millisecond, second, minute, hourly, daily, weekly, monthly, yearly, and custom, for ease of use. Using the `Custom` option, date/time oriented intervals such as 2 hours, days, weeks, and so on can be supplied. This histogram is ideal for analyzing time-series data. For example, finding the total number of incoming web requests per week/day.
- **Range**: This is similar to histogram aggregations, however rather than fixed intervals, ranges can be specified. Also, it not only works on numeric fields, but can work on dates and IP addresses also. Multiple ranges can be specified using `from` and `to` values. For example, finding the number of employees falling in the age range of 0-25, 25-35, 35-50, and 50 and higher.

 This aggregation includes the from value and excludes the to value for each range.

- **Terms**: This aggregation works by grouping the documents based on each unique term in the field. This aggregation is ideal for finding the top *n* values for a field. For example, finding the top five countries based on the number of incoming web requests.

 This aggregation works on `keyword` fields only.

- **Filters**: This aggregation is used to create buckets based on a filter condition. This aggregation allows for the comparison of specific values. For example, finding the average number of web requests in India compared to the US.
- **GeoHash Grid**: This aggregation works with fields containing `geo_point` values. This aggregation is used for plotting the `geo_points` on a map by grouping them into buckets. For example, visualizing web request traffic over different geographies.

Metric

This is used to compute metrics based on values extracted from the fields of the document. Metrics are used in conjunction with buckets. The different metrics that are available are:

- **Count**: The default metric in Kibana visualizations, returns the count of documents
- **Average**: Used to compute the average value (for a field) of all the documents in the bucket
- **Sum**: Used to compute the sum value (for a field) of all the documents in the bucket
- **Median**: Used to compute the median value (for a field) of all the documents in the bucket
- **Min**: Used to compute the minimum value (for a field) of all the documents in the bucket
- **Max**: Used to compute the maximum value (for a field) of all the documents in the bucket
- **Standard deviation**: Used to compute the standard deviation (for a field) of all the documents in the bucket
- **Percentiles**: Used to compute the number of percentile values
- **Percentile ranks**: For a set of percentiles, this is used to compute the corresponding values

Creating a visualization

The following are the steps to create visualizations:

1. Navigate to the **Visualize** page and click the **Create a new Visualization** button or the + button
2. Select a visualization type
3. Select a data source
4. Build the visualizations

The Visualize Interface looks as follows:

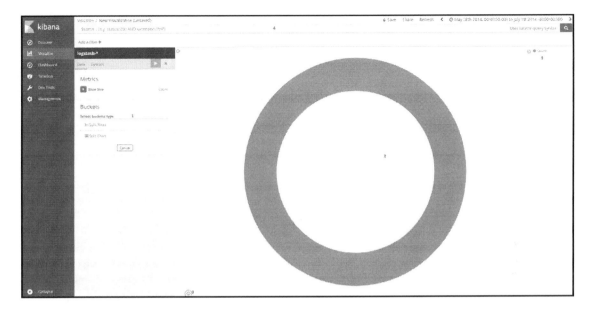

The following are the components of the visualize interface as depicted in the image:

- **Visualization designer**: This is used for choosing appropriate metrics and buckets for creating visualizations.
- **Visualization preview**: Based on the metrics, buckets, queries, filters, and time frame selected, the visualization is dynamically changed.
- **Spy Panel**: This allows you to inspect raw Elasticsearch requests, responses, tabular data, and HTTP request statistics.
- **Query Bar/Field filters**: This is used to filter the search results.
- **Label**: This reflects the metric type and bucket keys as labels. Colors in the visualization can be changed by clicking on Label and choosing the color from the color palette.
- **Toolbar/Time filter**: This provides the option to save or share the visualizations. Also, using the time filter, the user can restrict the time to filter the search results.

Time filters, the query bar, and field filters are explained in the *Discover* section.

Visualization types

Let us take a look at each visualization type in detail.

Line, area, and bar charts

These charts are used for visualizing the data distribution by plotting it against an X/Y axis. These charts are also used for visualizing the time-series data to analyze trends. Bar and area charts are very useful for visualizing stacked data (that is, when sub aggregations are used).

Kibana 5.5 onwards provides the option to dynamically switch the chart type, that is, the user can start off with a line chart but can change its type to either bar or area, thus allowing for the flexibility of choosing the right visualizations for analysis.

Data table

This is used to display aggregated data in a tabular format. This aggregation is useful for analyzing data that has a high degree of variance and which would be difficult to analyze using charts. For example, a data table is useful for finding the top 20 URLs or top 20 IP addresses. It helps identify the top *n* types of aggregations.

MarkDown widget

This visualization is used to create formatted text containing general information, comments, and instructions pertaining to a dashboard. This widget accepts GitHub-flavored Markdown text (`https://help.github.com/categories/writing-on-github/`).

Metric

Metric aggregations work only on numeric fields and display a single numeric value for the aggregations that are selected.

Goal

Goal is a metric aggregation that provides visualizations that display how the metric progresses towards a fixed goal. It is a new visualization that was introduced in Kibana 5.5.

Gauge

A gauge is a metric aggregation which provides visualizations that are used to show how a metric value relates to the predefined thresholds/ranges. For example, this visualization can be used to show whether a server load is within a normal range or instead has reached critical capacity. It is a new visualization that was introduced in Kibana 5.5.

Pie charts

This visualization is used to represent part to whole relationships. Parts are represented by slices in the visualization.

Co-ordinate maps

This visualization is used to display the geographical area mapped to the data determined by the specified buckets/aggregations. In order to make use of this visualization, the documents must have some fields mapped to the `geo_point` datatype. It uses a GeoHash grid aggregation and groups points into buckets that represent cells in a grid. This visualization was earlier named a tile map.

Region maps

Region maps are thematic maps in which boundary vector shapes are colored using a gradient; higher intensity colors indicate larger values, and lower intensity colors indicate smaller values. These are also known as **choropleth maps** (`https://en.wikipedia.org/wiki/Choropleth_map`). Kibana offers two vector layers by default, one for countries of the world and one for US shapes. It is a new visualization that was introduced in Kibana 5.5.

Tag cloud

A tag cloud is a visual representation of text data typically used to visualize free form text. Tags are usually single words, and the importance of each tag is shown with a font size or color. The font size for each word is determined by the metrics aggregation. For example, if a count (metric) is used, then the most frequently occurring word has the biggest font size and the least occurring word has the smallest font size.

Visualizations in action

Let's see how different visualizations can help us in doing the following:

- Analyzing the response codes over time
- Finding the top 10 URLs requested
- Analyzing the bandwidth usage of the top five countries over time
- Finding the most used user agent
- Analyzing the web traffic originating from different countries

 As the log events are from the period May 2014 to June 2014, set the appropriate date range in the time filter. Navigate to Time Filter | Absolute Time Range and set **From** as 2014-05-28 00:00:00.000 and **To** to 2014-07-01 00:00:00.000. Click **Go**.

Response codes over time

This can be visualized easily using a bar graph.

Create a new visualization:

1. Click on **New** and select **Vertical Bar**
2. Select **Logstash-*** under **From a New Search, Select Index**
3. In the X axis, select **Date Histogram** and **@timestamp** as the field
4. Click **Add sub-buckets** and select **Split Series**
5. Select **Terms** as the **sub aggregation**
6. Select **response.keyword** as the field

7. Click the **Play** (Apply Changes) button

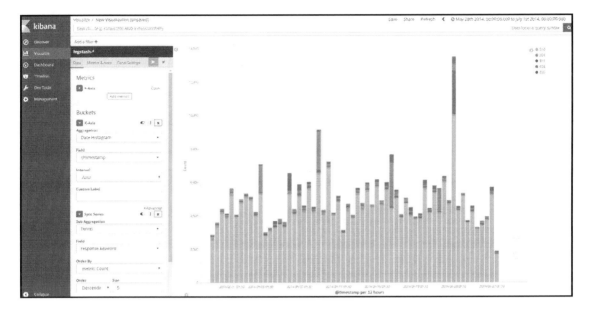

Save the visualization as **Response Codes By Time**

As seen in the visualization, on a few days, such as June 9th, June 16th, and so on, there is a significant amount of 404. Now, to analyze just the 404 events, from the labels/keys panel click on **404** and then click **positive filter**:

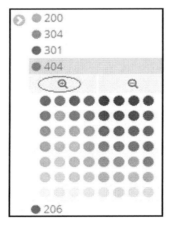

The resulting graph is shown as follows:

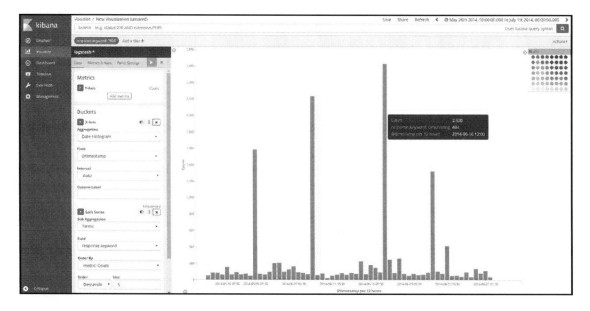

 You can expand the labels/keys and choose the colors from the color palette and thus change the colors in the visualization. Pin the filter and navigate to the **Discover** page to see the requests resulting in 404s.

Top 10 URLs requested

This can be visualized easily using a data table.

The steps are as follows:

1. Create a new visualization
2. Click on **New** and select **Data Table**
3. Select **Logstash-*** under **From a New Search, Select Index**
4. Select buckets type as the **Split Rows**
5. Select **Aggregation** as the **Terms**
6. Select the **request.keyword** field

7. Set the Size to 10
8. Click the **Play** (Apply Changes) button

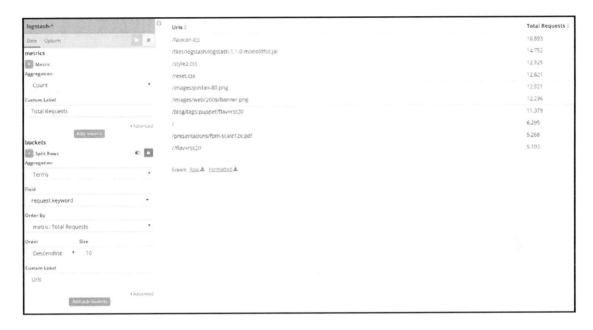

Save the visualization as **Top 10 URLs**.

`Custom Label` fields can be used to provide meaningful names to the aggregated results. Most of the visualizations support custom labels. Data table visualizations can be exported as `.csv` file by clicking **Raw** or **Formatted** links found under the data table visualization.

Bandwidth usage of top five countries over time

The steps to demonstrate this are as follows:

1. Create a new visualization
2. Click on **New** and select **Area Chart**
3. Select **Logstash-*** under **From a New Search, Select Index**
4. In **Y axis**, select Aggregation type as the **Sum** and **bytes** as the field
5. In **X axis**, select **Date Histogram** and **@timestamp** as the field

6. Click **Add sub-buckets** and select **Split Series**
7. Select **Terms** as the **sub aggregation**
8. Select **geoip.country_name.keyword** as the field
9. Click the **Play** (Apply Changes) button:

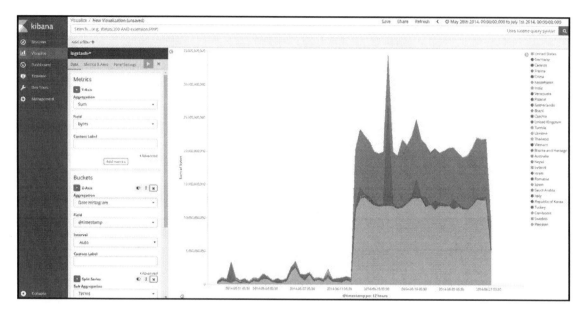

Save the visualization as **Top 5 Countries by Bandwidth Usage**.

What if we were not interested in finding only the top five countries? Rearrange the aggregation and click **Play**:

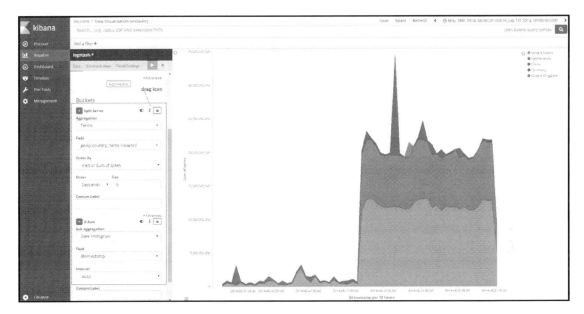

The order of aggregations is important.

Web traffic originating from different countries

This can be visualized easily using a coordinate map.

The steps are as follows:

1. Create a new visualization
2. Click on **New** and select **Coordinate Map**
3. Select **logstash-*** under **From a New Search, Select Index**
4. Set the bucket type to **Geo Coordinates**
5. Select the aggregation as **Geohash**
6. Select the **geoip.location** field
7. In the options tab select **Map Type** as **Heatmap**
8. Click the **Play (Apply Changes)** button:

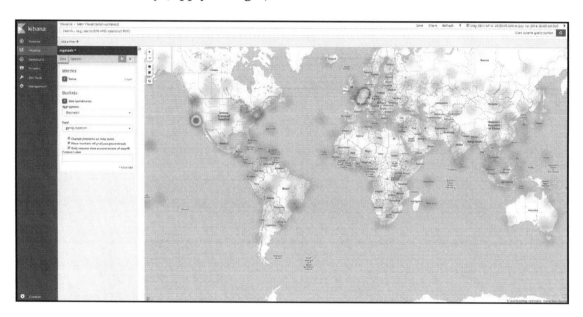

Save the visualization as **Traffic By Country**.

Based on this visualization, most of the traffic is originating from California.

For the same visualization, if the metric is changed to **bytes**, the resulting visualization is as follows:

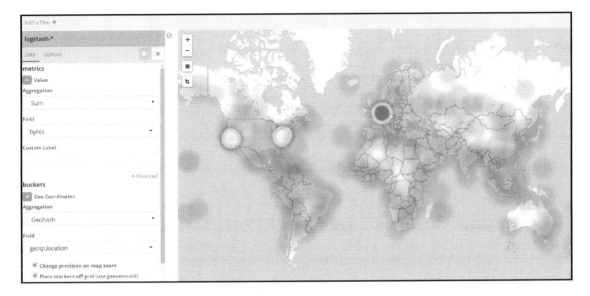

> You can click on the +/- button found at the top left of the map and zoom in/zoom out.

 Using the **Draw Rectangle** button found at the top left, below the zoom in and zoom out buttons, you can draw a region for filtering the documents. Then you can pin the filter and navigate to the **Discover** page to see the documents belonging to that region.

Most used user agent

This can be visualized easily using a variety of charts. Let's use tag cloud.

The steps are as follows:

1. Create a new visualization
2. Click on **New** and select **Tag Cloud**
3. Select **logstash-*** under **From a New Search, Select Index>**

4. Set the bucket type to Tags
5. Select the **Terms** aggregation
6. Select the **useragent.name.keyword** field
7. Set the Size to 10 and click the **Play** (**Apply Changes**) button:

Save the visualization as **Most used user agent**. Chrome, followed by Firefox, is the user agent the majority of traffic is originating from.

Dashboards

Dashboards help one bring different visualizations into a single page. By using the previously stored visualizations and saved queries, one can build a dashboard that tells a story about the data.

A sample dashboard would look like the following:

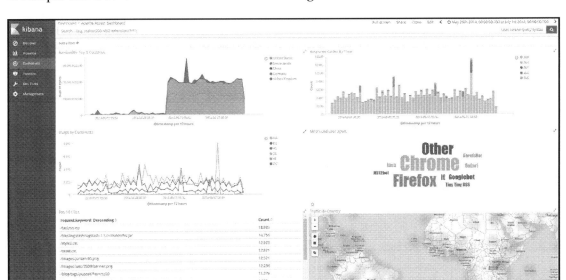

Let's see how we can build a dashboard for our log analysis use case.

Creating a dashboard

In order to create a new dashboard, navigate to the **Dashboard** page and click the **Create a Dashboard** button or the **+** button:

On the resulting page, the user can click the **Add** button which shows all the stored visualizations and saved searches that are available to be added. Clicking on the saved search/visualizations will result in them getting added to the page:

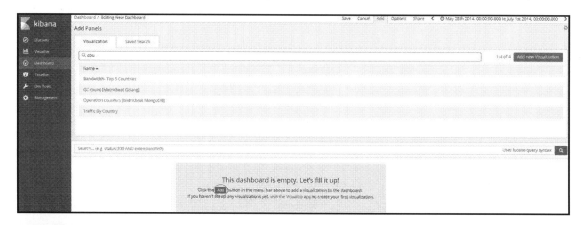

The user can expand, edit, rearrange, or remove the visualizations using the buttons available at the top corner of each visualization:

By using the query bar, field filters, and time filters, search results can be filtered. The dashboard reflects those changes via the changes to the embedded visualizations.

For example, you might be only interested in knowing the top user agents and top devices by country when the response code is 404.

Usage of the query bar, field filters, and time filters is explained in the *Discover* section.

Saving the dashboard

Once the required visualizations are added to the dashboard, make sure to save the dashboard by clicking the **Save** button available in the toolbar, and provide a title. When a dashboard is saved, all the query criteria and filters get saved, too. If one wants to save the time filters, then while saving the dashboard select the **Store time with dashboard** checkbox. Saving the time along with the dashboard might be useful when you want to share/reopen the dashboard in its current state:

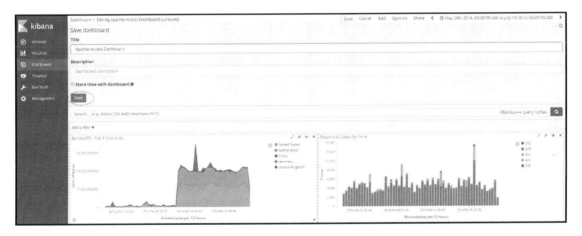

Cloning the dashboard

Using the Clone feature, you can copy the current dashboard, along with its queries and filters, and create a new dashboard. For example, you might want to create new dashboards for continents or countries:

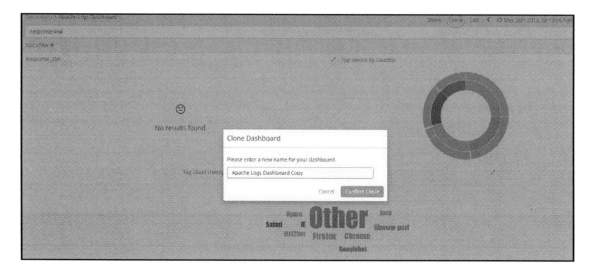

 The dashboard background theme can be changed from light to dark. When you click the **Edit** button in the toolbar, it provides a button called **Options** which provides the feature to change the dashboard theme.

Sharing the dashboard

Using the Share feature, you can either share a direct link to a Kibana dashboard with another user, or embed the dashboard in a web page as an Iframe:

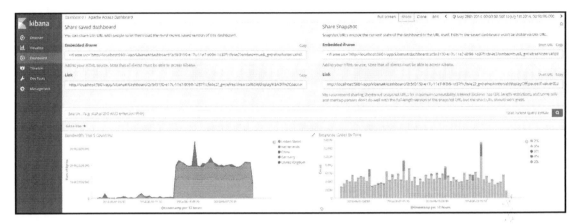

Timelion

Timelion is a visualization tool for analyzing time-series data in Kibana. It enables you to combine totally independent data sources within the same visualization. Using its simple expression language, you can execute advanced mathematical calculations, such as dividing and subtracting metrics, calculating derivatives and moving averages, and visualizing the results of these calculations.

Timelion UI

Timelion is present in the left pane of the Kibana UI, between the **Dashboard** and **Dev Tools** icons:

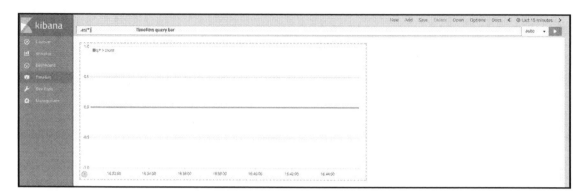

The main component/feature of the Timelion UI is the **Timelion query bar** that allows one to define expressions that influence the generation of the graphs. It allows one to define multiple expressions separated by commas, and also allows you to chain functions.

The Timelion UI also offers the following options:

- **New**: This is used to create a new Timelion sheet for creating graphs.
- **Add**: One can create multiple charts on the same same Timelion sheet using this option.
- **Save**: This is used to save the Timelion page. It provides two options, which are to save the Timelion sheet or save the current expression as a Kibana dashboard panel.
- **Open**: This is used to open the existing saved Timelion sheet.
- **Options**: This provides the option of specifying the number of rows and columns in the Timelion sheet.
- **Docs**: This provides the documentation for starting out with Timelion and also provides the documentation for all the supported functions in Timelion expressions.
- **Time Filter**: This provides the time-filter options for filtering the data.

Timelion expressions

The simplest Timelion expression used for generating graphs is as follows:

```
.es(*)
```

Timelion expressions always start with a dot followed by the function name which can accept one or more parameters. The `.es(*)` expression queries data from all the indexes present in Elasticsearch. By default, it will just count the number of documents, resulting in a graph showing the number of documents over time.

If you'd like to restrict Timelion to data within a specific index (for example, `logstash-*`), you can specify the index within the function as follows:

```
.es(index=logstash-*)
```

As Timelion is a time-series visualizer, it uses the `@timestamp` field present in the index as the time field for plotting the values on an *x* axis. One can change it by passing the appropriate time field as a value to the `timefield` parameter.

Timelion's helpful auto-completion feature will help you build the expression as you go along:

Let's see some examples in action to understand Timelion better.

As the log events are from the period May 2014 to June 2014, set the appropriate date range in the time filter. Navigate to **Time Filter** | **Absolute Time Range** and set **From** to 2014-05-28 00:00:00.000 and **To** to 2014-07-01 00:00:00.000. Click **Go**.

Let's find the average bytes usage over time for the US. The expression for this would be:

```
.es(q='geoip.country_code3:US',metric='avg:bytes')
```

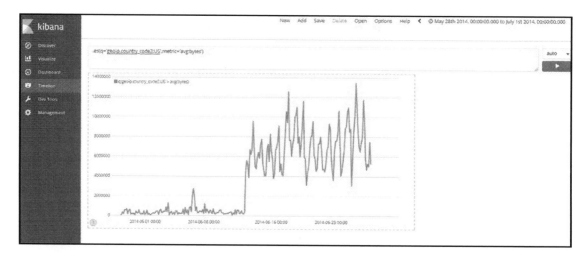

Timelion allows for the plotting of multiple graphs in the same chart as well. By separating the expressions with commas, one can plot multiple graphs.

Let's find the average bytes usage over time for the US and the average bytes usage over time for China. The expression for this would be:

```
.es(q='geoip.country_code3:US',metric='avg:bytes'),
.es(q='geoip.country_code3:CN',metric='avg:bytes')
```

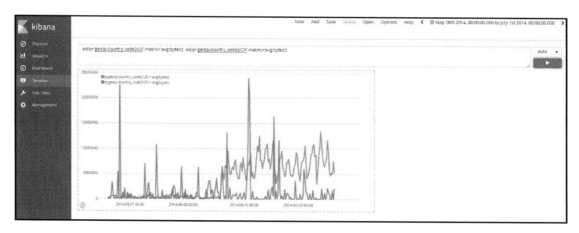

Timelion also allows for the chaining of functions. Let's change the label and color of the preceding graphs. The expression for this would be:

```
.es(q='geoip.country_code3:US',metric='avg:bytes').label('United
States').color('yellow'),
.es(q='geoip.country_code3:CN',metric='avg:bytes').label('China').color('re
d')
```

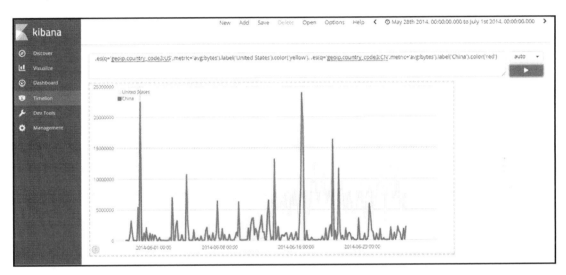

One more useful option in Timelion is using offsets to analyze old data. This is useful for comparing current trends with earlier patterns. Let's compare the sum of bytes usage over the previous week for the US. The expression for this would be:

```
.es(q='geoip.country_code3:US',metric='sum:bytes').label('Current Week'),
.es(q='geoip.country_code3:US',metric='sum:bytes',
offset=-1w).label('Previous Week')
```

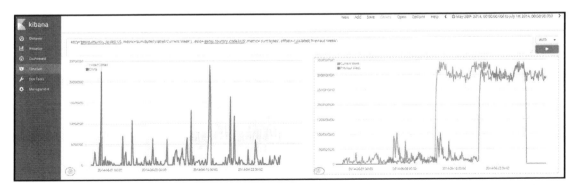

The preceding screenshot demonstrates the ability to add multiple charts to the same Timelion sheet. By clicking the **Add** button, one can add multiple charts. Selecting the chart changes the associated expression in the **Timelion Query Bar**.

Timelion also supports the pulling of data from external data sources using a public API. Timelion has a native API for pulling data from the World Bank, Quandl, and Graphite.

 Timelion expressions support around 50 different functions (`https://github.com/elastic/timelion/blob/master/FUNCTIONS.md`), which you can use to build expressions.

Using plugins

Plugins are a way to enhance the functionality of Kibana. All the plugins that are installed will be placed under the `$KIBANA_HOME/plugins` folder. Elastic, the company behind Kibana, provides many plugins that can be installed, and there are quite a number of public plugins that are not maintained by Elastic which can be installed, too.

Installing plugins

Navigate to `KIBANA_HOME` and execute the `install` command, as shown in the following code, to install any plugins. During installation, either the name of the plugin can be given (if it's hosted by Elastic itself), or the URL of the location where the plugin is hosted can be given:

```
$ KIBANA_HOME>bin/kibana-plugin install <package name or URL>
```

For example, to install `x-pack`, a plugin developed and maintained by Elastic, execute the following command:

```
$ KIBANA_HOME>bin/kibana-plugin install x-pack
```

To install a public plugin, for example LogTrail (`https://github.com/sivasamyk/logtrail`), execute the following command:

```
$ KIBANA_HOME>bin/kibana-plugin install
https://github.com/sivasamyk/logtrail/releases/download/v0.1.23/logtrail-6.0.0-0.1.23.zip
```

> LogTrail is a plugin to view, analyze, search, and tail log events from multiple hosts in real time with a developer friendly interface, inspired by Papertrail (`https://papertrailapp.com/`).

> A list of publicly available Kibana plugins can be found at `https://www.elastic.co/guide/en/kibana/6.0/known-plugins.html`.

Removing plugins

To remove a plugin, navigate to `KIBANA_HOME` and execute the `remove` command followed by the plugin name:

```
$ KIBANA_HOME>bin/kibana-plugin remove x-pack
```

Summary

In this chapter, we covered how to effectively use Kibana to build beautiful dashboards for effective storytelling about your data.

We learned how to configure Kibana to visualize data from Elasticsearch. We also looked at how to add custom plugins to Kibana.

In the next chapter, we will cover ElasticSearch, and the core components that help when building data pipelines. We will also cover visualizing data to add the extensions needed for specific use cases.

8
Elastic X-Pack

X-Pack is an Elastic Stack extension that bundles security, alerting, monitoring, reporting, machine learning, and graph capabilities into one easy-to-install package. It adds essential features to make Elastic Stack production ready. Unlike the components of Elastic Stack, which are open source, X-Pack is a commercial offering from Elastic.co, and so it requires a paid license for usage. When you install X-Pack for the first time, you are given a 30-day trial. The basic or free version will provide only monitoring and Dev Tools such as Search Profiler and Grok Debugger. Even though X-Pack comes as a bundle, it allows one to easily enable or disable the features one wants to use.

In this chapter, let's explore the following topics:

- Installing X-Pack on Elasticsearch and Kibana
- Securing Elasticsearch and Kibana
- Monitoring Elasticsearch
- Exploring alerting

Installing X-Pack

As X-Pack is an extension of Elastic Stack, prior to installing X-Pack, you need to have both Elasticsearch and Kibana installed. You must run the version of X-Pack that matches the version of Elasticsearch and Kibana.

Installing X-Pack on Elasticsearch

X-Pack is installed just like any plugin to extend Elasticsearch.

These are the steps to install X-Pack in Elasticsearch:

1. Navigate to the ES_HOME folder.
2. Install X-Pack using the following command:

   ```
   $ ES_HOME> bin/elasticsearch-plugin install x-pack
   ```

   During installation, it will ask you to grant extra permissions to X-Pack, which are required by Watcher to send email alerts and also to enable Elasticsearch to launch the machine learning analytical engine. Specify y to continue the installation or N to abort the installation.

   You should get the following logs/prompts during installation:

   ```
   -> Downloading x-pack from elastic
   [=================================================] 100%
   @@@@@@@@@@@@@@@@@@@@@@@@@@@@@@@@@@@@@@@@@@@@@@@@@@@@@@
   @ WARNING: plugin requires additional permissions @
   @@@@@@@@@@@@@@@@@@@@@@@@@@@@@@@@@@@@@@@@@@@@@@@@@@@@@@
   * java.io.FilePermission \\.\pipe\* read,write
   * java.lang.RuntimePermission
   accessClassInPackage.com.sun.activation.registries
   * java.lang.RuntimePermission getClassLoader
   * java.lang.RuntimePermission setContextClassLoader
   * java.lang.RuntimePermission setFactory
   * java.net.SocketPermission * connect,accept,resolve
   * java.security.SecurityPermission createPolicy.JavaPolicy
   * java.security.SecurityPermission getPolicy
   * java.security.SecurityPermission putProviderProperty.BC
   * java.security.SecurityPermission setPolicy
   * java.util.PropertyPermission * read,write
   * java.util.PropertyPermission sun.nio.ch.bugLevel write
   See
   http://docs.oracle.com/javase/8/docs/technotes/guides/security/perm
   issions.html
   for descriptions of what these permissions allow and the associated
   risks.

   Continue with installation? [y/N]y
   @@@@@@@@@@@@@@@@@@@@@@@@@@@@@@@@@@@@@@@@@@@@@@@@@@@@@@
   @ WARNING: plugin forks a native controller @
   @@@@@@@@@@@@@@@@@@@@@@@@@@@@@@@@@@@@@@@@@@@@@@@@@@@@@@
   This plugin launches a native controller that is not subject to the
   ```

```
Java
security manager nor to system call filters.

Continue with installation? [y/N]y
Elasticsearch keystore is required by plugin [x-pack], creating...
-> Installed x-pack
```

3. Restart Elasticsearch:

```
$ ES_HOME> bin/elasticsearch
```

4. Generate the passwords for the default/reserved users—elastic, kibana, and logstash_system—by executing this command:

```
$ ES_HOME>bin/x-pack/setup-passwords interactive
```

You should get the following logs/prompts to enter the password for the reserved/default users:

```
Initiating the setup of reserved user
elastic,kibana,logstash_system passwords.
You will be prompted to enter passwords as the process progresses.
Please confirm that you would like to continue [y/N]y
Enter password for [elastic]: elastic
Reenter password for [elastic]: elastic
Enter password for [kibana]: kibana
Reenter password for [kibana]:kibana
Enter password for [logstash_system]: logstash
Reenter password for [logstash_system]: logstash
Changed password for user [kibana]
Changed password for user [logstash_system]
Changed password for user [elastic]
```

Please make a note of the passwords set for the reserved/default users. You can choose any password of your liking. We have chosen the passwords as elastic, kibana, and logstash for elastic, kibana, and logstash_system users, respectively, and we will be using them throughout this chapter.

To verify the X-Pack installation and enforcement of security, point your web browser to `http://localhost:9200/` to open Elasticsearch. You should be prompted to log in to Elasticsearch. To log in, you can use the built-in `elastic` user and the password `elastic`. Upon a successful log in, you should see the following response:

```
{
name: "fwDdHSI",
cluster_name: "elasticsearch",
cluster_uuid: "08wSPsjSQCmeRaxF4iHizw",
version: {
number: "6.0.0",
build_hash: "8f0685b",
build_date: "2017-11-10T18:41:22.859Z",
build_snapshot: false,
lucene_version: "7.0.1",
minimum_wire_compatibility_version: "5.6.0",
minimum_index_compatibility_version: "5.0.0"
},
tagline: "You Know, for Search"
}
```

A typical cluster in Elasticsearch is made up of multiple nodes, and X-Pack needs to be installed on each node belonging to the cluster.

To skip the install prompt, use the—batch parameters during installation: `$ES_HOME>bin/elasticsearch-plugin install x-pack --batch`.

You installation of X-Pack will have created folders named `x-pack` in `bin`, `config`, and `plugins` found under `ES_HOME`. We shall explore these in later sections of the chapter.

Installing X-Pack on Kibana

X-Pack is installed just like any plugins to extend Kibana.

The following are the steps to install X-Pack in Kibana:

1. Navigate to the `KIBANA_HOME` folder.

2. Install X-Pack using the following command:

   $KIBANA_HOME>bin/kibana-plugin install x-pack

   You should get the following logs/prompts during installation:

   ```
   Attempting to transfer from x-pack
   Attempting to transfer from
   https://artifacts.elastic.co/downloads/kibana-plugins/x-pack/x-pack
   -6.0.0.zip
   Transferring 120307264 bytes...................
   Transfer complete
   Retrieving metadata from plugin archive
   Extracting plugin archive
   Extraction complete
   Optimizing and caching browser bundles...
   Plugin installation complete
   ```

3. Add the following credentials in the `kibana.yml` file found under
   `$KIBANA_HOME/config` and save it:

   ```
   elasticsearch.username: "kibana"
   elasticsearch.password: "kibana"
   ```

If you have chosen a different password for the `kibana` user during
password setup, use that value for
the `elasticsearch.password` property.

4. Start Kibana:

   $KIBANA_HOME>bin/kibana

To verify the X-Pack installation, go to `http://localhost:5601/` to open Kibana. You should be prompted to log in to Kibana. To log in, you can use the built-in `elastic` user and the password `elastic`.

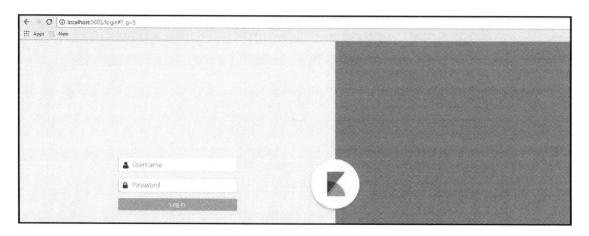

 Your installation of X-Pack will have created a folder named `x-pack` in the plugins folder found under `KIBANA_HOME`.
You can also optionally install X-Pack on Logstash. However, X-Pack currently supports only monitoring of Logstash.

Uninstalling X-Pack

To uninstall X-Pack:

1. Stop Elasticsearch.
2. Remove X-Pack from Elasticsearch:

   ```
   $ES_HOME>bin/elasticsearch-plugin remove x-pack
   ```

3. Restart Elasticsearch and stop Kibana 2. Remove X-Pack from Kibana:

```
$KIBANA_HOME>bin/kibana-plugin remove x-pack
```

4. Restart Kibana.

Configuring X-Pack

X-Pack comes bundled with security, alerting, monitoring, reporting, machine learning, and graph capabilities. By default, all of these features are enabled. However, one might not be interested in all the features it provides. One can selectively enable and disable the features that they are interested in from the `elasticsearch.yml` and `kibana.yml` configuration files.

Elasticsearch supports the following features and settings in the `elasticsearch.yml` file:

Feature	Setting	Description
Machine Learning	`xpack.ml.enabled`	Set this to false to disable X-Pack machine learning features
Monitoring	`xpack.monitoring.enabled`	Set this to false to disable Elasticsearch's monitoring features
Security	`xpack.security.enabled`	Set this to false to disable X-Pack security features
Watcher	`xpack.watcher.enabled`	Set this to false to disable Watcher

Kibana supports these features and settings in the `kibana.yml` file:

Feature	Setting	Description
Machine learning	`xpack.ml.enabled`	Set to false to disable X-Pack machine learning features
Monitoring	`xpack.monitoring.enabled`	Set to false to disable Kibana's monitoring features
Security	`xpack.security.enabled`	Set to false to disable X-Pack security features
Graph	`xpack.graph.enabled`	Set to false to disable X-Pack graph features
Reporting	`xpack.reporting.enabled`	Set to false to disable X-Pack reporting features

If X-Pack is installed on Logstash, you can disable the monitoring by setting the `xpack.monitoring.enabled` property to `false` in the `logstash.yml` configuration file.

Security

Components of Elastic Stack are unsecured, as it doesn't contain inherent security built into it and can be accessed by anyone. This poses a security risk when running Elastic Stack in production. In order to prevent unauthorized access in production, different mechanisms of imposing security such as running Elastic Stack behind a firewall and securing via reverse proxies (such as nginx, HAProxy, and so on) are employed. Elastic.co offers a commercial product to secure Elastic Stack. The offering is part of X-Pack and the module is called Security.

The X-Pack Security module provides the following ways to secure Elastic Stack:

- User authentication and User authorization
- Node/Client Authentication and Channel Encryption
- Auditing

User authentication

User authentication is a process of validating the user and thus preventing unauthorized access to Elastic Cluster. In the X-Pack Security module, the authentication process is handled by one or more authentication services called **realms**. The Security module provides two types of realms, namely internal realms and external realms.

Two types of built-in internal realms are native and file. The native realm is the default realm and the user credentials are stored in a special index called **.security-6** on Elasticsearch itself. The users are managed using the **User Management API** or the Management page of the Kibana UI. We will be exploring more of this in a later section of this chapter.

If the realm is of type `file`, then the user credentials are stored in a file on each node. The users are managed via dedicated tools that are provided by X-Pack on installation. These tools can be found at `$ES_HOME\bin\x-pack`. The files are stored under the `$ES_HOME\config\x-pack` folder. As the credentials are stored in a file, it is the responsibility of the administrator to create users with the same credentials on each node.

Built-in external realms are `ldap`, `active_directory`, and `pki`, which use external LDAP server, external Active Directory Server, and Public Key Infrastructure respectively to authenticate users.

Depending on the realms configured, the user credentials need to be attached to the requests sent to Elasticsearch. Realms live within a realm chain. The realms order configured in the `elasticsearch.yml` file determines the order in which realms are consulted during the authentication process. Each realm is consulted one by one based on the order defined until the authentication is successful. Once one of the realms successfully authenticates the request, the authentication is considered to be successful. If none of the realms is able to authenticate the user, then the authentication is considered unsuccessful and an authentication error (HTTP 401) will be returned to caller. The default realm chain consists of internal realm types, that is, `native` and `file`.

If none of the realms are specified in `elasticsearch.yml`, then the default realm used is native. To use the `file` type realm or external realms, they need to be specified in the `elasticsearch.yml` file.

For example, the following snippet shows the configuration for the realm chain containing `native`, `file`, and `ldap`:

```
xpack.security.authc:
  realms:
    native:
      type: native
      order: 0
    file:
      type: file
      order: 1
    ldap_server:
      type: ldap
      order: 2
      url: 'url_to_ldap_server'
```

> To disable a specific realm type, use the `enabled:false` property, as shown in the following example:
> ```
> ldap_server:
>     type: ldap
>     order: 2
>     enabled: false
>     url: 'url_to_ldap_server'
> ```

User authorization

Once the user is successfully authenticated, the authorization process kicks in. Authorization determines whether the user behind the request has enough permissions to execute a particular request.

In X-Pack security, **Secured Resources** are the foundation of user-based security. A secured resource is a resource that needs access, such as indexes, documents, fields or access, to perform Elasticsearch cluster operations. X-Pack Security enables authorization by assigning permissions to roles that are assigned to users. A permission is one or more privileges against a secured resource. A privilege is a named group representing one or more actions that a user may execute against a secured resource. A user can have one or more roles and the total set of permissions that a user has is defined as a union of the permissions in all its roles:

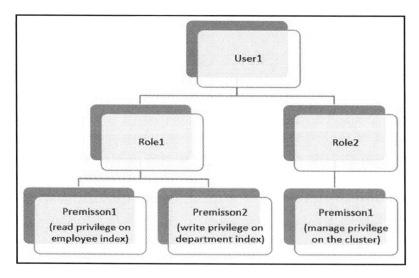

The X-Pack security module provides three types of privileges:

1. **Cluster Privileges**: Cluster Privileges provide privileges for performing various operations on the cluster. For example:

   - **all**: Allows one to execute cluster administration operations settings, update, rerouting, or managing users and roles
   - **monitor**: Allows one to execute all cluster read-only operations, such as fetching cluster health, cluster state, nodes' state, and so on, for monitoring purposes
   - **manage**: This allows one to execute and perform cluster operations that can update the cluster, such as rerouting and updating cluster settings

2. **Index Privileges**: Indices Privileges provide privileges for performing various operations on indices. For example:

   - **all**: Allows you to execute any operation on an index
   - **read**: Allows you to execute read-only operations on an index, such as invoking search, get, suggest, and many more APIs
   - **create_index**: This privilege allows you to create a new index
   - **create**: This privilege allows you to index new documents into an index

3. **Run As Privilege**: This provides the ability to perform user impersonation; that is, it enables an authenticated user to test out another users' access rights without knowing their credentials.

 The complete list of privileges can be obtained at `https://www.elastic.co/guide/en/x-pack/master/security-privileges.html`.

4. **Node/Client Authentication and Channel Encryption**: By encrypting the communication, X-Pack security prevents network-based attacks. It provides the ability to encrypt traffic to and from the Elasticsearch cluster to outside applications as well as encrypt the communication between nodes in the cluster. To prevent unintended nodes from joining the cluster, one can configure the nodes to authenticate as they join the cluster using SSL certificates. X-Pack security IP filtering can prevent unintended application clients, node clients, or transport clients from joining the cluster.

5. **Auditing**: Auditing allows us to capture suspicious activity in our cluster. One can enable auditing to keep track of security-related events, such as authentication failures and refused connections. Logging these events enables one to monitor the cluster for suspicious activity and provides evidence in the event of an attack.

Security in action

In this section, let's look into creating new users, creating new roles, and associating roles with users. Let's import sample data and use it to understand how security works.

Save the following data to a file named data.json:

```
{"index" : {"_index":"employee","_type":"employee"}}
{ "name":"user1", "email":"user1@packt.com","salary":5000, "gender":"M",
"address1":"312 Main St", "address2":"Walthill", "state":"NE"}
{"index" : {"_index":"employee","_type":"employee"}}
{ "name":"user2", "email":"user2@packt.com","salary":10000, "gender":"F",
"address1":"5658 N Denver Ave", "address2":"Portland", "state":"OR"}
{"index" : {"_index":"employee","_type":"employee"}}
{ "name":"user3", "email":"user3@packt.com","salary":7000, "gender":"F",
"address1":"300 Quinterra Ln", "address2":"Danville", "state":"CA"}
{"index" : {"_index":"department","_type":"department"}}
{ "name":"IT", "employees":50 }
{"index" : {"_index":"department","_type":"department"}}
{ "name":"SALES", "employees":500 }
{"index" : {"_index":"department","_type":"department"}}
{ "name":"SUPPORT", "employees":100 }
```

The _bulk API requires the last line of the file to end with the newline character, \n. While saving the file, make sure you have a newline as the last line of the file.

Navigate to the directory where the file is stored and execute the following command to import the data into Elasticsearch:

```
$ directoy_of_data_file> curl -s -H "Content-Type: application/json" -u
elastic:elastic -XPOST http://localhost:9200/_bulk --data-binary @data.json
```

To check whether the import was successful, execute the following command and validate the count of documents:

```
D:\packt\book>curl -s -H "Content-Type: application/json" -u
elastic:elastic -XGET http://localhost:9200/employee,department/_count
{"count":6,"_shards":{"total":10,"successful":10,"skipped":0,"failed":0}}
```

New user creation

Let's explore the creation of a new user in this section. Log in to Kibana
(`http://locahost:5601`) as the `elastic` user:

- To create a new user, Navigate to **Management** UI and select **Users** in the
  Security Section:

- The **Users** screen displays the available users and their roles. By default, it displays the default/reserved users that are part of the X-Pack security native realm:

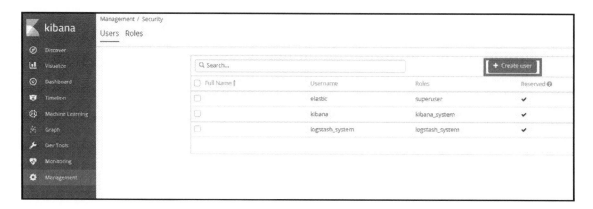

- To create a new user, click on the **Create User** button and enter the details as shown in the following screenshot. Click on **Save**:

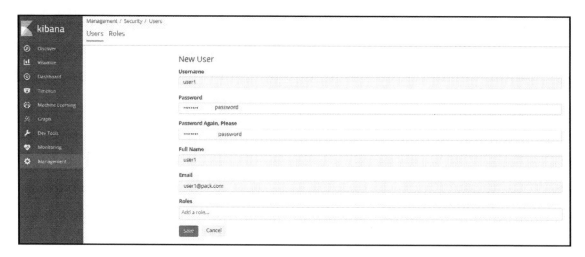

Now that the user is created, let's try to access some Elasticsearch REST APIs with the new user credentials and see what happens. Execute the following command and check the response returned. As the user is not having any role associated, even the authentication is successful. The user gets HTTP status code 403, stating that the user is not authorized to carry out the operation:

```
D:\packt\book>curl -s -H "Content-Type: application/json" -u
user1:password -XGET http://localhost:9200
```
Response:
```
{"error":{"root_cause":[{"type":"security_exception","reason":"acti
on [cluster:monitor/main] is unauthorized for user
[user1]"}],"type":"security_exception","reason":"action
[cluster:monitor/main] is unauthorized for user
[user1]"},"status":403}
```

- Similarly, go ahead and create one more user called user2 as shown in the following screenshot:

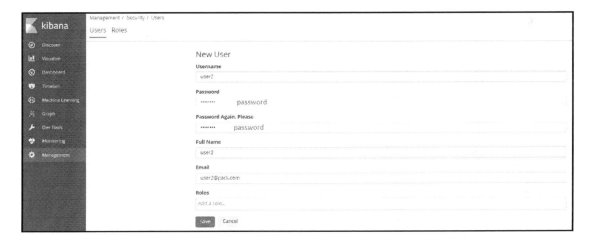

Deleting a user

To delete a role, navigate to **Users** UI, select the custom users created and click on the **Delete** button. One cannot delete built-in users:

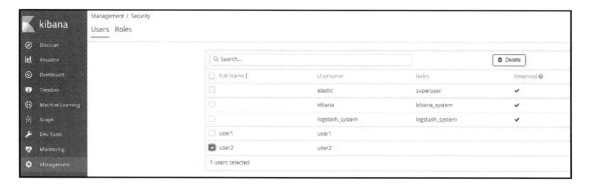

Changing the password

Navigate to **Users** UI and select the custom user for whom the password needs to be changed. This will take you to the `User Details` page. One can edit the user details, change the password, or delete the user from the user details screen. To change the password, click on the **Change Password** link and enter the new password details. Click on the **Save** button:

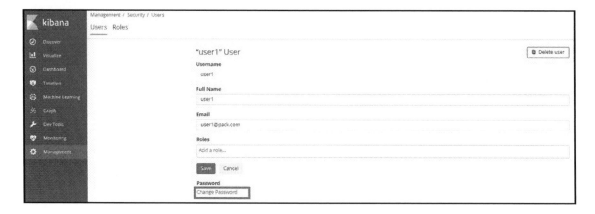

The passwords must be at minimum 6 characters long.

New role creation

To create a new user, navigate to the **Management** UI and select **Roles** in the **Security** Section, or if you are currently on the **Users** screen, click on the **Roles** tab. The **Roles** screen displays all the roles that are defined/available. By default, it displays the built-in/reserved roles that are part of the X-Pack Security native realm:

X-Pack security also provides a set of built-in roles that can be assigned to users. These roles are reserved and the privileges associated to these roles cannot be updated. Some of the built-in roles are:

- `kibana_system`: This role grants the necessary access to read from and write to Kibana indices, manage index templates, and check the availability of the Elasticsearch cluster. This role also grants read access for monitoring (`.monitoring-*`) and read-write access to reporting (`.reporting-*`) indices. The default user `kibana`, has these privileges.

- `superuser`: This role grants access to perform all operations on clusters, indices, and data. This role also grants rights to create/modify users or roles. The default user `elastic`, has superuser privileges.
- `ingest_admin`: This role grants permissions to manage all pipeline configurations and all index templates.

> To find the complete list of built-in roles and their descriptions, please refer to `https://www.elastic.co/guide/en/x-pack/master/built-in-roles.html`.

Users with the superuser role one can create custom roles and assign them to the users using the Kibana UI.

Let's create a new role with cluster privilege **monitor** and assign it to **user1** so that the user can cluster read-only operations such as cluster state, cluster health, nodes info, nodes stats, and so on.

Click on the **Create Role** button in the **Roles** page/tab and fill in the details as shown in the following screenshot:

To assign the newly created role to **user1**, click on the **Users** Tab and select **user1**. In the
User Details page, from the roles dropdown, select the **monitor_role** role and click on
the **Save** button, as shown in this screenshot:

 A user can be assigned multiple roles.

Now let's validate that `user1` can access some cluster/node details APIs:

```
curl -u user1:password "http://localhost:9200/_cluster/health?pretty"
{
  "cluster_name" : "elasticsearch",
  "status" : "yellow",
  "timed_out" : false,
  "number_of_nodes" : 1,
  "number_of_data_nodes" : 1,
  "active_primary_shards" : 53,
  "active_shards" : 53,
  "relocating_shards" : 0,
  "initializing_shards" : 0,
  "unassigned_shards" : 52,
  "delayed_unassigned_shards" : 0,
  "number_of_pending_tasks" : 0,
  "number_of_in_flight_fetch" : 0,
  "task_max_waiting_in_queue_millis" : 0,
  "active_shards_percent_as_number" : 50.476190476190474
}
```

Let's also execute the same command that we executed when we created `user1` but without assigning any roles to it, and let's see the difference:

```
curl -u user1:password "http://localhost:9200"
{
  "name" : "fwDdHSI",
  "cluster_name" : "elasticsearch",
  "cluster_uuid" : "08wSPsjSQCmeRaxF4iHizw",
  "version" : {
    "number" : "6.0.0",
    "build_hash" : "8f0685b",
    "build_date" : "2017-11-10T18:41:22.859Z",
    "build_snapshot" : false,
    "lucene_version" : "7.0.1",
    "minimum_wire_compatibility_version" : "5.6.0",
    "minimum_index_compatibility_version" : "5.0.0"
  },
  "tagline" : "You Know, for Search"
}
```

How to Delete/Edit a role

To delete a role, navigate to the **Roles** UI/Tab, select the custom roles created, and click on **Delete**. One cannot delete built-in roles:

To edit a role, navigate to the **Roles** UI/Tab and click on the custom role that needs to be edited. The user is taken to the **Roles Details** page. Make the required changes in the privileges section and click on the **Save** button. One can also delete the role from this page:

Document-level security or field-level security

Now that we know how to create a new user, create a new role, and assign roles to a user, let's explore how security can be imposed on documents and fields for a given index/document.

The sample data that we imported before, at the beginning of this chapter, contained two indexes: employee and department.

Use Case 1: When a user searches for employee details, the user should not be able to find the salary/address details contained in the documents belonging to the `employee` index.

This is where field-level security helps. Let's create a new role (`employee_read`) with `read` index privileges on the `employee` index. To restrict the fields, choose the fields that are allowed to be accessed by the user in the **Granted Fields** section shown in the following screenshot:

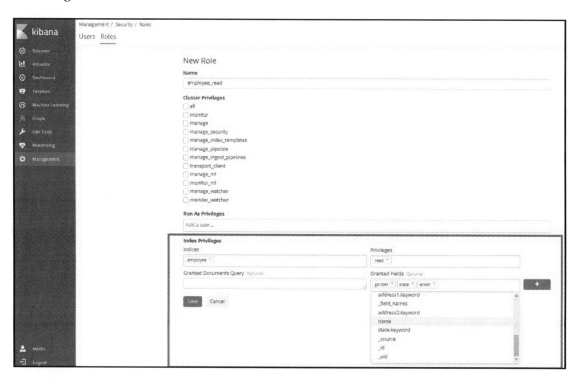

When creating a role, one can specify the same set of privileges on multiple indexes by adding one or more index names to the `Indices` field, or one can specify different privileges for different indexes by clicking on the **+** button found in the `Index Privileges` section.

Assign the newly created role to **user2**:

Now let's search in the employee index and check what all fields were returned in the response. As seen in the following response, we have successfully restricted the user from accessing salary and address details:

```
curl -u user2:password "http://localhost:9200/employee/_search?pretty"
{
  "took" : 20,
  "timed_out" : false,
  "_shards" : {
    "total" : 5,
    "successful" : 5,
    "skipped" : 0,
    "failed" : 0
  },
  "hits" : {
    "total" : 3,
    "max_score" : 1.0,
    "hits" : [
      {
        "_index" : "employee",
        "_type" : "employee",
        "_id" : "3QuULGABsx353N7xt4k6",
        "_score" : 1.0,
        "_source" : {
          "gender" : "F",
          "name" : "user2",
          "state" : "OR",
          "email" : "user2@packt.com"
```

```
        }
      },
      {
        "_index" : "employee",
        "_type" : "employee",
        "_id" : "3guULGABsx353N7xt4k6",
        "_score" : 1.0,
        "_source" : {
          "gender" : "F",
          "name" : "user3",
          "state" : "CA",
          "email" : "user3@packt.com"
        }
      },
      {
        "_index" : "employee",
        "_type" : "employee",
        "_id" : "3AuULGABsx353N7xt4k6",
        "_score" : 1.0,
        "_source" : {
          "gender" : "M",
          "name" : "user1",
          "state" : "NE",
          "email" : "user1@packt.com"
        }
      }
    ]
  }
}
```

Use Case 2: We want to have a multi-tenant index and restrict certain documents to certain users. Say, **user1** should be able to search in the department index and retrieve only documents belonging to the IT department.

Let's create a role, `department_IT_role`, and provide the `read` privilege for the index `department`. To restrict the documents, specify the query in the `Granted Documents Query` section. The query should be in the `Elatsicsearch Query DSL` format:

Associate the newly created role with **user1**:

Lets verify that it is working as expected by executing a search against the `department` index, using the `user1` credentials:

```
curl -u user1:password "http://localhost:9200/department/_search?pretty"
{
  "took" : 1,
  "timed_out" : false,
  "_shards" : {
    "total" : 5,
    "successful" : 5,
    "skipped" : 0,
    "failed" : 0
  },
  "hits" : {
    "total" : 1,
    "max_score" : 1.0,
    "hits" : [
      {
        "_index" : "department",
        "_type" : "department",
        "_id" : "3wuULGABsx353N7xt4k6",
        "_score" : 1.0,
        "_source" : {
          "name" : "IT",
          "employees" : 50
        }
      }
    ]
  }
}
```

X-Pack security APIs

In the previous section, we learned how to manage users and roles using the Kibana UI. However, many times we would like to carry out these operations programmatically from our applications. This is where the X-Pack Security APIs come in handy. X-Pack Security APIs are REST APIs that can be used for user/role management, role mapping to users, performing authentication, and checking whether the authenticated user has specified list of privileges. These APIs perform operations on the `native` realm. The Kibana UI internally makes use of these APIs for user/role management. In order to execute these APIs, the user should have `superuser` or the latest `manage_security` privileges. Let's explore some of these APIs in this section.

User management APIs

This provides a set of APIs to create, update, or delete users from the `native` realm.

The list of APIs available:

```
GET /_xpack/security/user                          -- To list all the
user
GET /_xpack/security/user/<username>               -- To get the details
of a specific user
DELETE /_xpack/security/user/<username>            --  To Delete a user
POST /_xpack/security/user/<username>              -- To Create a new
user
PUT /_xpack/security/user/<username>               -- To Update an
existing user
PUT /_xpack/security/user/<username>/_disable      -- To disable an
existing user
PUT /_xpack/security/user/<username>/_enable       -- To enable an
existing disabled user
PUT /_xpack/security/user/<username>/_password     -- to Change the
password
```

The `username` in the path parameter specifies the user against which the operation is carried out. The body of the request accepts parameters such as `email`, `full_name`, and `password` as string and `roles` as list.

Example 1: Create a new user, `user3`, with `monitor_role` assigned to it:

```
curl -u elastic:elastic -X POST
http://localhost:9200/_xpack/security/user/user3 -H 'content-type:
application/json' -d '
{
  "password" : "randompassword",
  "roles" : [ "monitor_role"],
  "full_name" : "user3",
  "email" : "user3@packt.com"
}'
```

Response:
```
user":{"created":true}}
```

Example 2: Get the list of all users:

```
curl -u elastic:elastic -XGET
http://localhost:9200/_xpack/security/user?pretty
```

Example 3: Delete `user3`:

```
curl -u elastic:elastic -XDELETE
http://localhost:9200/_xpack/security/user/user3
Response:
{"found":true}
```

Example 4: Change the password:

```
curl -u elastic:elastic -XPUT
http://localhost:9200/_xpack/security/user/user2/_password  -H "content-
type: application/json" -d "{ \"password\": \"newpassword\"}"
```

 When using `curl` commands on Windows machines, note that they don't work if they have single quotes (') in them. The preceding example showed the use of a `curl` command on a Windows machine. Also make sure you escape double quotes within the body of the command as shown in the preceding example.

Role management APIs

This provides a set of APIs to create, update, remove, and retrieve roles from the `native` realm.

The list of APIs available is as follows:

```
GET /_xpack/security/role                          -- To retrieve the
list of all roles
GET /_xpack/security/role/<rolename>                 -- To retrieve
details of a specific role
POST /_xpack/security/role/<rolename>/_clear_cache     -- To
evict/clear roles from the native role cache
POST /_xpack/security/role/<rolename>                 -- To create a
role
PUT /_xpack/security/role/<rolename>                 -- To update an
existing role
```

The `rolename` in the path parameter specifies the role against which the operation is carried out. The body of the request accepts parameters such as `cluster`, which accepts a list of cluster privileges; `indices`, which accepts a list of objects that specify the indices privileges ; and `run_as`, containing a list of users that the owners of this role can impersonate.

The `indices` contains an object with parameters such as `names`, which accepts a list of index names; `field_security`, which accepts a list of fields to provide read access; `privileges`, which accepts a list of index privileges; and the `query` parameter, which accepts the query to filter the documents.

Example 1: Create a new role with field-level security imposed on the employee index:

```
curl -u elastic:elastic -X POST
http://localhost:9200/_xpack/security/role/employee_read_new -H 'content-
type: application/json' -d '{

  "indices": [
    {
      "names": [ "employee" ],
      "privileges": [ "read" ],
      "field_security" : {
        "grant" : [ "*" ],
        "except": [ "address*","salary" ]
      }
    }
  ]
}'
```

Response:
```
role":{"created":true}}
```

Unlike the Kibana UI, which doesn't have any way to exclude fields from user access, using the security API, one can easily exclude or include fields as part of field-level security. In the preceding example, we have restricted access to the `salary` field and any fields starting with the `address` text/string.

Example 2: Get the details of a specific role:

```
curl -u elastic:elastic -XGET
http://localhost:9200/_xpack/security/role/employee_read_new?pretty
```
Response:
```
{
  "employee_read" : {
    "cluster" : [ ],
    "indices" : [
      {
        "names" : [
          "employee"
        ],
        "privileges" : [
          "read"
```

```
        ],
        "field_security" : {
          "grant" : [
            "*"
          ],
          "except" : [
            "address*",
            "salary"
          ]
        }
      }
    ],
    "run_as" : [ ],
    "metadata" : { },
    "transient_metadata" : {
      "enabled" : true
    }
  }
}
```

Example 3: Delete a role:

```
curl -u elastic:elastic -XDELETE
http://localhost:9200/_xpack/security/role/employee_read
```

Response:
```
{"found":true}
```

Similar to User Management and Role Management APIs, using Role Mapping APIs, one can associate roles to users. Details about Role Mapping APIs can be found at `https://www.elastic.co/guide/en/elasticsearch/reference/master/security-api-role-mapping.html`.

Monitoring Elasticsearch

Elasticsearch exposes a rich set of APIs known as **stats** APIs to monitor Elasticsearch at cluster, node, and indices levels. Some of those APIs are `_cluster/stats`, `_nodes/stats`, and `myindex/stats`. These APIs provide state/monitoring information in real time and the statistics presented in these APIs is point-in-time and in `.json` format. As an administrator/developer, when working with Elasticsearch, one would be interested in both real-time statistics as well as historical statistics, which would help them in understanding/analyzing the behavior (health or performance) of a cluster better.

Also, reading through a set of numbers for a period of time (say, for example, to find out the JVM utilization over time) would be very difficult. Rather, a UI that pictorially represents these numbers as graphs would be very useful in visualizing and analyzing the current and past trends/behaviors (health or performance) of the Elasticsearch cluster. This is where the monitoring feature of X-Pack comes in handy.

The X-Pack monitoring components enable you to easily monitor the Elastic Stack (Elasticsearch, Kibana, and Logstash) from Kibana. X-Pack consists of a monitoring agent that runs on each of the instances (Elasticsearch, Kibana, and Logstash) and periodically collects and indexes the health and performance metrics. These can then be easily visualized using the Monitoring UI component of Kibana. The Monitoring UI of Kibana comes with predefined dashboards, which let you easily visualize and analyze real-time and past performance data.

By default, the metrics collected by X-Pack are indexed within the cluster you are monitoring. However, in production, it is strongly recommended to have a separated dedicated cluster to store these metrics. A dedicated cluster for monitoring has the following benefits:

- Enables you to monitor multiple clusters from a central location
- Reduces the load and storage on your production clusters as the metrics are stored in a dedicated monitoring cluster
- There is access to Monitoring even when some clusters are unhealthy or down
- Separate security levels from Monitoring and production clusters can be enforced:

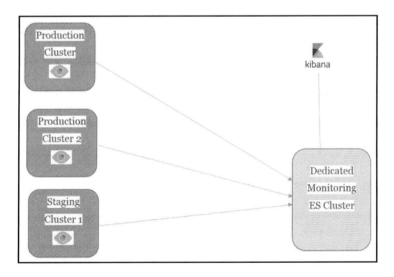

As stated earlier, the metrics collected by X-Pack are indexed within the cluster you are monitoring. If a dedicated monitoring cluster is set up, then we need to configure where to send/ship the metrics to in the monitored instances. This can be configured in the `elasticsearch.yml` file of each node, as shown in the following code:

```
xpack.monitoring.exporters:
    id1:
    type: http
    host: ["http://dedicated_monitoring_cluster:port"]
```

 It's optional to have X-Pack installed on a dedicated monitoring cluster; however, it is recommended to have it installed there too. If X-Pack is installed on a dedicated monitoring cluster, then make sure you provide the user credentials (`auth.username` and `auth.password`) as well while configuring the monitored instances. Monitored metrics are stored in a system-level index that has the index pattern `.monitoring-*`.

Monitoring UI

To access the Monitoring UI, log in to Kibana and click on **Monitoring** from the side navigation. The resulting page will be as shown in the following screenshot:

This page provides a summary of the metrics available for Elasticsearch and Kibana. By clicking on links such as **Overview, Nodes, Indices** or **Instances**, one can get additional/detailed information. The metrics displayed on the page are automatically refreshed every 10 seconds, and by default, one can view the data of the past 1 hour, which can be changed in the **Time Filter** found towards the top left of the screen. Also, one can see the cluster name, which in this case is only one—**elasticsearch**.

The monitoring agent installed on the instances being monitored sends metrics every 10 seconds by default. This can be changed in the configuration file (`elasticsearch.yml`) by setting the appropriate value to the `pack.monitoring.collection.interval` property.

Elasticsearch metrics

One can monitor the Elasticsearch performance data at a cluster level, node level, and index level. The Elasticsearch Monitoring UI provides three tabs, each displaying the metrics at cluster, node, and index levels. The three tabs are **Overview, Nodes,** and **Indices**. To navigate to the Elasticsearch Monitoring UI, click on one of the links (**Overview, Nodes,** and **Indices**) found under the Elasticsearch section.

Overview tab

Cluster-level metrics provide aggregated information across all the nodes and is the first place one should look when monitoring an Elasticsearch cluster. Cluster-level metrics are displayed in the **Overview** tab and can be navigated to by clicking on the **Overview** link under the Elasticsearch section found in the landing page of the Monitoring UI.

The **Overview** tab provides key metrics that indicate the overall health of an Elasticsearch cluster:

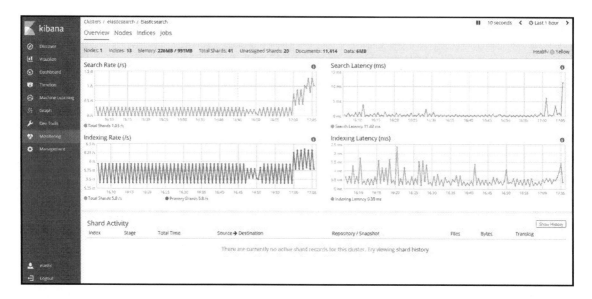

The key metrics that are displayed are cluster status, number of nodes and number of indices present, memory used, total number of shards present, total number of unassigned shards, total number of documents present in the indices, the disk space used for storing the documents, uptime, and version of Elasticsearch. The **Overview** tab also displays charts that show the search and indexing performance over time, and the table at the bottom shows information about any shards that are being recovered.

Clicking on the information icon present at the top right of each chart provides a description of the metrics.

In the **Overview** Tab, the metrics are aggregated at the cluster level; so when monitoring the Elasticsearch cluster, one might miss out some vital parameters that might eventually affect the overall cluster state. For example, the **Memory Used** metric showcases the average memory used by combining the memory used across all the nodes. However, one node might be running with full memory utilization and an other nodes memory might have hardly been used. Hence, as an administrator, one should always monitor at the **Node** level too.

Nodes tab

Clicking on the **Nodes** tab displays the summary details of each node present in the cluster, as shown in this screenshot:

For each node, it provides information such as the name of the node, status of the node, CPU usage (average, min, and max usage), load average (average, min, and max usage), JVM memory (average, min, and max usage), disk free space (average, min, and max usage), and total number of assigned Shards. It also provides information such as whether a node is a Master node or not (indicated by a star next to the node name) and details about the transport host and port.

Clicking on the **Node** name provides detailed information about the node. This detailed information of the node is displayed in two tabs, namely **Overview** and **Advanced**. The Node **Overview** tab looks like this:

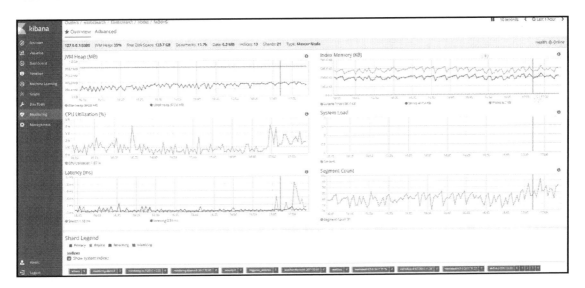

The node **Overview** tab provides information in the top pane, such as the status of the node, transport IP address of the node, JVM Heap Utilization in percent, free disk space available, total number of documents present on the node (this number includes documents present in both replica and primary shards), total disk space used, total number of indices in the node, total number of shards, and type of node (master, data, ingest, and coordinating node).

The Node **Overview** tab also provides visualizations for JVM Heap usage, Index Memory, CPU utilization in percent, system load average, Latency (in ms) and Segment Count. The statuses of shards of various indices are provided under the **Shard Legend** section.

> If the **Show system indices** checkbox is checked, then the shard status of all the indexes created by X-Pack can be seen.

The Node **Advanced** tab provides visualizations of other metrics such as **garbage collection (GC)** count and duration, detailed Index Memory usage at Lucene and Elasticsearch levels, Indexing Time (in ms), Request rate, Indexing, Read Threads, and Cgroup stats.

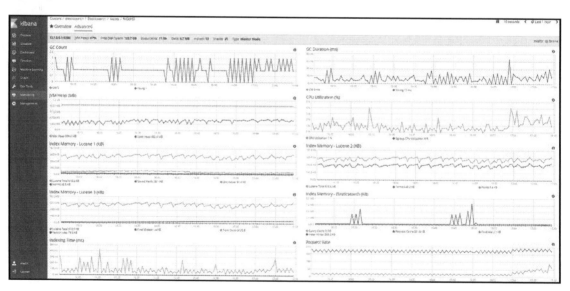

The Indices tab

Clicking on the **Indices** tab displays the summary details of each index present in the cluster, as shown in the following screenshot:

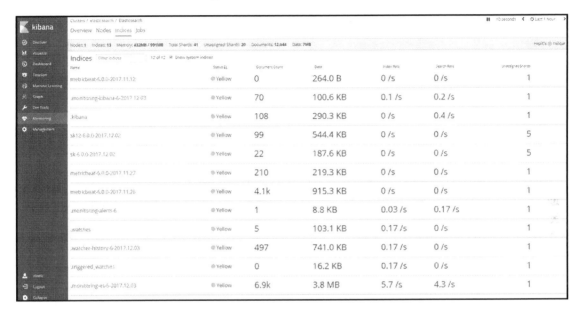

> **TIP**
>
> If the **Show system indices** checkbox is checked, then the shard status of all indexes created by X-Pack can be seen.

For each index, it provides information such as the name of the index, status of the index, total count of documents present, disk space used, index rate per second, search rate per second, and number of unassigned shards.

Clicking on an **Index** name provides detailed information about the Index. The detailed information is displayed in two tabs, namely **Overview** and **Advanced**. The Index **Overview** tab looks like this:

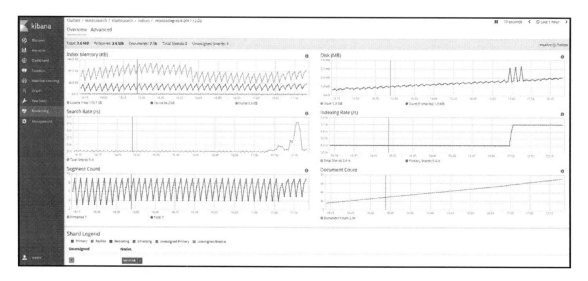

This tab provides information in the top pane, such as the status of the index, total number of documents present in the index, disk space used, total number of shards (primary + replicas), and unassigned shards.

The Index **Overview** tab also provides visualizations for Index Memory (in KB), Index size (in MB), Search rate per second, Indexing rate per second, total count of segments and total count of documents. **Shard Legend** displays the status of shards belonging to the index and the information of the nodes the shards are assigned to.

The Index **Advanced** tab provides visualizations of other metrics such as detailed Index Memory usage at Lucene and Elasticsearch levels, Indexing Time (in ms), Request rate and time, Refresh Time (in ms), Disk usage, and Segment counts:

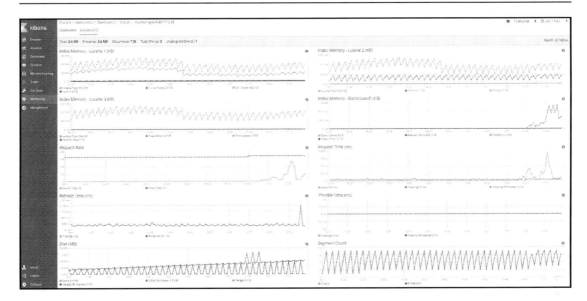

 From the landing page of the Monitoring UI, by clicking on **Overview** or **Instances** under the Kibana section, the metrics of Kibana can be visualized/monitored in a similar way.

Alerting

Kibana UI provides beautiful visualizations that help in analyzing and detecting anomalies in data in real time. However, as an administrator or an analyst, it wouldn't be possible to sit in front of dashboards for hours together to detect anomalies and take appropriate action. Wouldn't it be nice if the administrator gets notified when, for example, the following events occur?

- There is an outage in one of the servers being monitored
- Elasticsearch Cluster turns red/yellow due to some nodes leaving the cluster
- Disk space/CPU utilization crosses a specific threshold
- There is an intrusion in the network
- There are errors reported in the logs

This is where the X-Pack Alerting component comes to the rescue. The X-Pack Alerting component, named `Watcher`, provides the ability to automatically watch for changes/anomalies in data stored on Elasticsearch and take the required action. X-Pack Alerting is enabled by default as part of the X-Pack default installation.

`Watcher` provides a set of REST APIs for creating, managing, and testing watches. Kibana also provides a **Watcher UI** for creating, managing, and testing. Watcher UI internally makes use of Watcher REST APIs for management of watches.

Anatomy of a watch

A **Watch** is made of the following components:

- `schedule`: This is used to specify the time interval for scheduling/triggering the watch.
- `query`: Used to specify a query to retrieve data from Elasticsearch and run as input to the condition. Elasticsearch Query DSL/Lucene queries can be used to specify the queries.
- `condition`: This is used to specify conditions against the input data obtained from the query and check whether any action needs to be taken or not.
- `action`: This is used to specify actions such as sending an email, sending a slack notification, logging the event to a specific log, and much more on meeting the condition.

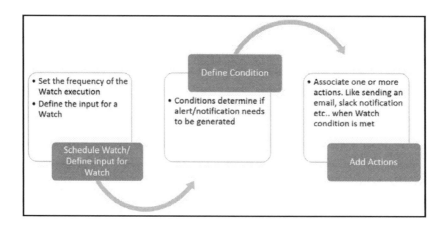

Let's look into a sample watch and understand the building blocks of a watch in detail. The following code snippet creates a watch:

```
curl -u elastic:elastic -X POST
http://localhost:9200/_xpack/watcher/watch/logstash_error_watch    -H
'content-type: application/json'    -d '{

    "trigger" : { "schedule" : { "interval" : "30s" }},
    "input" : {
      "search" : {
        "request" : {
          "indices" : [ "logstash*" ],
          "body" : {
            "query" : {
              "match" : { "message": "error" }
            }
          }
        }
      }
    },
    "condition" : {
      "compare" : { "ctx.payload.hits.total" : { "gt" : 0 }}
    },
    "actions" : {
      "log_error" : {
        "logging" : {
          "text" : "The number of errors in logs is
{{ctx.payload.hits.total}}"
        }
      }
    }
}'
```

> In order to create a watch, the user should have watcher_admin cluster privileges.

- trigger: This section is used to provide a schedule to specify how often the watch needs to be executed. Once the watch is created, Watcher immediately registers its trigger with the scheduler trigger engine and the trigger engine evaluates the trigger and runs the watch accordingly.

Several types of schedule triggers can be defined to specify when the watch execution should start. The different types of schedule triggers are interval, hourly, daily, weekly, monthly, yearly, and cron.

In the preceding code snippet, a trigger was specified with a schedule of 30 seconds, which meant the watch is executed every 30 seconds.

Example to specify hourly trigger: The following snippet shows how to specify an hourly trigger that triggers the watch every 45th minute of an hour:

```
{
  "trigger" : {
    "schedule" : {
      "hourly" : { "minute" : 45 }
    }
  }
}
```

One can specify an array of minutes too. The following snippet shows how to specify an hourly trigger that triggers the watch every 15th and 45th minute of an hour:

```
{
  "trigger" : {
    "schedule" : {
      "hourly" : { "minute" : [ 15, 45 ] }
    }
  }
}
```

An example to specify the watch to trigger daily at 8 pm:

```
{
  "trigger" : {
    "schedule" : {
      "daily" : { "at" : "20:00" }
    }
  }
}
```

An example to specify a watch to trigger weekly on Mondays at 10 a.m. and on Friday at 8 pm:

```
{
  "trigger" : {
    "schedule" : {
```

```
        "weekly" : [
          { "on" : "monday", "at" : "10:00" },
          { "on" : "friday", "at" : "10:00" }
        ]
      }
    }
  }
```

An example to specify a schedule using `cron` syntax. The following snippet specifies a watch to be triggered hourly at the 45th minute:

```
{
  "trigger" : {
    "schedule" : {
      "cron" : "0 45 * * * ?"
    }
  }
}
```

- `input`: This section is used to specify the input to load the data into the Watcher execution context. This data is refereed as **Watcher Payload** and this payload will be available/accessible in subsequent phases of the watcher execution so that it can be used to create conditions on it or used when generating actions. The payload can be accessed using the `ctx.payload.*` variable:

```
"input" : {
    "search" : {
      "request" : {
        "indices" : [ "logstash*" ],
        "body" : {
          "query" : {
            "match" : { "message": "error" }
          }
        }
      }
    }
  }
```

As seen in the preceding code snippet, an input of type `search` is used to specify the query to be executed against Elasticsearch to load the data into Watcher Payload. The query fetches all the documents present in the indices of pattern `logstash*` containing `error` in the `message` field.

Inputs of type `simple` to load static data, `http` to load an `http` response, and `chain` to provide a series of inputs can also be used in the `input` section.

- `condition`: This section is used to specify a condition against the payload in order to determine whether an action needs to be executed or not:

```
"condition" : {
    "compare" : { "ctx.payload.hits.total" : { "gt" : 0 }}
}
```

As seen in the preceding code snippet, it uses a condition of type `compare` to determine whether the payload has any documents, and if it finds any, then the action will be invoked.

A condition of type `compare` is used to specify simple comparisons `eq`, `not-eq`, `gt`, `gte`, `lt`, and `lte` against a value in the watch payload.

Conditions of type `always`, which always evaluates watch condition to `true` and `never` which always evaluates watch condition to `false`, `array_compare` to compare against a array of values to determine the watch condition, and `script` to script that used to be used to determine the watch condition are also supported.

- `actions`: This section is used to specify one or more actions that need to be taken when the watch condition evaluates to `true`:

```
"actions" : {
    "log_error" : {
        "logging" : {
            "text" : "The number of errors in logs is
{{ctx.payload.hits.total}}"
        }
    }
}
```

As seen in the preceding code snippet, it uses logging action to log the specified text when the watch condition is met. The logs would be logged into Elasticsearch logs. The number of errors found is dynamically obtained using the field (`hits.total`) of the payload. The payload is accessed using the variable `ctx.payload.*`.

Watcher supports the following types of actions: `email`, `webhook`, `index`, `logging`, `hipchat`, `Slack`, and `pagerduty`.

During the watch execution, once the condition is met, a decision is made per configured action as to whether it should be throttled or to continue executing the action. The main purpose of action throttling is to prevent too many executions of the same action for the same watch.

Watcher supports two types of throttling:

- **Time Based Throttling**: One can define a throttling period using the parameter `throttle_period` as part of the action configuration or a the watch level (which applies to all actions) to limit how often the action is executed. The global default throttle period is 5 seconds.

- **Ack-based Throttling**: Using ACK Watch APIs, one can prevent watch actions from being executed again while the watch condition remains `true`.

Watches are stored in a special index named `.watches`. Every time a watch is executed, a `watch_record` containing details such as watch details, the time of watch execution, watch payload, and the result of the condition is stored in the watch history index, named `.watches-history-6-*`.

A user with the `watcher_user` privilege can view watches and watch history.

Alerting in action

Now that we know what a **Watch** is made up of, in this section, let's explore how to create, delete, and manage watches.

One can create/delete/manage **watches** using:

- Kibana Watcher UI
- X-Pack Watcher REST APIs

Watcher UI internally makes use of **Watcher** REST APIs for management of watches. In this section, let's explore the creation, deletion, and managing of watches using Kibana **Watcher UI**.

Create a new alert

To create a watch, log in to Kibana (`http://localhost:5601`) as elastic/elastic and navigate to **Management** UI; click on **Watcher** in the **Elasticsearch** Section:

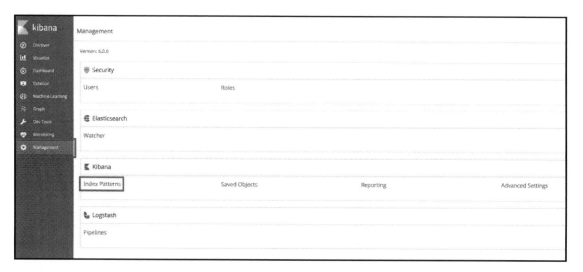

Clicking on **Create New Watch** provides two options for creating alerts:

- Threshold Alert
- Advanced Watch

Using the **Threshold Alert** option, one can create a threshold-based alert to get notified when a metric goes above or below a given threshold. Using this UI, users can easily create threshold-based alerts without worrying about directly working with raw JSON requests. This UI provides options for creating alerts on time-based indices only (that is, the index has a timestamp).

Using **Advanced Watch** options, one can create watches by directly working with the raw .json required for the watches API.

 The Watcher UI requires a user with kibana_user and watcher_admin privileges to create, edit, delete, and deactivate a watch.

Threshold Alert

Click on **Create New Watch** and choose the **Threshold Alert** option. This brings up the **Threshold Alert** UI.

Specify the name of the alert; choose the index to be used to query against, time field, and trigger frequency in the **Threshold Alert** UI:

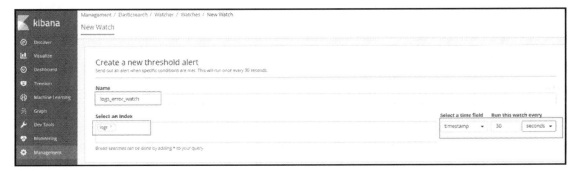

Then specify the condition that will cause the alert to trigger. As the expressions/conditions are changed or modified, the visualization is updated automatically to show the threshold value and data as red and blue lines respectively:

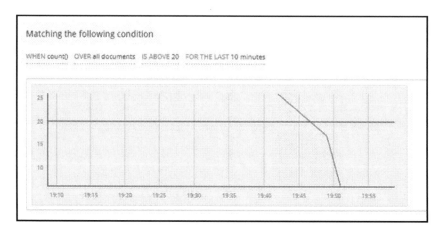

Finally specify the action that needs to be triggered when the action is met by clicking on the **Add new action** button. It provides for creation of three types of actions, that is, email, slack and logging actions. One or more actions can be configured:

Finally, click on the **Save** button to create the watch.

Clicking on **Save** will save the watch in the `watches` index, as shown in the following screenshot:

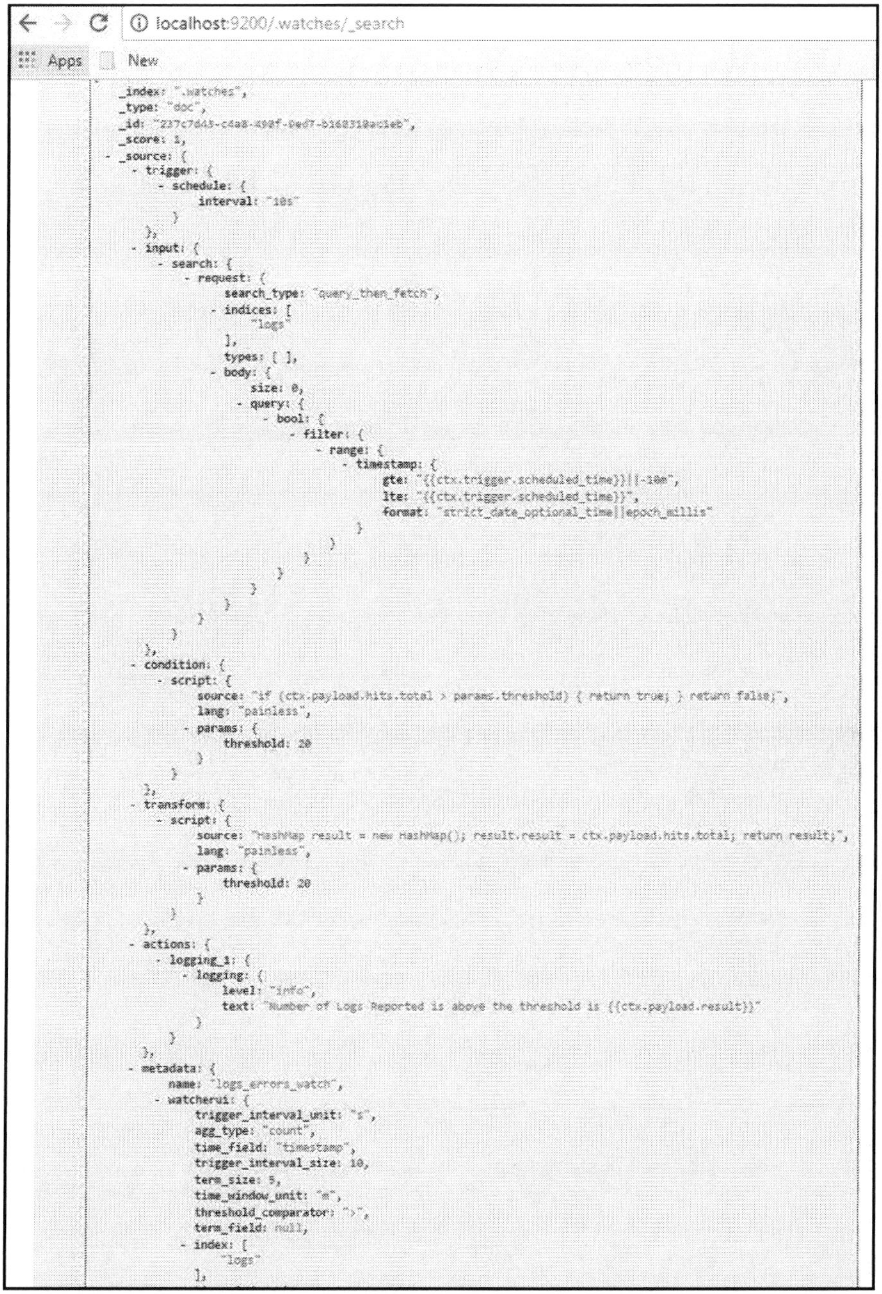

Advanced Watch

Click on the **Create New Watch** button and choose the **Advanced Watch** option. This brings up the **Advanced Watch** UI.

Specify the Watch ID and watch name and paste the JSON to create a watch in the **Watch JSON** box; click on **Save** to create a watch. Watch ID refers to the identifier used by Elasticsearch when creating a Watch, whereas name is the more user-friendly way to identify the watch:

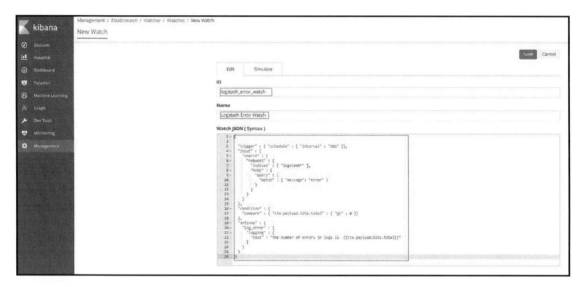

The **Simulate** Tab provides a UI to override parts of the watch and then run a simulation of it:

Watch Name will be stored in the metadata section of the watch body. One can use the metadata section when creating the watch to store custom metadata, tags, or information to represent/identify a watch.

Clicking on **Save** will save the watch in the `watches` index, as shown in the following screenshot:

```
←  →  C   ⓘ localhost:9200/.watches/_search

Apps    New

        },
     - {
          _index: ".watches",
          _type: "doc",
          _id: "logstash_error_watch",
          _score: 1,
        - _source: {
           - trigger: {
              - schedule: {
                   interval: "30s"
                }
             },
           - input: {
              - search: {
                 - request: {
                      search_type: "query_then_fetch",
                    - indices: [
                         "logstash*"
                      ],
                      types: [ ],
                    - body: {
                       - query: {
                          - match: {
                               message: "error"
                             }
                          }
                       }
                    }
                 }
              }
             },
           - condition: {
              - compare: {
                 - ctx.payload.hits.total: {
                      gt: 0
                    }
                 }
             },
           - actions: {
              - log_error: {
                 - logging: {
                      level: "info",
                      text: "The number of errors in logs is {{ctx.payload.hits.total}}"
                    }
                 }
             },
           - metadata: {
                name: "Logstash Error Watch",
              - xpack: {
                   type: "json"
                }
             },
           + status: {…}
        }
     },
```

How to Delete/Deactivate/Edit a Watch

To delete a watch, navigate to the **Management** UI and click on **Watcher** in the **Elasticsearch** Section. From the **Watches** list, select one or more watches that need to be deleted and click on the **Delete** button:

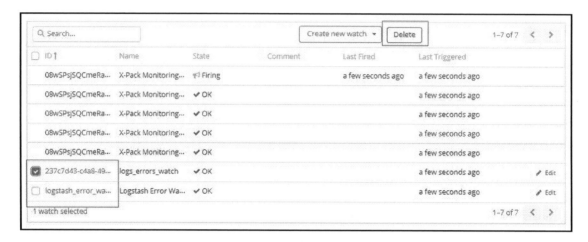

To deactivate a watch (that is, to temporarily disable watch execution), navigate to the **Management** UI and click on **Watcher** in the **Elasticsearch** section. From the **Watches** list, click on the custom watch. On Clicking, it displays the watch history. Click on the **Deactivate** Button. One can also delete a watch from this screen too.

Clicking on a execution time (link) in the watch history displays the details of a particular `watch_record`:

To edit a watch, click on the **Edit** tab and modify the watch details; click on the **Save** button to save your changes.

Summary

In this chapter, we explored how to install and configure the X-Pack components in Elastic Stack and how to to secure the elastic cluster by creating users and roles. We also learned how to monitor the ElasticSearch server and alerting for generating notifications when there are changes or anomalies in the data.

In the next chapter, we'll put together a complete application using Elastic Stack for sensor data analytics with the concepts learned so far.

Running Elastic Stack in Production

9

In our quest to learn Elastic Stack, we have covered good ground and have a solid footing in all of its components. We have a solid foundation of the core Elasticsearch with its search and analytics capabilities, and we have covered how to effectively use Logstash and Kibana to build a powerful platform that can deliver analytics on big data. We have also seen how X-Pack makes it easy to secure and monitor big data, generate alerts, and perform graph analysis and machine learning.

Taking the Elastic Stack components to production requires that you be aware of some common pitfalls, patterns, and strategies that can help you run your solution smoothly in production. In this chapter, we will see some common patterns, tips, and tricks to run Elasticsearch, Logstash, Kibana, and other components in production.

We will start with Elasticsearch and then move on to other components. There are various ways one could run Elasticsearch in production. There may be various factors that influence your decision on how you should deploy. We will cover the following topics to help you take your next Elastic Stack project to production:

- Hosting Elastic Stack on a managed cloud
- Hosting Elastic Stack on your own, that is, self-hosting
- Backing up and restoring
- Setting up index aliases
- Setting up index templates
- Modeling time series data

Let's first understand how we can go about taking the Elastic Stack to production with one of the managed cloud providers. This option requires a minimum amount of work to set up a production-ready cluster.

Hosting Elastic Stack on a managed cloud

Cloud providers make the process of setting up a production ready cluster much easier. As a user, we don't have to do low-level configuration or the selection and management of hardware, an operating system, and many of the Elasticsearch and Kibana configuration parameters.

There are multiple cloud providers that provide managed clusters for Elastic Stack, such as Elastic Cloud, QBox.io, Bonsai, and many more. In this section, we will go through how to get started with **Elastic Cloud**. Elastic Cloud is the official cloud offering by the company Elastic.co, which is the main company contributing to the development of Elasticsearch and other Elastic Stack components. We will cover the following topics while working with Elastic Cloud:

- Getting up and running on Elastic Cloud
- Using Kibana
- Overriding configuration
- Recovering from a snapshot

Getting up and running on Elastic Cloud

Sign up for Elastic Cloud using `https://www.elastic.co/cloud/as-a-service/signup`, provide your email address, and verify your email. You will be asked to set your initial password.

After your initial password is set, you can log in to the Elastic Cloud console at `https://cloud.elastic.co`. The Elastic Cloud console offers an easy to use user interface to manage your clusters. Since you just signed up for a trial account, you get a free cluster with 4 GB RAM and a 96 GB storage capacity for the initial trial period.

We can choose **AWS** (**Amazon Web Services**) or **GCE** (**Google Compute Engine**) while launching the cluster. Upon logging in, you can create a cluster from the following screen:

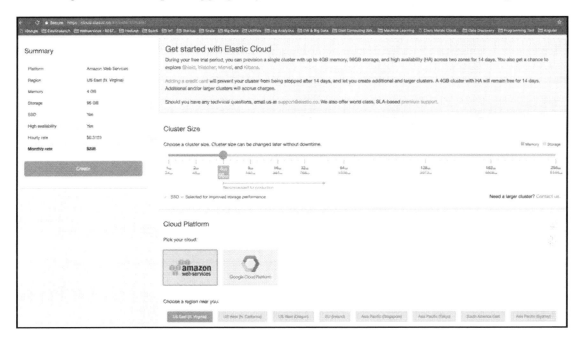

Fig-9.1 Creating a new cluster on Elastic Cloud

You can choose RAM and storage space, and decide whether you want to replicate your cluster in multiple availability zones. It also allows you to configure additional plugins that you want to install to your Elasticsearch cluster. Select the version to be the latest 6.x version that is available. At the time of writing this book, the 6.0.0 version is the latest version available on Elastic Cloud.

When you enter a name for the cluster, hit the **Create** button; your cluster will be created and started with production-grade configuration. The cluster will be secured. It will also start with a Kibana instance. At this point, it should provide you with a username/password to be used for logging into your Elasticsearch and Kibana nodes. Please note it down. It also provides a **Cloud ID**, which is a helpful string when connecting to your cloud cluster from your beats agents and Logstash servers.

You should see the following page when viewing the cluster:

Fig-9.2 - Cluster Overview screen on Elastic Cloud

As you can see, the cluster is up and running. It also has a Kibana instance set up, which is accessible at the given URL. The Elasticsearch cluster is available at the given secured HTTPS URL.

The cluster has two nodes: one in each AWS availability zone and one tiebreaker node. The tiebreaker node helps to elect a master node. Tiebreaker nodes are special nodes on Elastic Cloud that help in the re-election of masters whenever some nodes become unreachable in the cluster.

Now that we have the cluster up and running with a Kibana instance, let's use it!

Using Kibana

The link to the Kibana instance is already made available to us on the cluster overview page on Elastic Cloud. You can click on it to launch the Kibana UI. Unlike the local instance of Kibana that we initially created, this instance is secured by X-Pack security. You will have to log in using the credentials provided to you after you created the Elastic Cloud cluster in the previous section.

After logging in, you should see the Kibana UI as follows:

Fig-9.3 Kibana UI on Elastic Cloud after logging in

You can view all indexes, analyze data on your Elasticsearch cluster, and monitor your Elasticsearch cluster from this Kibana UI.

Overriding configuration

It is possible to override the configuration of your Elasticsearch nodes via the **Configuration** tab in Elastic Cloud. Elastic Cloud doesn't allow you to edit the elasticsearch.yml file directly. However, it provides a section called **User Settings** which allows you to override a subset of the configuration parameters.

The configuration parameters that can be overridden are documented in the Elastic Cloud reference documentation at https://www.elastic.co/guide/en/cloud/current/cluster-config.html#user-settings.

Recovering from a snapshot

Elastic Cloud automatically creates a snapshot of all indices in your cluster periodically (every 30 minutes) and keeps them for recovery purposes, if required. This happens automatically without doing any additional setup or code. You can visit the **Snapshots** tab to view the available list of snapshots, as follows:

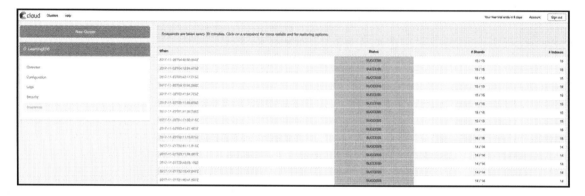

Fig-9.4-Listing of snapshots on Elastic Cloud

You can choose the snapshot that you want to restore from and you will be presented with the following screen:

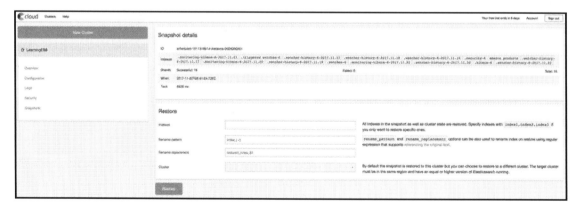

Fig-9.5 - Restoring from a specific snapshot

The snapshot contains the saved state for all indices in the cluster. It is possible to choose a subset of the indices for restoring and also to rename it while restoring it. It is also possible to restore the snapshot on a separate cluster.

Next, we will see how to get started with Elastic Stack if you are planning to manage the Elastic Stack components yourself. This is also called **self-hosting**, in the context that you will be hosting and managing it on your own.

Hosting Elastic Stack on your own

Hosting Elastic Stack on your own, that is, self-hosting Elastic Stack, requires you to install, configure, and manage your Elasticsearch and other Elastic Stack products. This can be done in one of two ways:

- Self-hosting on-premise
- Self-hosting on a cloud

Regardless of whether you run Elastic Stack on-premise (in your own data center) or run it on one of the cloud providers, such as AWS, Azure, or GCE, there are some common aspects that you should take into consideration. While self-hosting, you will be faced with the following choices:

- Selecting hardware
- Selecting the operating system
- Configuring Elasticsearch nodes
- Managing and monitoring Elasticsearch nodes
- Special considerations while self-hosting on a cloud

Except for the last item, which is applicable only if you are self-hosting on a cloud, the others are equally applicable for cloud as well as on-premise deployments.

Selecting hardware

Elasticsearch primarily has memory-bound tasks which rely on the inverted index. The more data that it can fit in the RAM, the faster the performance will be. But this statement can not always be generalized. It depends on the nature of your data and the type of operations or workload that you are going to have.

Using Elasticsearch doesn't mean that it has to perform all operations in-memory. Elasticsearch also uses on-disk data very efficiently, especially for aggregation operations.

 All datatypes (except analyzed strings) support a special data structure called `doc_values`, which organizes the data on the disk in a columnar fashion. `doc_values` is useful for sorting and aggregation operations. Since `doc_values` are enabled by default for all datatypes except analyzed strings, they make sort and aggregations run mostly off the disk. Those fields do not need to be loaded in memory for aggregating or sorting by them.

As Elasticsearch can scale horizontally, this is a relatively easy decision to make. It is fine to start with nodes of around 16 or 32 GB RAM, with around 8 CPU cores. As we will see in the coming sections, you cannot have Elasticsearch JVM with more than 32 GB of heap; effectively, there is no point in having a machine with more than 64 GB RAM. SSD hard disks are recommended if you are planning to do heavy aggregations.

It is important to benchmark with the initial hardware and then add more nodes or upgrade your nodes.

Selecting an operating system

Linux is the preferred choice when deploying Elasticsearch and the Elastic Stack components. Your choice of operating system will mostly depend on the preferred technologies of your organization. Elastic Stack can also be deployed on Windows if your organization prefers the Microsoft stack.

Configuring Elasticsearch nodes

Elasticsearch, which is the heart of the Elastic Stack, needs some configuration before starting it in production. Most of the configuration should work out of the box, but will require the following things to be reviewed on the OS level or JVM level.

JVM heap size

Set -Xms and -Xmx to be the same. More heap means Elasticsearch can keep more data in memory for faster access. But more heap also means that when the Java heap is close to full, the JVM's garbage collector will run a full garbage collection. At that point, all other processing within the Elasticsearch node experiences a pause. So, the larger the heap size, the longer the pauses will be. The maximum heap size that one can configure is around 32 GB. Another recommendation to keep in mind is that we should allocate no more than 50% of the total available RAM on the machine to the Elasticsearch JVM. The reason behind it is that the system needs enough memory for the filesystem cache for Apache Lucene. Ultimately, all the data stored on the Elasticsearch node is managed as Apache Lucene indexes, which needs RAM for fast access to the files.

So, if you are planning to store huge amounts of data in Elasticsearch, there is no point in having one single node with more than 64 GB RAM (50% of which is 32 GB, the max heap size). Instead, add more nodes if you want to scale.

Disable swapping

When swapping is enabled, an OS generally has a tendency to reclaim the memory from an application by swapping the data to disk to make more memory available for other programs.

On the Elasticsearch node, this can result in the OS swapping out the heap memory of Elasticsearch. This process of swapping out from memory to disk and then swapping back from disk to memory can slow down the process. This is why swapping should be disabled on the node that is running Elasticsearch.

File descriptors

On the Linux and macOS operating systems, there is a limit to the number of open file handles or file descriptors that a process can keep. This often needs to be increased in the case of Elasticsearch, as the default value is generally quite low for the open file descriptor limit.

Thread pools and garbage collector

Elasticsearch does many types of operations, such as indexing, searching, sorting, and aggregations, and uses the JVM thread pools to accomplish its tasks. It is advisable to not tune the settings related to thread pools in Elasticsearch. They generally do more harm than help to improve performance. Another thing not to tune in Elasticsearch is the garbage collector settings.

Managing and monitoring Elasticsearch

When you self-host Elasticsearch, the entire monitoring and management activities for the cluster are on you. It is necessary to monitor your Elasticsearch node process status, memory, and disk space on the node. If a node crashes for any reason, or becomes unavailable, it needs to be started back again.

The Snapshots of the Elasticsearch indexes need to be taken regularly for taking backups. We will discuss the snapshot/restore functionalities for backing up. Most of the monitoring part can be achieved via X-Pack and Kibana, but management processes need to be set up manually.

Running in Docker containers

Docker is a popular way of containarizing and shipping software. The advantage of docker is that the software that is dockerized, runs inside a light-weight container which has minimum overhead as compared to a virtual machine. As a result of its very less overhead and large pool of publicly available docker images, docker is a great way to run software in production in a predictable way without the need of much configuration.

Official Elasticsearch docker images are available for download in different flavours.

- Elasticsearch with basic X-Pack license
- Elasticsearch with full X-Pack license and 30-day evaluation
- Open source version of Elasticsearch without X-Pack

Getting started with an Elasticsearch instance running inside docker is as easy as installing docker and running the `docker pull` command with the Elasticsearch image of your choice. The following simple commands will get your single-node Elasticsearch 6.0.0 up and running if you have docker installed on your system.

```
docker pull docker.elastic.co/elasticsearch/elasticsearch:6.0.0

docker run -p 9200:9200 -p 9300:9300 -e "discovery.type=single-node"
docker.elastic.co/elasticsearch/elasticsearch:6.0.0
```

Docker is a highly recommended way of running applications in a predictable way in production. You can find out more about how to run Elasticsearch in docker in a production environment in the reference documentation—`https://www.elastic.co/guide/en/elasticsearch/reference/6.0/docker.html`.

Special considerations while deploying to a cloud

While self-hosting on a cloud, you may choose one of the cloud providers, such as AWS, Microsoft Azure, GCE, and so on. They provide compute resources, networking capabilities, virtual private clouds, and much more, to get control over your servers. Using a cloud provider as opposed to running on your own hardware comes with the following advantages:

- No upfront investment in hardware
- Ability to upgrade/downgrade servers
- Ability to add or remove servers as and when needed

It is typical to not be sure how much CPU, RAM, and so on, is required for your nodes when you start. Choosing the cloud gives the flexibility to benchmark on one type of configuration and then upgrade/downgrade or add/remove nodes as needed without incurring upfront costs. We will take EC2 as an example and try to understand the considerations to take into account. Most of the considerations should remain similar for other cloud providers as well. The following are some of the aspects to consider on AWS EC2:

- Choosing instance type
- Changing the ports; do not expose ports!
- Proxy requests
- Binding HTTP to local addresses
- Installing EC2 discovery plugin

- Installing S3 repository plugin
- Setting up periodic snapshots

Let's focus on them one by one.

Choosing instance type

EC2 offers different types of instances to meet different requirements. A typical starting point for Elasticsearch is to consider the `m3.2xlarge` instance; it has 8 CPU cores, 30 GB RAM, and 2 SSD disks with 80 GB. It is always good to benchmark on your data and monitor the resource usage on your nodes. You can upgrade or downgrade the nodes as per your findings.

Changing default ports; do not expose ports!

Running any type of service in a cloud involves different security risks. It is important that none of the ports used by Elasticsearch are exposed and accessible from the public internet. EC2 allows detailed control over which ports are accessible and from which IP addresses or subnets. Generally, you should not need to make any ports accessible from outside anywhere other than port `22` in order to log in remotely.

By default, Elasticsearch uses port `9200` for HTTP traffic and `9300` for inter-node communication. It is advisable to change these default ports by editing `elasticsearch.yml` on all nodes.

Proxy requests

Use a reverse proxy such as nginx (pronounced **engine x**) or Apache to proxy your requests to Elasticsearch/Kibana.

Binding HTTP to local addresses

You should run your Elasticsearch nodes in a **VPC (Virtual Private Cloud)**. More recently, AWS creates all nodes in a VPC. The nodes which do not need to interface with the clients, that is, accept the queries from clients over HTTP. This can be done by setting `http.host` in `elasticsearch.yml`. You can find out more about the HTTP host/port bindings in the reference documentation at `https://www.elastic.co/guide/en/elasticsearch/reference/current/modules-http.html`.

Installing EC2 discovery plugin

Elasticsearch nodes discover their peers via multicast when they are in the same network. This works very well in a regular LAN. When it comes to EC2, the network is shared and the node to node communication and automatic discovery don't work. It requires the installation of the EC2 discovery plugin on all nodes to be able to discover new nodes.

To install the EC2 discovery plugin, follow the instructions `https://www.elastic.co/guide/en/elasticsearch/plugins/current/discovery-ec2.html` and install it on all nodes.

Installing S3 repository plugin

It is important to back up your data in Elasticsearch regularly to restore the data if a catastrophic event occurs or if you want to revert to a last known healthy state. We will look at how to backup and restore using the snapshot/restore APIs of Elasticsearch in the next section. In order to take regular backups and store them in centralized and resilient data storage, we need to set up a snapshot mechanism. When you are running Elasticsearch in EC2, it makes sense to store snapshots in an AWS S3 bucket.

> **S3** stands for **Simple Storage Service**. It is a scalable, durable, and reliable storage service to store large amounts of data. It provides comprehensive security for your data and accessibility from many different platforms. It can meet very stringent compliance requirements due to its comprehensive security support. It is often the preferred solution for storing long-term data, especially when systems that generate the data are hosted on AWS.

The S3 repository plugin can be installed using the following command; it needs to be installed on every node of your Elasticsearch cluster:

```
sudo bin/elasticsearch-plugin install repository-s3
```

Setting up periodic snapshots

Once you have a repository set up on S3, we need to ensure that actual snapshots are taken periodically. What this means is that we need a scheduled job that triggers the command to take a snapshot at regular intervals. The interval could be 15 minutes, 30 minutes, one hour, and so on, depending on the sensitivity of your data. We will see how to establish the snapshot/restore process for your cluster in depth later in this chapter.

These are some of the considerations that you have to address while running Elasticsearch in production on AWS or other clouds.

So far, we have covered how to get your production up and running on a managed cloud or self-hosted environment. If you opted to self-host, you will need to set up a back-up and restore process so that you don't lose your data. The next section is only applicable if you are self-hosting your Elasticsearch cluster.

Backing up and restoring

Taking regular backups of your data to recover in the event of catastrophic failures is absolutely critical. It is important that all of your data is saved periodically at fixed time intervals and a sufficient number of such backups are preserved.

A common strategy is to take a full backup of your data at regular intervals and keep a fixed number of backups. Your cluster may be deployed on-premise in your own data center or it may be deployed on a cloud hosted service such as AWS, where you may be managing the cluster yourself.

We will look at the following topics on how to manage your backups and restore a specific backup if it is needed:

- Setting up a repository for snapshots
- Taking snapshots
- Restoring a specific snapshot

Let's look at how to do these one by one.

Setting up a repository for snapshots

The first step in setting up a regular backup process is setting up a repository for storing snapshots. There are different places where we could store snapshots:

- A shared filesystem
- Cloud or distributed filesystems (S3, Azure, GCS, or HDFS)

Depending upon where the Elasticsearch cluster is deployed, and which storage options are available, you may want to set up the repository for your snapshots in a certain way.

Let's first understand how you would do this in the simplest of scenarios, when you want to store it in a shared filesystem directory.

Shared filesystem

When your cluster has a shared filesystem accessible from all the nodes of the cluster, you have to ensure that the shared filesystem is accessible on a common path. You should mount that shared folder on all nodes and add the path of the mounted directory. The shared, mounted filesystem's path should be added to each node's elasticsearch.yml as follows:

```
path.repo: ["/mount/es_backups"]
```

If you are running a single node cluster and haven't set up a real distributed cluster, there is no need for a mounted shared drive. The path.repo parameter can be set to a local directory of your node. It is not recommended to run a production server on a single node cluster.

Once this setting is added to config/elasticsearch.yml on all nodes, please restart all the nodes of your cluster.

The next step is to register a named repository under this registered folder. This is done using the following curl command, where we are registering a named repository with the name backups:

```
curl -XPUT 'http://localhost:9200/_snapshot/backups' -H 'Content-Type:
application/json' -d '{
    "type": "fs",
    "settings": {
        "location": "/mount/es_backups/backups",
        "compress": true
    }
}'
```

You will need to replace `localhost` with the hostname or IP address of one of the nodes on your cluster. The `type` parameter set to `fs` is for the shared filesystem. The `settings` parameter's body depends on the `type` parameter's value.

Since we are currently looking at a shared filesystem snapshot repository, the body of the `settings` parameter has specific parameters to set up the shared filesystem based repository. If the `location` parameter is specified as an absolute path, it must be under one of the folders registered with the `path.repo` parameter in `elasticsearch.yml`. If the `location` parameter is not an absolute path, Elasticsearch will assume it is a relative path from the `path.repo` parameter. The parameter `compress` saves the snapshots in compressed format.

Cloud or distributed filesystems

When you are running your Elasticsearch cluster on AWS, Azure, or Google Cloud, it makes sense to store the snapshots in one of the alternatives provided by the cloud platform to store the data in robust, fault tolerant storage, rather than storing it on a shared drive.

Elasticsearch has official plugins that allow you to store the snapshots in S3. All you need to do is install the repository—s3 plugin on all nodes of your cluster and set up the repository settings in a similar way to how we set up the shared filesystem repository:

```
curl -XPUT 'http://localhost:9200/_snapshot/backups' -H 'Content-Type:
application/json' -d '{
    "type": "s3",
    "settings": {
        "bucket": "bucket_name",
        "region": "us-west",
        ...
    }
}'
```

The `type` should be s3 and `settings` would have relevant values for s3.

Taking snapshots

Once the repository is set up, we can take named snapshots under a specific repository:

```
curl -XPUT
'http://localhost:9200/_snapshot/backups/backup_201710101930?pretty' -H
'Content-Type: application/json' -d'
{
  "indices": "bigginsight,logstash-*",
  "ignore_unavailable": true,
  "include_global_state": false
}
'
```

In this command, we specified that we want a snapshot to be taken in the repository `backups` with the name `backup_201710101900`. The name of the snapshot could be anything, but it should help you identify the snapshot at a later stage. One typical strategy would be to take a snapshot every 30 minutes and set snapshot names with prefixes like `backup_yyyyMMddHHmm`. In the event of any failure, you could then identify the snapshot that can be restored.

Snapshots are incremental by default. They don't store all the redundant data in all snapshots.

Having taken the snapshots periodically, you would want to list all the snapshots that exist in a repository. This can be done using the following command:

```
curl -XGET 'http://localhost:9200/_snapshot/backups/_all?pretty'
```

Restoring a specific snapshot

If the need arises, you can restore the state from a specific snapshot using the following command:

```
curl -XPOST
'http://localhost:9200/_snapshot/backups/backup_201710101930/_restore'
```

This will restore the snapshot `backup_201710101930` from the backups repository.

Once we have set up a periodic job that takes and stores a snapshot, we are safe in the event of any failure. We now have a cluster that is recoverable from any disaster-like situation. Remember, the output of snapshots should be stored in resilient storage. At least, it should not be saved on the same Elasticsearch cluster; it should be saved on different storage, preferably a robust filesystem that is highly available, such as S3, HDFS, and so on.

So far in this chapter, we have got up and running with a cluster that is reliable and is backed up regularly. In the upcoming sections, we will see how to address some common scenarios in data modeling. We will see some common strategies for setting up aliases for indexes, index templates, modeling time-series data, and so on.

Setting up index aliases

Index aliases let you create aliases for one or more indexes or index name patterns. We will cover the following topics in order to learn how index aliases work:

- Understanding index aliases
- How index aliases can help

Understanding index aliases

An index alias just provides an extra name to refer to an index; it can be defined in the following way:

```
POST /_aliases
{
  "actions" : [
    { "add" : { "index" : "index1", "alias" : "current_index" } }
  ]
}
```

Here, `index1` can be referred to with the alias `current_index`. Similarly, the index alias can be removed with the remove action of the `_aliases` REST API:

```
POST /_aliases
{
  "actions" : [
    { "remove" : { "index" : "index1", "alias" : "current_index" } }
  ]
}
```

The preceding call will remove the alias `current_index`. Two actions can be combined in a single invocation of the `_aliases` API. When two calls are combined, the operations are done automatically. For example, the following call would be completely transparent to the client:

```
POST /_aliases
{
  "actions" : [
    { "remove" : { "index" : "index1", "alias" : "current_index" } },
    { "add" : { "index" : "index2", "alias" : "current_index" } }
  ]
}
```

Before the call, the alias `current_index` was referring to the index `index1`, and after the call, the alias will refer to the index `index2`.

How index aliases can help

Once in production, it often happens that we need to reindex data from one index to another. We might have one or more applications developed in JAVA, Python, .NET, or other programming environments that may be referring to these indexes. In the event that the production index needs to be changed from `index1` to `index2`, it will require a change in all client applications.

Aliases come to the rescue here. They offer extra flexibility, and hence, they are a recommended feature to use in production. The key thing is to create an alias for your production index and use the alias instead of the actual index name in the client applications that use them.

In the event that the current production index needs to change, we just need to update the alias to point to the new index instead of the old one. Using this feature, we can achieve zero downtime in production in the case of data migration or the need for reindexing. Aliases use a famous principle in computer science—an extra layer of indirection can solve most problems in computer science—https://en.wikipedia.org/wiki/Indirection.

Apart from the ones discussed here, there are more features that aliases offer; these include the ability to use index patterns, routing, the ability to specify filters, and many more. We will see how index aliases can be leveraged when creating time-based indices later in the chapter.

Setting up index templates

One important step while setting up your index is defining the mapping for the types, number of shards, replica, and other configurations. Depending upon the complexity of the types within your index, this step can involve a substantial amount of configuration.

Index templates allow you to create indexes based on a given template, rather than creating each index manually beforehand. Index templates allow you to specify settings and mappings for the index to be created. Let's understand this by going through the following points:

- Defining an index template
- Creating indexes on the fly

Let's say we want to store sensor data from various devices and we would like to create one index per day. At the beginning of every day, we want a new index to be created whenever the first sensor reading is indexed for that day. We will look into the details as to why we should use such time-based indices in the next section.

Defining an index template

We start by defining an index template:

```
PUT _template/readings_template                    1
{
  "index_patterns": ["readings*"],                 2
  "settings": {                                    3
    "number_of_shards": 1
  },
  "mappings": {                                    4
    "reading": {
      "properties": {
        "sensorId": {
          "type": "keyword"
        },
        "timestamp": {
          "type": "date"
        },
        "reading": {
          "type": "double"
        }
      }
    }
  }
}
```

}

In this `_template` call, we define the following things:

- A template with the name `readings_template`.
- The index name patterns that will match this template. We configured `readings*` as the one and only index pattern. Any attempt to index into an index that does not exist but matches this pattern would use this template.
- The settings to be applied to the newly created index from this template.
- The mappings to be applied to the newly created index from this template.

Let's try to index data into this new index.

Creating indexes on the fly

When any client tries to index the data for a particular sensor device, it should use the index name with the current day appended in yyyy-mm-dd format after `readings`. A call to index data for `2017-01-01` would look like the following:

```
POST /readings-2017-01-01/reading
{
    "sensorId": "a11111",
    "timestamp": 1483228800000,
    "reading": 1.02
}
```

When the first record for the date `2017-01-01` is being inserted, the client should use the index name `readings-2017-01-01`. Since this index doesn't exist yet, and we have an index template in place, Elasticsearch creates a new index using the index template we defined. As a result, the settings and mappings defined in our index template get applied to this new index.

This is how we create indexes based on index templates. In the next section, let's understand why these types of time-based indices are useful and how to use them in production with your time-series data.

Modeling time series data

Often, we have a need to store time series data in Elasticsearch. Typically, one would create a single index to hold all documents. This typical approach of one big index to hold all documents has its own limitations, especially for the following reasons:

- Scaling the index with an unpredictable volume over time
- Changing the mapping over time
- Automatically deleting older documents

Let's look at how each problem manifests itself when we choose a single monolithic index.

Scaling the index with unpredictable volume over time

One of the most difficult choices when creating an Elasticsearch cluster and its indices is deciding how many primary shards should be created and how many replica shards should be created.

Let's understand how the number of shards becomes important in the following sub sections:

- Unit of parallelism in Elasticsearch:
    - The effect of the number of shards on the relevance score
    - The effect of the number of shards on the accuracy of aggregations

Unit of parallelism in Elasticsearch

We have to decide the number of shards at the time of creating the index. The number of shards cannot be changed once the index is created. There is no golden rule that will help you decide how many shards should be created at the time of creating an index. The number of shards actually decides the level of parallelism in the index. Let's understand this by taking an example of how a search query might be executed.

When a search or aggregation query is sent by a client, it is first received by one of the nodes in the cluster. That node acts as a coordinator for that request. The coordinating node sends requests to all the shards on the cluster and waits for the response from all shards. Once the response is received by the coordinating node from all shards, it collates the response and sends it back to the original client.

What this means is, when we have a greater number of shards, each shard has to do relatively less work and parallelism can be increased.

But can we choose an arbitrarily big number of shards? Let's look at this in the next couple of subsections.

The effect of the number of shards on the relevance score

A large number of small shards is not always the solution, as it can affect the relevance of the search results. In the context of search queries, the relevance score is calculated within the context of a shard. The relative frequencies of documents are calculated within the context of each shard and not across all shards. This is why the number of shards can affect the overall scores observed for a query. In particular, having too many shards to address the future scalability problem is not a solution.

The effect of the number of shards on the accuracy of aggregations

Similar to the execution of the search query, an aggregation query is also coordinated by a coordinating node. Let's say that the client has requested terms aggregation on a field that can take a large number of unique values. By default, the terms aggregation returns the top 10 terms to the client.

For coordinating the execution of terms aggregation, the coordinator node does not request all the buckets from all shards. All shards are requested to give their top n buckets. By default, this number, n, is equal to the `size` parameter of the terms aggregation, that is, the number of top buckets that the client has requested. So, if the client requested the top 10 terms, the coordinating node in turn requests the top 10 buckets from each shard.

Since the data can be skewed across the shards to a certain extent, some of the shards may not even have certain buckets, even though those buckets might be one of the top buckets in some shards. If a particular bucket is in the top n buckets returned by one of the shards and that bucket is not one of the top n buckets by one of the other shards, the final count aggregated by the coordinating node will be off for that bucket. A large number of shards, just to ensure future scalability, does not help the accuracy of aggregations.

We have understood why the number of shards is important and how deciding the number of shards upfront is difficult. Next, we will see how changing the mapping of indices becomes difficult over a period of time.

Changing the mapping over time

Once an index is created and documents start getting stored, the requirements can change. There is only one thing that is constant, **change**.

When the schema changes, the following types of change may happen with respect to the schema:

- New fields get added
- Existing fields get removed

New fields get added

When the first document with a new field gets indexed, the new field's mapping is automatically created if it doesn't already exist. Elasticsearch infers the datatype of the field based on the value of that field in the first document in order to create the mapping. The mappings of one particular type of document can grow over a period of time.

Once a document with a new field is indexed, the mapping is created for that new field and its mapping remains.

Existing fields get removed

Over a period of time, the requirements of a project can change. Some fields might become obsolete and may no longer be used. In the case of Elasticsearch indexes, the fields that are no longer used are not removed automatically; the mapping remains in the index for all the fields that were ever indexed. Each extra field in the Elasticsearch index carries an overhead; this is especially true if you have hundreds or thousands of fields. If, in your use case, you have a very high number of fields that are not used, it can increase the burden on your cluster.

Automatically deleting older documents

No cluster has infinite capacity to retain data forever. With the volume growing over a period of time, you may decide to only store necessary data in Elasticsearch. Typically, you may want to retain data for the past few weeks, months, or years in Elasticsearch, depending on your use case.

Prior to Elasticsearch 2.x, this was achieved using **TTL (Time to Live)** set on individual documents. Each document could be configured to remain in the index for a configurable amount of time. But, the TTL feature was deprecated with the 2.x version because of its overheads in maintaining time-to-live on a per-document basis.

We have seen some problems that one might face while dealing with time series data. Now, let's look at how the use of **time-based indices** addresses these issues. Time-based indices are also called **index-per-timeframe**.

- How index-per-timeframe solves these issues
- How to set up index-per-timeframe

How index-per-timeframe solves these issues

Instead of going with one big monolithic index, we now create one index per timeframe. The timeframe could be one day, one week, one month, or any arbitrary time duration. For example, in our example in the *Index Template* section, we had chosen index-per-day. The names of the index would reflect that—we had indexes like `readings-2017-01-01`, `readings-2017-01-02`, and so on. If we had chosen index-per-month, the index names would look like `readings-2017-01`, `readings-2017-02`, `readings-2017-03`, and so on.

Let's look at how this scheme solves the issues we saw earlier one by one.

Scaling with index-per-timeframe

Since we no longer have a monolithic index that needs to hold all historic data, scaling-up or scaling-down according to the recent volumes becomes easier. The choice of the number of shards is not an upfront and permanent decision. Start with an initial estimated number of shards for the given time period. This number, the chosen number of shards, can be put in the index template.

Since that choice of shards can be changed before the next timeframe begins, you are not stuck with a bad choice. With each time period, it gives a chance to adjust the index template to increase or decrease the number of shards for the next index to be created.

Changing the mapping over time

Changing the mapping becomes easier, as we could just update the *index template* that is used for creating new indices. When the index template is updated, the new index that is created for the new timeframe uses the new mappings in the template.

Again, each timeframe gives us an opportunity to change.

Automatically deleting older documents

With time-based indices, deleting the older documents becomes easier. We could just drop older indices rather than deleting individual documents. If we were using monthly indices and wanted to enforce six-month retention of data, we could delete all indices older than 6 months. This may be set up as a scheduled job to look for and delete older indices.

As we have seen in this section, setting up index-per-timeframe has obvious advantages when we are dealing with time-series data.

Summary

In this chapter, we have seen essential techniques necessary to take your next Elastic Stack application to production. We have seen various deployment options, including cloud-based and on-premise. We have seen how to use a managed cloud service provider like Elastic Cloud and have also covered how to self-host Elastic Stack. We have covered some common concerns and decision choices that you will face, whether you self-host or use a managed cloud provider.

Additionally, we have seen various techniques useful in a production grade Elastic Stack deployment. These include the usage of index aliases, index templates, and modeling time-series data. This is definitely not a comprehensive guide covering all the nuances of running Elastic Stack in production, but we have definitely covered enough for you to comfortably take your next Elastic Stack project to production.

Equipped with all these techniques, we will build a sensor data analytics application in the next chapter, Chapter 10, *Building a Sensor Data Analytics Application*.

10
Building a Sensor Data Analytics Application

In the previous chapter, we saw how you can take an Elastic Stack application to production. Armed with all the knowledge of Elastic Stack and the techniques for taking applications to production, we are ready to apply these concepts in a real-world application. In this chapter, we will build one such application using Elastic Stack that can handle a large amount of data applying the techniques that we have learnt so far.

In this chapter, we will cover the following topics as we build a sensor data analytics application:

- Introduction to the application
- Modeling data in Elasticsearch
- Setting up the metadata database
- Building the Logstash data pipeline
- Sending data to Logstash over HTTP
- Visualizing the data in Kibana

Let's go through the topics.

Introduction to the application

IoT (**Internet of things**) has found a wide range of applications in modern times. IoT can be defined as follows:

> *The Internet of things (IoT) is the collective web of connected smart devices that can sense and communicate with each other by exchanging data via the Internet.*

IoT devices are connected to the Internet; they **sense** and **communicate**. They are equipped with different types of sensors that collect the data they observe and transmit it over the Internet. This data can be stored, analyzed, and often acted upon in near-real time. The number of such connected devices is projected to rise rapidly; according to Wikipedia, there will be an estimated 30 billion connected devices by 2020. Since each device can capture the current value of a metric and transmit it over the Internet, this can result in massive amounts of data.

A plethora of types of sensors have emerged in recent times for temperature, humidity, light, motion, and airflow; these can be used in different types of applications. Each sensor can be programmed to take a current reading and send it over the Internet.

Let's consider the following diagram for our understanding:

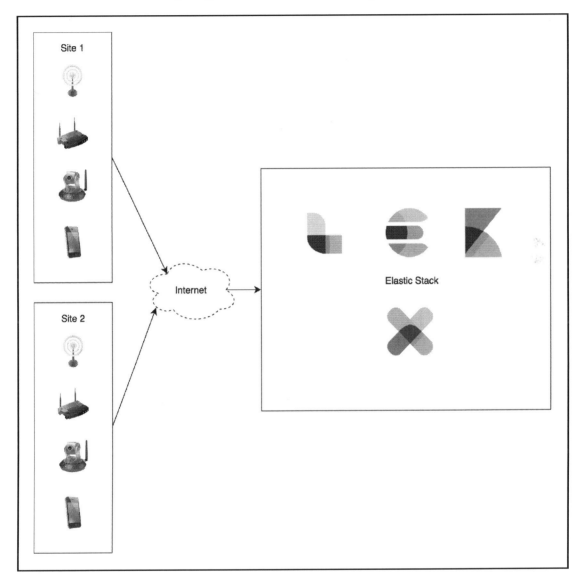

Fig-9.1: Connected devices and sensors sending data to Elastic Stack

Figure 9.1 provides an idea of the high-level architecture of the system that we will discuss in this chapter. The left-hand side of the figure depicts various types of devices equipped with sensors. These devices are capable of capturing different metrics and sending the metrics over the Internet for long-term storage and analysis. In the right half of the figure, you see the server-side components on the other side of the Internet. The server-side components primarily consist of Elastic Stack.

In this chapter, we will look at an application where we want to store and analyze sensor data from two types of sensors: Temperature and Humidity sensors, placed at various locations.

Sensors can be deployed across multiple sites or locations, with each site connected to the internet as shown in the figure. Our example demonstrates two types of sensors, Temperature and Humidity, but the application can be extended to support any kind of sensor data.

We will cover the following points about the system in this section:

- Understanding the sensor-generated data
- Understanding the sensor metadata
- Understanding the final stored data

Let's go deep into the application by understanding each topic one by one.

Understanding the sensor-generated data

What does the data look like when it is generated by the sensor? The sensor sends JSON format data over the internet and each reading looks like the following one:

```
{
  "sensor_id": 1,
  "time": 1511935948000,
  "value": 21.89
}
```

Here:

- The `sensor_id` field is the unique identifier of the sensor that has emitted the record
- The `time` field is the time of the reading in milliseconds since the epoch, i.e. 00:00:00 on 1 January, 1970
- The `value` field is the actual metric value emitted by the sensor

This type of JSON payload is generated every minute by all the sensors in the system. Since all sensors are registered in the system, the server-side system has the associated metadata with each sensor. Let us look at the sensor-related metadata that is available to us on the server side in a database.

Understanding the sensor metadata

The metadata about all the sensors across all locations is available to us in a relational database. In our example, we have stored it in MySQL. This type of metadata can be stored in any relational database other than MySQL. It can also be stored in Elasticsearch in an index.

The metadata about sensors contains primarily the following details:

- **Type of sensor**: What type of sensor is it? It can be a temperature sensor, Humidity sensor, and so on.
- **Location-related metadata**: Where is the sensor with the given sensor ID physically located? Which customer is it associated with?

This information is stored in the following three tables in MySQL:

- `sensor_type`: Defines various sensor types and their `sensor_type_id`:

sensor_type_id	sensor_type
1	Temperature
2	Humidity

- location: This defines locations with their latitude/longitude and address within a physical building:

location_id	customer	department	building_name	room	floor	location_on_floor	latitude	longitude
1	Abc Labs	R & D	222 Broadway	101	1	C-101	40.710936	-74.008500

- sensors: This maps sensor_id with sensor types and locations:

sensor_id	sensor_type_id	location_id
1	1	1
2	2	1

Given this database design, it is possible to look up all the of metadata associated for the given sensor_id using the following SQL query:

```
select
    st.sensor_type as sensorType,
    l.customer as customer,
    l.department as department,
    l.building_name as buildingName,
    l.room as room,
    l.floor as floor,
    l.location_on_floor as locationOnFloor,
    l.latitude,
    l.longitude
from
    sensors s
        inner join
    sensor_type st ON s.sensor_type_id = st.sensor_type_id
        inner join
    location l ON s.location_id = l.location_id
where
    s.sensor_id = 1;
```

The result of the previous query will look like this:

sensorType	customer	department	buildingName	room	floor	locationOnFloor	latitude	longitude
Temperature	Abc Labs	R & D	222 Broadway	101	Floor1	C-101	40.710936	-74.0085

Up until now, we have seen the format of incoming sensor data from the client side. We have also established a mechanism to look up the associated metadata for the given sensor.

Next, we will see what the final enriched record should look like.

Understanding the final stored data

By combining the data that is coming from the client side and contains the sensor's metric value for a given metric at a given time, we can construct an enriched record of the following fields:

- sensorId
- sensorType
- customer
- department
- buildingName
- room
- floor
- locationOnFloor
- latitude
- longitude
- time
- reading

Fields number 1, 11, and 12 are present in the payload sent by the sensor to our application. The remaining fields are looked up or enriched using the SQL query that we saw in the previous section—using the sensorId. This way, we can generate a denormalized sensor reading record for every sensor for every minute.

We have understood what the application is about and what the data represents. As we start developing the application, we will start the solution from the inside out. It is better to attack the problem at hand at the very heart and try to piece together its core. In the Elastic Stack, Elasticsearch is at the core of the stack, and so we will start defining our solution from the very heart of it by first building the data model in Elasticsearch. Let us do that in the next section.

Modeling data in Elasticsearch

We have seen the structure of the final record after enriching the data. That should help us model the data in Elasticsearch. Given that our data is time series data, we can apply some of the techniques mentioned in `Chapter 9`, *Running Elastic Stack in Production*, to model the data:

- Defining an index template
- Understanding the mapping

Let us look at the index template that we will define.

Defining an index template

Since we are going to be storing time series data that is immutable, we do not want to create one big monolithic index. We'll use the techniques discussed in the section *Modeling time series data* in `Chapter 9`, *Running Elastic Stack in Production*.

The source code of the application in this chapter is within the GitHub repository at `https://github.com/pranav-shukla/learningelasticstack/tree/master/chapter-10`. As we go through the chapter, we will perform the steps mentioned in the `README.md` file located at that path.

Please create the index template mentioned in *Step 1* of `README.md` or execute the following script in your Kibana Dev Tools Console:

```
POST _template/sensor_data_template
{
  "index_patterns": ["sensor_data*"],
  "settings": {
      "number_of_replicas": "1",
      "number_of_shards": "5"
  },
  "mappings": {
    "doc": {
      "properties": {
        "sensorId": {
          "type": "integer"
        },
        "sensorType": {
          "type": "keyword",
          "fields": {
            "analyzed": {
              "type": "text"
```

```
        }
      }
    },
    "customer": {
      "type": "keyword",
      "fields": {
        "analyzed": {
          "type": "text"
        }
      }
    },
    "department": {
      "type": "keyword",
      "fields": {
        "analyzed": {
          "type": "text"
        }
      }
    },
    "buildingName": {
      "type": "keyword",
      "fields": {
        "analyzed": {
          "type": "text"
        }
      }
    },
    "room": {
      "type": "keyword",
      "fields": {
        "analyzed": {
          "type": "text"
        }
      }
    },
    "floor": {
      "type": "keyword",
      "fields": {
        "analyzed": {
          "type": "text"
        }
      }
    },
    "locationOnFloor": {
      "type": "keyword",
      "fields": {
        "analyzed": {
          "type": "text"
```

```
                }
              }
            },
            "location": {
              "type": "geo_point"
            },
            "time": {
              "type": "date"
            },
            "reading": {
              "type": "double"
            }
          }
        }
      }
    }
```

This index template will create a new index with the name `sensor_data-YYYY.MM.dd` when any client attempts to index the first record in this index. We will see later in this chapter how this can be done from Logstash under *Building the Logstash data pipeline*.

Understanding the mapping

The mapping that we defined in the index template contains all the fields that will be present in the denormalized record after lookup. A few things to notice in the index template mapping are as follows:

- All the fields that contain text type of data are stored as the `keyword` type; additionally, they are stored as `text` in an analyzed field. For an example, please have a look at the `customer` field.
- The latitude and longitude fields that we had in the enriched data are now mapped to a `geo_point` type of field with the field name as `location`.

At this point, we have defined an index template that will trigger the creation of an index with the mapping we defined in the template.

Setting up the metadata database

We need to have a database that has metadata about the sensors. This database will hold the tables that we discussed in the *Introduction to the application* section.

We are storing the data in a relational database MySQL, but you can use any other relational database equally well. Since we are using MySQL, we will be using the MySQL JDBC driver to connect to the database. Please ensure that you have following things set up on your system:

1. MySQL database community version 5.5, 5.6, or 5.7. You can use an existing database if you already have it on your system.
2. Install the downloaded MySQL database and log in with the root user. Execute the script at this path: `https://github.com/pranav-shukla/learningelasticstack/tree/master/chapter-10/files/create_sensor_metadata.sql`.
3. Log in to the newly created `sensor_metadata` database and verify that the three tables—`sensor_type`, `locations`, and `sensors`—exist in the database.

You can verify that the database was created and populated successfully by executing the following query:

```
select
    st.sensor_type as sensorType,
    l.customer as customer,
    l.department as department,
    l.building_name as buildingName,
    l.room as room,
    l.floor as floor,
    l.location_on_floor as locationOnFloor,
    l.latitude,
    l.longitude
from
    sensors s
        inner join
    sensor_type st ON s.sensor_type_id = st.sensor_type_id
        inner join
    location l ON s.location_id = l.location_id
where
    s.sensor_id = 1;
```

The result of the previous query will look like this:

sensorType	customer	department	buildingName	room	floor	locationOnFloor	latitude	longitude
Temperature	Abc Labs	R & D	222 Broadway	101	Floor1	C-101	40.710936	-74.0085

Our `sensor_metadata` database is ready to look up the necessary sensor metadata. In the next section, let us build the Logstash data pipeline.

Building the Logstash data pipeline

Having set up the mechanism to automatically create the Elasticsearch index and also the metadata database, we can now focus on building the data pipeline using Logstash. What should our data pipeline do? It should perform the following steps:

- Accept JSON requests over the web (over HTTP)
- Enrich the JSON with the metadata we have in the MySQL database
- Store the resulting documents in Elasticsearch

These three main functions that we want to perform correspond exactly to the Logstash data pipeline's input, filter, and output plugins respectively. The full Logstash configuration file for this data pipeline is in the code base at `https://github.com/pranav-shukla/learningelasticstack/tree/master/chapter-10/files/logstash_sensor_data_http.conf`.

Let us look at how to achieve the end goal of our data pipeline by following the aforementioned steps. We will start with accepting JSON requests over the web (over HTTP).

Accept JSON requests over the web

This function is achieved by the input plugin. Logstash has support for the `http` input plugin, which does precisely that. It builds an HTTP interface using which different types of payloads can be submitted to Logstash as an input.

The relevant part from `logstash_sensor_data_http.conf` that has the input filter is as follows:

```
input {
  http {
    id => "sensor_data_http_input"
  }
}
```

Here, the `id` field is a string that can uniquely identify this input filter later in the file if needed. We will not need to reference this name in the file; we just chose a name `sensor_data_http_input`.

The reference documentation of the HTTP input plugin is available here: `https://www.elastic.co/guide/en/logstash/current/plugins-inputs-http.html`. In this instance, since we are using the default configuration of the `http` input plugin, we have just specified `id`. We should secure this HTTP endpoint as it will be exposed over the internet to allow sensors to send data from anywhere. We can configure `user` and `password` to protect this endpoint with the desired username and password, as follows:

```
input {
  http {
    id => "sensor_data_http_input"
    user => "sensor_data"
    password => "sensor_data"
  }
}
```

When Logstash is started with this input plugin, it starts an HTTP server on port 8080, which is secured using basic authentication with the given username and password. We can send a request to this Logstash pipeline using a `curl` command, as follows:

```
curl -XPOST -u sensor_data:sensor_data --header "Content-Type:
application/json" "http://localhost:8080/" -d
'{"sensor_id":1,"time":1512102540000,"reading":16.24}'
```

Let us see how we will enrich the JSON payload with the metadata we have in MySQL.

Enrich the JSON with the metadata we have in the MySQL database

The enrichment and other processing part of the data pipeline can be done using filter plugins. We have built a relational database that contains the tables and the necessary lookup data for enriching the incoming JSON requests.

Logstash has a `jdbc_streaming` filter plugin that can be used to do lookups from any relational database and enrich the incoming JSON documents. Let us zoom into the filter plugin section in our Logstash configuration file:

```
filter {
  jdbc_streaming {
    jdbc_driver_library => "/path/to/mysql-connector-java-5.1.45-bin.jar"
    jdbc_driver_class => "com.mysql.jdbc.Driver"
    jdbc_connection_string => "jdbc:mysql://localhost:3306/sensor_metadata"
    jdbc_user => "root"
    jdbc_password => "<password>"
    statement => "select st.sensor_type as sensorType, l.customer as
customer, l.department as department, l.building_name as buildingName,
l.room as room, l.floor as floor, l.location_on_floor as locationOnFloor,
l.latitude, l.longitude from sensors s inner join sensor_type st on
s.sensor_type_id=st.sensor_type_id inner join location l on
s.location_id=l.location_id where s.sensor_id= :sensor_identifier"
    parameters => { "sensor_identifier" => "sensor_id"}
    target => lookupResult
  }

  mutate {
    rename => {"[lookupResult][0][sensorType]" => "sensorType"}
    rename => {"[lookupResult][0][customer]" => "customer"}
    rename => {"[lookupResult][0][department]" => "department"}
    rename => {"[lookupResult][0][buildingName]" => "buildingName"}
    rename => {"[lookupResult][0][room]" => "room"}
    rename => {"[lookupResult][0][floor]" => "floor"}
    rename => {"[lookupResult][0][locationOnFloor]" => "locationOnFloor"}
    add_field => {
      "location" =>
"%{lookupResult[0]latitude},%{lookupResult[0]longitude}"
    }
    remove_field => ["lookupResult", "headers", "host"]
  }

}
```

As you will notice, there are two filter plugins used in the file:

- `jdbc_streaming`
- `mutate`

Let us see what each filter plugin is doing.

The jdbc_streaming plugin

We essentially specify the whereabouts of the database that we want to connect to, username/password, JDBC driver `.jar` file, and class. We have already created the database in the *Setting up the metadata database* section.

Download the latest MySQL JDBC Driver, also known as **Connector/J**, from `https://dev.mysql.com/downloads/connector/j/`. At the time of writing this book, the latest version is 5.1.45, which works with MySQL 5.5, 5.6, and 5.7. Download the `.tar/.zip` file containing the driver and extract it into your system. The path of this extracted `.jar` file should be updated in the `jdbc_driver_library` parameter.

To summarize, you should review and update the following parameters in the Logstash configuration to point to your database and driver `.jar` file:

- `jdbc_connection_string`
- `jdbc_password`
- `jdbc_driver_library`

The `statement` parameter has the same SQL query that we saw earlier. It looks up the metadata for the given `sensor_id`. A successful query will fetch all additional fields for that `sensor_id`. The result of the lookup query is stored in a new field, `lookupResult`, as specified by the `target` parameter.

The resulting document up to this point should look like:

```
{
  "sensor_id": 1,
  "time": 1512102540000,
  "reading": 16.24,
  "lookupResult": [
    {
      "buildingName": "222 Broadway",
      "sensorType": "Temperature",
      "latitude": 40.710936,
      "locationOnFloor": "Desk 102",
```

```
            "department": "Engineering",
            "floor": "Floor 1",
            "room": "101",
            "customer": "Linkedin",
            "longitude": -74.0085
        }
    ],
    "@timestamp": "2017-12-07T12:12:37.477Z",
    "@version": "1",
    "host": "0:0:0:0:0:0:0:1",
    "headers": {
      "remote_user": "sensor_data",
      "http_accept": "*\/*",
      ...
    }
}
```

As you can see, the `jdbc_streaming` filter plugin added some fields apart from the `lookupResult` field. These fields were added by Logstash and the `headers` field was added by the HTTP input plugin.

In the next section, we will use the `mutate` filter plugin to modify this JSON to the desired end result that we want in Elasticsearch.

The mutate plugin

As we have seen in the previous section, the output of the `jdbc_streaming` filter plugin has some undesired aspects. Our JSON payload needs the following modifications:

- Move the looked-up fields that are under `lookupResult` directly in JSON
- Combine the latitude and longitude fields under lookupResult as a location field
- Remove the unnecessary fields

```
mutate {
    rename => {"[lookupResult][0][sensorType]" => "sensorType"}
    rename => {"[lookupResult][0][customer]" => "customer"}
    rename => {"[lookupResult][0][department]" => "department"}
    rename => {"[lookupResult][0][buildingName]" => "buildingName"}
    rename => {"[lookupResult][0][room]" => "room"}
    rename => {"[lookupResult][0][floor]" => "floor"}
    rename => {"[lookupResult][0][locationOnFloor]" =>
"locationOnFloor"}
    add_field => {
        "location" =>
"%{lookupResult[0]latitude},%{lookupResult[0]longitude}"
```

```
        }
        remove_field => ["lookupResult", "headers", "host"]
    }
```

Let us see how the `mutate` filter plugin achieves these objectives.

Move the looked-up fields that are under lookupResult directly in JSON

As we have seen, `lookupResult` is an array with just one element, the element at index 0 in the array. We need to move all the fields under this array element directly under the JSON payload. This is done field by field using the `rename` operation.

For example, the following operation renames the existing `sensorType` field directly under the JSON payload:

```
rename => {"[lookupResult][0][sensorType]" => "sensorType"}
```

We do this for all the looked-up fields that are returned by the SQL query.

Combine the latitude and longitude fields under lookupResult as a location field

Remember when we defined the index template mapping for our index? We had defined the `location` field to be of `geo_point` type. The `geo_point` type accepts a value that is formatted as a string with latitude and longitude appended together, separated by a comma.

This is achieved by using the `add_field` operation to construct the `location` field, as follows:

```
add_field => {
  "location" => "%{lookupResult[0]latitude},%{lookupResult[0]longitude}"
}
```

By now, we should have a new field called `location` added to our JSON payload, exactly as desired. Next, we will remove the undesirable fields.

Remove the unnecessary fields

After moving all the elements from the `lookupResult` field directly in the JSON, we don't need that field anymore. Similarly, we don't want to store the `headers` and the `host` fields in the Elasticsearch index. So, we remove them all at once using the following operation:

```
remove_field => ["lookupResult", "headers", "host"]
```

We finally have the JSON payload in the structure that we want in the Elasticsearch index. Next, let us see how to send it to Elasticsearch.

Store the resulting documents in Elasticsearch

We use the Elasticsearch output plugin that comes with Logstash to send data to Elasticsearch. The usage is very simple; we just need to have `elasticsearch` under the output tag:

```
output {
  elasticsearch {
    hosts => ["localhost:9200"]
    index => "sensor_data-%{+YYYY.MM.dd}"
  }
}
```

We have specified `hosts` and `index` to send the data to the right index within the right cluster. Notice that the index name has `%{YYYY.MM.dd}`. It calculates the index name to be used by using the event's current time and formats the time in this format.

Remember that we had defined an index template with the index pattern `sensor_data*`. When the first event on 1st December 2017 is sent, the output plugin defined here will send the event to index `sensor_data-2017.12.01`.

If you want to send events to a secured Elasticsearch cluster as we did using X-Pack in Chapter 8, *Elastic X-Pack*, you can configure the user and password as follows:

```
output {
  elasticsearch {
    hosts => ["localhost:9200"]
    index => "sensor_data-%{+YYYY.MM.dd}"
    user => "elastic"
    password => "elastic"
  }
}
```

This way, we will have one index for every day, where each day's data will be stored within its index. We had learned index per time frame in Chapter 9, *Running Elastic Stack in Production*.

Now that we have our Logstash data pipeline ready, let us send some data.

Sending data to Logstash over HTTP

At this point, sensors can start sending their readings to the Logstash data pipeline that we have created in the previous section. They just need to send data as follows:

```
curl -XPOST -u sensor_data:sensor_data --header "Content-Type:
application/json" "http://localhost:8080/" -d
'{"sensor_id":1,"time":1512102540000,"reading":16.24}'
```

Since we don't have real sensors, we will simulate the data by sending these types of requests. The simulated data and script that sends this data are incorporated in the code at https://github.com/pranav-shukla/learningelasticstack/tree/master/chapter-10/data.

If you are on Linux or macOS, open the terminal and change the directory to your Learning Elasticstack workspace that was checked out from GitHub.

If your machine has a Windows operating system, you will need a Linux-like shell that supports the `curl` command and basic **BASH (Bourne Again SHell)** commands. As you may already have a GitHub workspace checked out, you may be using *Git for Windows*, which has Git BASH. This can be used to run the script that loads data. If you don't have Git BASH, please download and install *Git for Windows* from https://git-scm.com/download/win and launch Git BASH to run the commands mentioned in this section.

Now, go to the chapter-10/data directory and execute load_sensor_data.sh:

```
$ pwd
/Users/pranavshukla/workspace/learningelasticstack
$ cd chapter-10/data
$ ls
load_sensor_data.sh sensor_data.json
$ ./load_sensor_data.sh
```

The `load_sensor_data.sh` script reads the `sensor_data.json` line by line and submits to Logstash using the curl command we just saw.

We have just played 1 days worth of sensor readings, taken every minute from different sensors across a few geographical locations, to Logstash. The Logstash data pipeline that we had built earlier should have enriched and sent the data to our Elasticsearch.

It is time to switch over to Kibana and get some insights from the data.

Visualizing the data in Kibana

We have successfully set up the Logstash data pipeline and also loaded some data using the pipeline into Elasticsearch. It is time to explore the data and build a dashboard that will help us gain some insights into the data.

Let's start by doing a sanity check to see if the data is loaded correctly. We can do so by going to Kibana **Dev Tools** and executing the following query:

```
GET /sensor_data-*/_search?size=0
{
   "query": {"match_all": {}}
}
```

This query will search data across all indices matching the `sensor_data-*` pattern. There should be a good number of records in the index if the data was indexed correctly.

We will cover the following topics:

- Set up an index pattern in Kibana
- Build visualizations
- Create a dashboard using the visualizations

Let us go through each step.

Chapter 10

Set up an index pattern in Kibana

Before we can start building visualizations, we need to set up the index pattern for all indexes that we will potentially have for the Sensor Data Analytics application. We need to do this because our index names are dynamic. We will have one index per day, but we want to be able to create visualizations and dashboards that work across multiple indices of Sensor Data even when there are multiple indices. To do this, go to the **Management** tab on Kibana and click on the **Index Patterns** link:

Fig-10.6: Create an Index Pattern

Click on the **Create Index Pattern** button and add the `sensor_data*` index pattern as shown in the following screenshot. In **Time Filter Field Name**, choose the `time` field as follows and click on **Create**:

Fig-10.7: Create an Index Pattern

[365]

We have successfully created the index pattern for our sensor data. Next, we will start building some visualizations.

Build visualizations

Before we embark on an analytics project, we often already have some questions that we want to get answered quickly from visualizations. These visualizations, which answer different questions, may be packaged as a dashboard or may be used as and when needed. We will also start with some questions and try to build visualizations to get answers to those questions.

We will try to answer the following questions:

- How does the average temperature change over time?
- How does the average humidity change over time?
- How do temperature and humidity change at each location over time?
- Can I visualize temperature and humidity over a map?
- How are the sensors distributed across departments?

Let us build visualizations to get the answers, starting with the first question.

How does the average temperature change over time?

Here, we are just looking for an aggregate statistic. We want to know the average temperature across all temperature sensors regardless of their location or any other criteria. As we saw in `Chapter 7`, *Visualizing Data with Kibana*, we should go to the **Visualize** tab to create new visualizations and click on the button with a + sign.

Choose **Basic Charts**, and then choose the **Line** chart item. In the next screen, to configure the line chart, follow *Steps 1* to *5* as shown in the following screenshot:

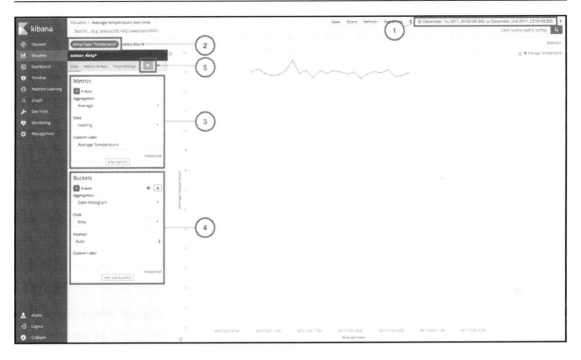

Fig-10.8: Create the visualization for Average temperature over time

1. Click on the small clock icon at the top-right corner, choose **Absolute**, and select the date range as 1st December 2017 to 2nd December 2017. We have to do this because our simulated sensor data is from 1st December 2017.

2. Click on **Add a filter** as shown in Fig-10.8; choose the **Filter** as follows— sensorType is Temperature. Click on the **Save** button. We have two types of sensors, Temperature and Humidity. In the current visualization that we are building, we are only interested in the temperature readings. This is why we've added this filter.

3. From the Metrics section, choose the values as shown in Figure 10.8. We are interested in the average value of the readings. We have also modified the label to be Average Temperature.

4. From the Buckets section, choose the Date Histogram aggregation and the time field, with the other options left as is.

5. Click on the triangular **Apply changes** button.

The result is the average temperature across all temperature sensors over the selected time period. This is what we were looking for when we started building this visualization. From the preceding graph, we can quickly see that on 1st December 2017 at 15:00 IST, the temperature became unusually high. The time may be different on your machine. We may want to find out which underlying sensors reported higher-than-normal temperatures that caused this peak.

We can click on the Save link at the top bar and give this visualization a name. Let's call it **Average temperature over time**. Later, we will use this visualization in a dashboard.

Let us proceed to the next question.

How does the average humidity change over time?

This question is very similar to the previous question. We can reuse the previous visualization, make a slight modification, and create another copy to answer this question. We will start by opening the first visualization, which we saved with the name **Average temperature over time**.

Execute the steps mentioned as follows to update the visualization:

1. Hover on the filter with label **sensorType: "Temperature"** and click on the Edit icon as shown in figure 10.8.
2. Change the Filter value from **Temperature** to **Humidity** and click on **Save**.
3. Modify **Custom Label** from **Average Temperature** to **Average Humidity** and click on the **Apply changes** button.

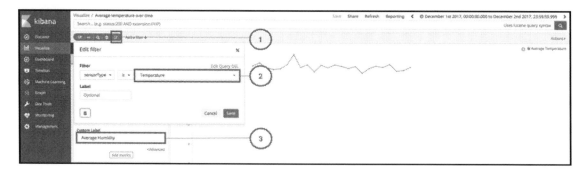

Fig-10.9: Create the visualization for Average humidity over time

As you will see, the chart gets updated for the Humidity sensors. You can click on the **Save** link at the top navigation bar. You can give a new name to the visualization as **Average humidity over time**, check the **Save as a new visualization** box, and click on **Save**. This completes our second visualization and answers our second question.

How do temperature and humidity change at each location over time?

This time, we are looking to get more details than the first two questions. We want to know how the temperature and humidity vary at each location over time. We will solve it for temperature.

Go to the **Visualizations** tab in Kibana and create a new **Line** chart visualization, the same as how we did before:

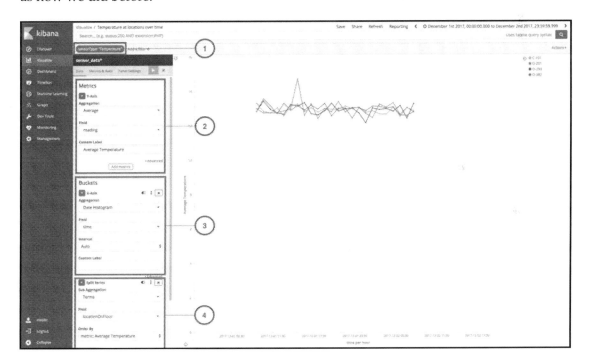

Fig-10.10: Create the visualization for Temperature at locations over time

1. Add a filter for **sensorType: "Temperature"** as we have done before.
2. Set the Metrics section as shown in fig-10.10 to do Average aggregation on the `reading` field.
3. Since we are aggregating the data over the `time` field, we need to choose the **Date Histogram** aggregation in the Buckets section. Here we should choose the `time` field and leave the aggregation **Interval** to be **Auto.**
4. Up to this point, this visualization is the same as **Average temperature over time**. We don't just want to see the average temperature over time; we want to see it per `locationOnFloor`, which is our most fine-grained unit of identifying a location. This is why we are splitting the series using Terms aggregation on the field `locationOnFloor` in this step. We select Order By to be `metric:` `Average Temperature` and keep 5 as the Order Size to keep only the top five locations.

We have now built a visualization that shows how the temperature changes for each value of `locationOnFloor` in our data. You can clearly see that there is spike in O-201 on 1st December 2017 at 15:00 IST. Because of this spike, we had seen the average temperature in our first visualization spike at that time. This is an important insight that we have uncovered.

A visualization for humidity can be created by following the same steps but just replacing Temperature with Humidity.

Can I visualize temperature and humidity over a map?

We can visualize temperature and humidity over the map using the the Coordinate Map visualization. Create a new **Coordinate Map** visualization and perform the following steps:

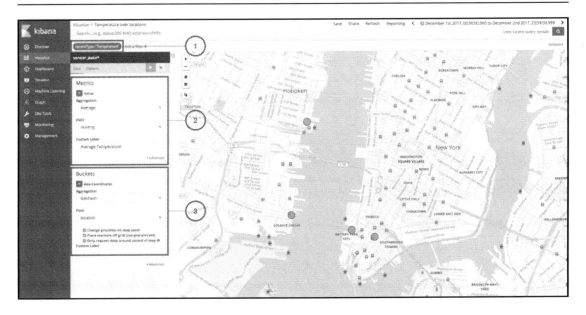

Fig-10.11: Create a visualization to view sensor locations over a map

1. As in previous visualizations, add a filter for **sensorType: "Temperature"**
2. In the **Metrics** section, choose **Average** aggregation on the `reading` field as done previously
3. Since this is a **Coordinate Map**, we need to choose the GeoHash Grid aggregation and then select the `geo_point` field that we have in our data—`location` is the field to aggregate

As you can see, it helps in visualizing our data on the map. We can immediately see the average temperature at each site when we hover over a specific location. Focus on the relevant part of the map and save the visualization with the name **Temperature over locations**.

You can create a similar Coordinate Map visualization for the humidity sensors.

How are the sensors distributed across departments?

What if we want to see how the sensors distributed across different departments? Remember, we have the `department` field in our data, which we had got after enriching the data using the `sensor_id`. Pie charts are particularly useful to visualize how data is distributed across multiple values of a `keyword` type of field, such as `department`. We will start by creating a new **Pie** chart visualization.

Follow the steps as shown in Fig-10.12:

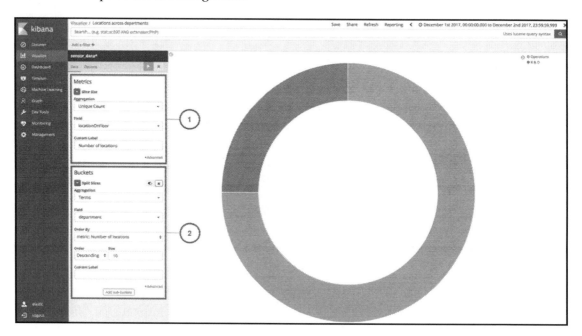

Fig-10.12: Creating a visualization for Locations across departments

1. In the **Metrics** section, choose **Unique Count** aggregation and `locationOnFloor` field. You may modify the **Custom Label** to Number of locations.
2. In the **Buckets** section, we need to choose **Terms** aggregation on the `department` field as we want to aggregate the data across different departments.

Click on **Apply changes** and save this visualization as `Locations across departments`. You can also create another similar visualization to visualize Locations across different buildings. Lets call that visualization `Locations across buildings`. That will help us see how many locations are being monitored in each building.

Next, we will create a dashboard to bring together all the visualizations we have built.

Create a dashboard

A dashboard lets you organize multiple visualizations together, save, and share with other people. The ability to look at multiple visualizations has its own benefits. You can filter the data using some criteria and all visualizations will show the data filtered by the same criteria. This ability lets you uncover some powerful insights. It can also answer more complex questions.

Let us build a dashboard from the visualizations that we have created so far. Please click on the **Dashboard** tab from the left-hand-side navigation bar in Kibana. Click on the + button to create a new dashboard.

Click on the Add menu bar item at the top to add visualizations to your newly created dashboard. As you click, you will see all the visualizations we have built in a drop-down selection. You can add all the visualizations one by one and drag/resize to create a dashboard that suits your requirements.

Let us see what a dashboard may look like for the application that we are building:

fig-10.13: Dashboard for Sensor Data Analytics application

With dashboard, you can add filters by clicking on the Add a filter link near the top-left corner of the dashboard. The selected filter will be applied to all the charts.

The visualizations are interactive; for example, clicking on one of the pies of the donut charts will apply that filter globally. Let's see how it can be helpful.

When you click on the pie for 222 Broadway building in the donut chart at the bottom-right corner, you will see the filter for **buildingName: "222 Broadway"** added to the filters. This lets you see all of the data from the perspective of all the sensors in that building:

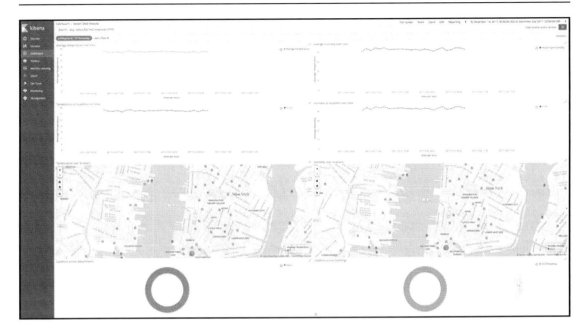

Fig-10.13 - Interacting with the visualizations in a dashboard

Let us delete that filter by hovering over the **buildingName: "222 Broadway"** filter and clicking on the trash icon. Next, we will try to interact with one of the line charts, that is, the **Temperature at locations over time** visualization.

As we observed earlier, there was a spike on 1st December 2017 at 15:00 IST. It is possible to zoom into a particular time period by clicking, dragging, and drawing a rectangle around the time interval that we want to zoom into within any line chart. In other words, just draw a rectangle around the spike, dragging your mouse while it is clicked. The result is that the time filter applied on the entire dashboard (which is displayed in the top-right corner) is changed.

Let's see whether we get any new insights from this simple operation to focus on that time period:

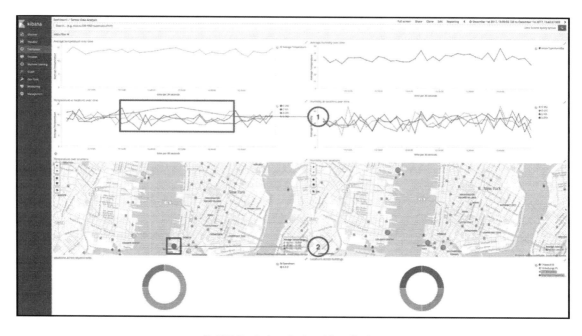

Fig-10.15: Zooming into a time interval from a line chart

We uncover the following facts:

1. The temperature sensor at location O-201 (pink legend in fig-10.15) is steadily rising around this time.
2. In the Coordinate Map visualization, you can see that the highlighted circle is red, compared to the other locations, which are yellow. This highlights that the location has an abnormally high temperature compared to the other locations.

Interacting with charts and applying different filters can provide powerful insights like the ones we just saw.

This concludes our application and demonstration of what we can do using the Elastic Stack components.

Summary

In this chapter, we built a sensor data analytics application that has a wide variety of applications, as it is related to the emerging IoT field. We understood the problem domain and the data model, including metadata related to sensors. We wanted to build an analytics application using only Elastic Stack components, without using any other tools and programming languages, to get a powerful tool that can handle large volumes of data.

We started at the very core by designing the data model for Elasticsearch. Then we designed a data pipeline that is secured and can accept data over the internet using HTTP. We enriched the incoming data using the metadata that we had in a relational database and stored in Elasticsearch. We sent some test data over HTTP just like real sensors send over the internet. We built some meaningful visualizations that will give answers to some typical questions. Then we put together all visualizations in a powerful, interactive dashboard.

In Chapter 11, *Monitoring Server Infrastructure*, we will build another real-world application where Elastic Stack excels.

11
Monitoring Server Infrastructure

In the previous chapter, we covered how to effectively run Elastic Stack in a production environment, and the best practices to follow when running Elastic Stack in production.

In this chapter, we will be covering how to use the Beats platform for monitoring server infrastructure. We will learn in detail about Metricbeat, a Beat which helps IT administrators and application support teams in monitoring their applications and server infrastructure, and in responding in a timely manner in case of infrastructure outage.

In this chapter, we will cover:

- Metricbeat, a Beat used for collecting system and application metrics
- Installation and configuration of Metricbeat
- Deployment architectures

Metricbeat

Metricbeat is a lightweight shipper that periodically collects metrics from the operating system and from services running on the server. It helps one to monitor servers by collecting metrics from the system and services such as Apache, MongoDB, Redis, and so on, running on the server. Metricbeat can push the collected metrics directly into Elasticsearch or send them to Logstash, Redis, or Kafka. To monitor services, Metricbeat can be installed on the edge server where services are running, but it also provides the ability to collect metrics from remote servers, as well. However, it's recommended to have it installed on the edge servers where the services are running.

Downloading and installing Metricbeat

Navigate to `https://www.elastic.co/downloads/beats/metricbeat` and, depending on your operating system, download the ZIP/TAR file as shown in the following screenshot. The installation of Metricbeat is simple and straightforward:

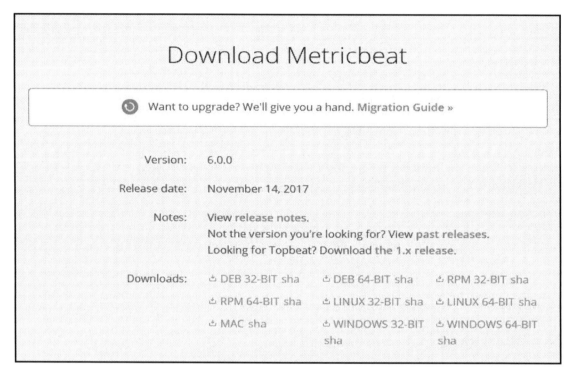

 Beats version 6.0.x is compatible with Elasticsearch 5.6.x and 6.0.x, and Logstash 5.6.x and 6.0.x. The compatibility matrix can be found at `https:/ /www.elastic.co/support/matrix#matrix_compatibility`. When you come across Elasticsearch and Logstash examples or usages with Beats in this chapter, make sure you have compatible versions of Elasticsearch and Logstash installed.

Installing on Windows

Unzip the downloaded file and navigate to the extracted location, as follows:

```
D:>cd D:\packt\metricbeat-6.0.0-windows-x86_64
```

To install Metricbeat as a service on Windows, refer to the following steps:

1. Open Windows PowerShell as an administrator and navigate to the extracted location
2. From the PowerShell prompt, run the following commands to install Metricbeat as a Windows service:

```
PS >cd D:\packt\metricbeat-6.0.0-windows-x86_64
PS D:\packt\metricbeat-6.0.0-windows-x86_64>.\install-
service-metricbeat.ps1
```

If script execution is disabled on your system, you need to set the execution policy for the current session to allow the script to run. For example, PowerShell.exe -ExecutionPolicy UnRestricted -File .\install-service-metricbeat.ps1.

Installing on Linux

Unzip the tar.gz package and navigate to the newly created folder as shown in the following code snippet:

```
$> tar -xzf metricbeat-6.0.0-linux-x86_64.tar.gz
$>cd metricbeat
```

To install using dep/rpm, execute the appropriate commands in the terminal:

deb:
```
curl -L -O
https://artifacts.elastic.co/downloads/beats/metricbeat/m
etricbeat-6.0.0-amd64.deb
sudo dpkg -i metricbeat-6.0.0-amd64.deb
```

rpm:
```
curl -L -O
https://artifacts.elastic.co/downloads/beats/metricbeat/m
etricbeat-6.0.0-x86_64.rpm
sudo rpm -vi metricbeat-6.0.0-x86_64.rpm
```

Metricbeat will be installed in the `/usr/share/metricbeat` directory. The configuration files will be present in `/etc/metricbeat`. The `init` script will be present in `/etc/init.d/metricbeat`. The log files will be present within the `/var/log/metricbeat` directory.

Architecture

Metricbeat is made up of two components. One is **modules** and the other is **metricsets**. A Metricbeat module defines the basic logic of collecting data from a specific service such as MongoDB, Apache, and so on. The module specifies details about the service, including how to connect, how often to collect metrics, and which metrics to collect.

Each module has one or more metricsets. A metricset is the component which collects the list of related metrics from services or the operating system using a single request. It structures the event data and ships it to the configured outputs, such as Elasticsearch or Logstash.

Metricbeat collects the metrics periodically based on the interval specified in the `metricbeat.yml` configuration file, and publishes the event to the configured output asynchronously. As the events are published asynchronously, just like in Filebeat which guarantees delivery at least once, if the configured output is not available then the events will be lost.

For example, the MongoDB module provides the `status` and `dbstats` metricsets, which collect the information and statistics by parsing the returned response obtained from running the `db.serverStatus()` and `db.stats()` commands on MongoDB, as shown in the following figure:

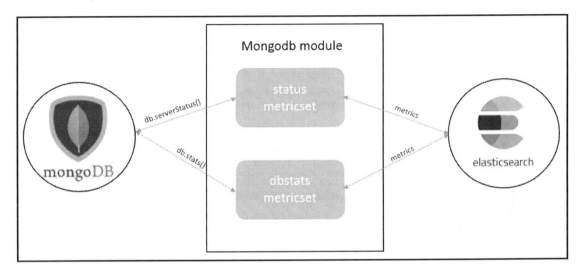

The key benefits of Metricbeat are as follows:

- **Metricbeat sends error events too**: When the service is not reachable or down, Metricbeat will still send the events containing full error messages obtained during fetching from the host systems. This is beneficial for troubleshooting or identifying the reason behind the outage of the service.
- **Combines multiple related metrics into a single event**: Metricbeat fetches all the related metrics from the host system, making a single request rather than making multiple requests for fetching each metrics one by one, thus resulting in less load on the services/host systems. Fetched metrics are combined into a single event and sent to the configured output.

- **Sends metadata information**: Metrics sent by Metricbeat contain both numbers as well as strings contacting the status information. It also ships basic metadata information about each metric as part of each event. This is helpful for mapping appropriate data types during storage and helps with querying/filtering data, identifying events based on meta data information, and so on.
- **Sends raw data as it is**: Metricbeat sends the obtained raw data as it is without performing any processing or any aggregation operations on it, thus reducing the complexity of Metricbeat.

Event structure

Metricbeat sends two type of events:

- Regular events containing the fetched metrics
- Error events when the service is down/unreachable

Irrespective of the type of event, all the events have the same basic structure and contain at minimum the following fields, irrespective of the type of module enabled:

- `@timestamp`: Time when the event was captured
- `beat.hostname`: Hostname of the server on which the Beat is running
- `beat.name`: Name given to the Beat (defaults to hostname)
- `beat.version`: Version of the Beat
- `metricset.module`: Name of the module that the data is from
- `metricset.name`: Name of the metricset that the data is from
- `metricset.rtt`: Round trip time of the request in microseconds
- `@metadata.beat`: Beat type (that is, Metricbeat)
- `@metadata.type`: Defaults to `doc`
- `@metadata.version`: Version of the Beat

In case of error events, an error field such as `error.message`, `error.code`, and `error.type`, containing the error message, code, and type, will be appended to the event.

An example of a regular event is as follows:

```
{
    "@timestamp": "2017-11-25T11:48:33.269Z",
    "@metadata": {
        "beat": "metricbeat",
        "type": "doc",
        "version": "6.0.0"
    },
    "system": {
        "fsstat": {
            "total_size": {
                "free": 189415194624,
                "used": 305321828352,
                "total": 494737022976
            },
            "count": 2,
            "total_files": 0
        }
    },
    "metricset": {
        "name": "fsstat",
        "rtt": 2000,
        "module": "system"
    },
    "beat": {
        "version": "6.0.0",
        "name": "SHMN-IN",
        "hostname": "SHMN-IN"
    }
}
```

An example of an error event when `mongodb` is not reachable is as follows:

```
{
    "@timestamp": "2017-11-25T11:53:08.056Z",
    "@metadata": {
        "beat": "metricbeat",
        "type": "doc",
        "version": "6.0.0"
    },
    "metricset": {
        "host": "localhost:27017",
        "rtt": 1003057,
        "module": "mongodb",
        "name": "status"
    },
    "error": {
```

```
    "message": "no reachable servers"
},
"mongodb": {
  "status": {}
}
```

Along with the minimum fields (basic structure of the event) that the Metricbeat ships, depending on the modules enabled, it ships fields related to the module. The complete list of fields it ships per module can be obtained at https://www.elastic.co/guide/en/beats/metricbeat/current/exported-fields.html.

Configuring Metricbeat

The configurations related to Metricbeat are stored in a configuration file named `metricbeat.yml`, and it uses YAML syntax.

The `metricbeat.yml` file contains the following:

- Module configuration
- General settings
- Output configuration
- Processor configuration
- Path configuration
- Dashboard configuration
- Logging configuration

Let's explore some of these sections.

 The location of the `metricbeat.yml` file will be present in the installation directory if `.zip` or `.tar` files are used for installation. If `.dep` or `.rpm` is used for installation, then it will be present in the `/etc/metricbeat` location.

Module configuration

Metricbeat comes bundled with various modules to collect metrics from the system and applications such as Apache, MongoDB, Redis, MySQL, and so on.

Metricbeat provides two ways of enabling modules and metricsets:

- Enabling module configs in the `modules.d` directory
- Enabling module configs in the `metricbeat.yml` file

Enabling module configs in the modules.d directory

The `modules.d` directory contains default configurations for all the modules available in Metricbeat. The configuration specific to a module is stored in a `.yml` file with the name of the file being the name of the module. For example, the configuration related to the MySQL module would be stored in the `mysql.yml` file. By default, excepting the `system` module, all other modules are disabled. To list the modules that are available in Metricbeat, execute the following command:

```
Windows:
D:\packt\metricbeat-6.0.0-windows-x86_64>metricbeat.exe modules list

Linux:
[locationOfMetricBeat]$./metricbeat modules list
```

The `modules list` command displays all the available modules and also lists which modules are currently enabled/disabled.

 If a module is disabled, then in the `modules.d` directory, the configuration related to the module will be stored with the `.disabled` extension.

As each module comes with the default configurations, make the appropriate changes in the module configuration file.

The basic configuration for `mongodb` module will look as follows:

```
- module: mongodb
  metricsets: ["dbstats", "status"]
  period: 10s
  hosts: ["localhost:27017"]
  username: user
  password: pass
```

To enable it, execute the `modules enable` command, passing one or more module name. For example:

```
Windows:
D:\packt\metricbeat-6.0.0-windows-x86_64>metricbeat.exe modules enable
redis mongodb

Linux:
[locationOfMetricBeat]$./metricbeat modules enable redis mongodb
```

Similar to disable modules, execute the `modules disable` command, passing one or more module names to it. For example:

```
Windows:
D:\packt\metricbeat-6.0.0-windows-x86_64>metricbeat.exe modules disable
redis mongodb

Linux:
[locationOfMetricBeat]$./metricbeat modules disable redis mongodb
```

> To enable dynamic config reloading, set `reload.enabled` to true and to specify the frequency to look for config file changes. Set the `reload.period` parameter under the `metricbeat.config.modules` property.

For example:
```
#metricbeat.yml

metricbeat.config.modules:
path: ${path.config}/modules.d/*.yml
reload.enabled: true
reload.period: 20s
```

Enabling module config in the metricbeat.yml file

If one is used to earlier versions of Metricbeat, one can enable the modules and metricsets in the `metricbeat.yml` file directly by adding entries to the `metricbeat.modules` list. Each entry in the list begins with a dash (–) and is followed by the settings for that module. For example:

```
metricbeat.modules:
#------------------ Memcached Module ---------------------------
- module: memcached
  metricsets: ["stats"]
  period: 10s
  hosts: ["localhost:11211"]

#------------------ MongoDB Module ---------------------------
- module: mongodb
  metricsets: ["dbstats", "status"]
  period: 5s
```

> It is possible to specify the module multiple times and specify a different period to use for one or more metricset. For example:
>
> ```
> #------- Couchbase Module ---------------------------
> - module: couchbase
> metricsets: ["bucket"]
> period: 15s
> hosts: ["localhost:8091"]
>
> - module: couchbase
> metricsets: ["cluster", "node"]
> period: 30s
> hosts: ["localhost:8091"]
> ```

General settings

This section contains configuration options and some general settings to control the behavior of Metricbeat.

Some of the configuration options/settings are:

- `name`: The name of the shipper that publishes the network data. By default, hostname is used for this field:

  ```
  name: "dc1-host1"
  ```

- `tags`: The list of tags that will be included in the `tags` field of every event Metricbeat ships. Tags make it easy to group servers by different logical properties and help when filtering events in Kibana and Logstash:

  ```
  tags: ["staging", "web-tier","dc1"]
  ```

- `max_procs`: The maximum number of CPUs that can be executing simultaneously. The default is the number of logical CPUs available in the system:

  ```
  max_procs: 2
  ```

Output configuration

This section is used to configure outputs where the events need to be shipped. Events can be sent to single or multiple outputs simultaneously. The allowed outputs are Elasticsearch, Logstash, Kafka, Redis, file, and console.

Some of the outputs that can be configured are as follows:

- `elasticsearch`: It is used to send the events directly to Elasticsearch. A sample Elasticsearch output configuration is shown in the following code snippet:

  ```
  output.elasticsearch:
    enabled: true
    hosts: ["localhost:9200"]
  ```

Using the `enabled` setting, one can enable or disable the output. `hosts` accepts one or more Elasticsearch node/server. Multiple hosts can be defined for failover purposes. When multiple hosts are configured, the events are distributed to these nodes in round robin order. If Elasticsearch is secured, then the credentials can be passed using the `username` and `password` settings:

```
output.elasticsearch:
  enabled: true
  hosts: ["localhost:9200"]
  username: "elasticuser"
  password: "password"
```

To ship the events to the Elasticsearch ingest node pipeline so that they can be pre-processed before being stored in Elasticsearch, the pipeline information can be provided using the `pipleline` setting:

```
output.elasticsearch:
  enabled: true
  hosts: ["localhost:9200"]
  pipeline: "ngnix_log_pipeline"
```

The default index the data gets written to is of the format `metricbeat-%{[beat.version]}-%{+yyyy.MM.dd}`. This will create a new index every day. For example if today is December 2, 2017 then all the events are placed in the `metricbeat-6.0.0-2017-12-02` index. One can override the index name or the pattern using the `index` setting. In the following configuration snippet, a new index is created for every month:

```
output.elasticsearch:
  hosts: ["http://localhost:9200"]
  index: "metricbeat-%{[beat.version]}-%{+yyyy.MM}"
```

Using the `indices` setting, one can conditionally place the events in the appropriate index that matches the specified condition. In the following code snippet, if the message contains the DEBUG string, it will be placed in the `debug-%{+yyyy.MM.dd}` index. If the message contains the ERR string, it will be placed in the `error-%{+yyyy.MM.dd}` index. If the message contains neither of these texts, then those events will be pushed to the `logs-%{+yyyy.MM.dd}` index as specified in the `index` parameter:

```
output.elasticsearch:
  hosts: ["http://localhost:9200"]
  index: "logs-%{+yyyy.MM.dd}"
  indices:
    - index: "debug-%{+yyyy.MM.dd}"
```

```
    when.contains:
      message: "DEBUG"
  - index: "error-%{+yyyy.MM.dd}"
    when.contains:
      message: "ERR"
```

When the `index` parameter is overridden, disable templates and dashboards by adding the following setting in:

```
setup.dashboards.enabled: false
setup.template.enabled: false
```

Alternatively, provide the value for `setup.template.name` and `setup.template.pattern` in the `metricbeat.yml` configuration file, or else Metricbeat will fail to run.

- `logstash`: It is used to send the events to Logstash.

To use Logstash as the output, Logstash needs to be configured with the Beats input plugin to receive incoming Beats events.

A sample Logstash output configuration is as follows:

```
output.logstash:
  enabled: true
  hosts: ["localhost:5044"]
```

Using the `enabled` setting, one can enable or disable the output. `hosts` accepts one or more Logstash servers. Multiple hosts can be defined for failover purposes. If the configured host is unresponsive, then the event will be sent to one of the other configured hosts. When multiple hosts are configured, the events are distributed in random order. To enable load balancing of events across the Logstash hosts, use the `loadbalance` flag, set to `true`:

```
output.logstash:
  hosts: ["localhost:5045", "localhost:5046"]
  loadbalance: true
```

- `console`: It is used to send the events to `stdout`. The events are written in JSON format. It is useful during debugging or testing.

  A sample console configuration is as follows:

  ```
  output.console:
    enabled: true
    pretty: true
  ```

Logging

This section contains the options for configuring the Filebeat logging output. The logging system can write logs to syslog or rotate log files. If logging is not explicitly configured, file output is used on Windows systems, and syslog output is used on Linux and OS X.

A sample configuration is as follows:

```
logging.level: debug
logging.to_files: true
logging.files:
 path: C:\logs\metricbeat
 name: metricbeat.log
 keepfiles: 10
```

Some of the configuration options are:

- `level`: To specify the logging level.
- `to_files`: To write all logging output to files. The files are subject to file rotation. This is the default value.
- `to_syslog`: To write the logging output to syslogs if this setting is set to true.
- `files.path`, `files.name`, and `files.keepfiles`: These are used to specify the location of the file, the name of the file, and the number of most recently rotated log files to keep on the disk.

Capturing system metrics

In order to monitor and capture metrics related to servers, Metricbeat provides the `system` module. The `system` module provides the following metricsets to capture server metrics:

- `core`: This metricset provides usage statistics for each CPU core.
- `cpu`: This metricset provides CPU statistics.
- `diskio`: This metricset provides disk IO metrics collected from the operating system. One event is created for each disk mounted on the system.
- `filesystem`: This metricset provides file system statistics. For each file system, one event is created.
- `process`: This metricset provides process statistics. One event is created for each process.
- `process_summary`: This metricset collects high-level statistics about the running processes.
- `fsstat`: This metricset provides overall file system statistics.
- `load`: This metricset provides load statistics.
- `memory`: This metricset provides memory statistics.
- `network`: This metricset provides network IO metrics collected from the operating system. One event is created for each network interface.
- `socket`: This metricset reports an event for each new TCP socket that it sees. This metricset is available on Linux only and requires kernel 2.6.14 or newer.

Some of the metricsets provide configuration options to fine tune the returned metrics. For example, the `cpu` metricset provides `cpu.metrics` configuration to control the CPU metrics reported. However, metricsets such as `memory` and `diskio` don't provide any configuration options. Unlike other modules, which can be monitored from other servers by configuring the hosts appropriately (not a highly recommended approach), `system` modules are local to the server and can collect the metrics of underlying hosts only.

 The complete list of fields per metricset exported by the `system` module can be found at `https://www.elastic.co/guide/en/beats/metricbeat/current/exported-fields-system.html`.

Running Metricbeat with the system module

Let's make use of Metricbeat and capture the system metrics.

Make sure Kibana 6.0 and Elasticsearch 6.0 are running:

1. Replace the content of `metricbeat.yml` with the following configuration and save the file:

```
############## Metricbeat Configuration Example ##############
#=============== Modules configuration ========================

metricbeat.config.modules:
  # Glob pattern for configuration loading
  path: ${path.config}/modules.d/*.yml

  # Set to true to enable config reloading
  reload.enabled: false

  # Period on which files under path should be checked for changes
  #reload.period: 10s

#=========== Elasticsearch template setting =================

setup.template.settings:
  index.number_of_shards: 1
  index.codec: best_compression
  #_source.enabled: false

#==================== General
Settings===============================
name: metricbeat_inst1

tags: ["system-metrics", "localhost"]

fields:
  env: test-env

#============================== Dashboards
===========================
setup.dashboards.enabled: true

#============================== Kibana Settings
===========================
setup.kibana:
  host: "localhost:5601"
  #username: "elastic"
```

```
#password: "changeme"

#------------------------- Elasticsearch output Settings ---------
-----------
output.elasticsearch:
  # Array of hosts to connect to.
  hosts: ["localhost:9200"]
  #username: "elastic"
  #password: "changeme"
```

 The `setup.dashboards.enabled: true` setting loads sample dashboards to the Kibana index during startup, and the dashboards are loaded via the Kibana API. If Elasticsearch and Kibana are secured, make sure to un-comment `username` and `password` parameters and set the appropriate values.

2. By default, the `system` module is enabled. Make sure it is enabled by executing the following command:

Windows:
```
D:\packt\metricbeat-6.0.0-windows-x86_64>metricbeat.exe modules
enable system
Module system is already enabled
```

Linux:
```
[locationOfMetricBeat]$./metricbeat modules enable system
Module system is already enabled
```

3. You can verify the metricsets that are enabled for the `system` module by opening the `system.yml` file, found under the `modules.d` directory:

```
#system.yml
- module: system
  period: 10s
  metricsets:
    - cpu
    #- load
    - memory
    - network
    - process
    - process_summary
    #- core
    #- diskio
    #- socket
  processes: ['.*']
  process.include_top_n:
    by_cpu: 5 # include top 5 processes by CPU
```

```
            by_memory: 5 # include top 5 processes by memory

  - module: system
    period: 1m
    metricsets:
      - filesystem
      - fsstat
    processors:
    - drop_event.when.regexp:
        system.filesystem.mount_point:
  '^/(sys|cgroup|proc|dev|etc|host|lib)($|/)'
```

As seen in the preceding code, the configuration module is defined twice with different periods to use for a set of metricsets.
The `cpu`, `memory`, `network`, `process`, `process_summary`, `filesystem`, and `fsstats` metricsets are enabled.

4. Start the Metricbeat by executing the following command:

   Windows:
   ```
   D:\packt\metricbeat-6.0.0-windows-x86_64>metricbeat.exe -e
   ```

   Linux:
   ```
   [locationOfMetricBeat]$./metricbeat -e
   ```

Once Metricbeat is started, it loads sample Kibana dashboards and starts shipping metrics to Elasticsearch. To validate, execute the following command:

```
curl -X GET 'http://localhost:9200/_cat/indices?v=&format=json'
```

Sample Response:
```
[
    {
        "health": "yellow",
        "status": "open",
        "index": "metricbeat-6.0.0-2017.11.26",
        "uuid": "w2WoP2IhQ9eG7vSU_HmgnA",
        "pri": "1",
        "rep": "1",
        "docs.count": "29",
        "docs.deleted": "0",
        "store.size": "45.3kb",
        "pri.store.size": "45.3kb"
    },
    {
        "health": "yellow",
        "status": "open",
```

```
        "index": ".kibana",
        "uuid": "sSzeYu-YTtWR8vr2nzKrbg",
        "pri": "1",
        "rep": "1",
        "docs.count": "108",
        "docs.deleted": "59",
        "store.size": "289.3kb",
        "pri.store.size": "289.3kb"
    }
]

curl -X GET 'http://localhost:9200/_cat/indices?v'

health status index uuid pri rep docs.count docs.deleted store.size
pri.store.size
yellow open metricbeat-6.0.0-2017.11.26 w2WoP2IhQ9eG7vSU_HmgnA 1 1
29 0 45.3kb 45.3kb
yellow open .kibana sSzeYu-YTtWR8vr2nzKrbg 1 1 108 59 289.3kb
289.3kb
```

Specifying aliases

Elasticsearch allows the user to create an alias—a virtual index name that can be used to refer to an index or multiple indices. The Elasticsearch index aliases API allows for aliasing an index with a name, with all APIs automatically converting the alias name to the actual index name.

Say, for example, we want to query against a set of similar indexes. Rather than specifying each of the index names in the query, we can make use of aliases and execute the query against the alias. The alias will internally point to all the indexes and perform a query against them. This will be highly beneficial if we added certain indexes dynamically on a regular basis, so that one application/user performing the query need not worry about including those indexes in the query as long as the index is updated with the alias (which can be done manually by an admin or specified during index creation).

Let's say the IT admin creates an alias pointing to all the indexes containing the metrics for a specific month. For example, as shown in the following code snippet, an alias called `november_17_metrics` is created for all indexes of the `metricbeat-6.0.0-2017.11.*` pattern, that is, the metricbeat indexes that are created on a daily basis in the month of November:

```
curl -X POST    http://localhost:9200/_aliases   -H 'content-type:
application/json' -d '
{
  "actions":
  [
    {"add":{ "index" : "metricbeat-6.0.0-2017.11.*", "alias":
"november_17_metrics"} }
    ]
 }'
```

Now, using the `november_17_metrics` alias name, the query can be executed against all the indexes of the `metricbeat-6.0.0-2017.11.*` pattern:

```
curl -X GET http://localhost:9200/november_17_metrics/_search
```

In the following example, the `"sales"` alias is created against the `"it_sales"` and `"retail_sales"` indexes. In future, if a new sales index gets created, then that index can also point to the `"sales"` index so that the end user/application can always make use of the `"sales"` endpoint for querying all sales data:

```
curl -X POST    http://localhost:9200/_aliases -d '{
"actions" : [
    { "add" : { "index" : "it_sales", "alias" : "sales" } },
    { "add" : { "index" : "retail_sales", "alias" : "sales" } }
] }
```

To remove an alias from an index, use the `"remove"` action of the aliases API:

```
curl -X POST    http://localhost:9200/_aliases -d '
{ "actions" : [ { "remove" : { "index" : "retail_sales", "alias" : "sales"
} }] }
```

Visualizing system metrics using Kibana

To visualize the system metrics using Kibana, execute the following steps:

1. Navigate to `http://localhost:5601` and open up Kibana.
2. Click on the **Dashboard** link found in the left navigation menu and select either **[Metricbeat System] Overview** or **[Metricbeat System] Host Overview** from the dashboard:

[Metricbeat System] Overview Dashboard: This dashboard provides an overview of all the systems that are being monitored. As we are monitoring only a single host, we will see that the number of hosts is 1:

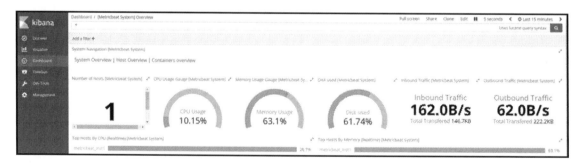

[Metricbeat Host] Overview Dashboard: This dashboard is useful for finding the detailed metrics of individual systems/hosts. In order to filter the metrics based on a particular host, enter the search/filter criteria in the search/query bar. In the following screenshot, the search criteria is `beat.name:metricbeat_inst1`. Any attribute that uniquely identifies a system/host can be used, for example, one can filter based on `beat.hostname`:

As the `diskio` and `load` metricsets were disabled in the system module configuration, we will see empty visualizations for diskio and system load visualizations:

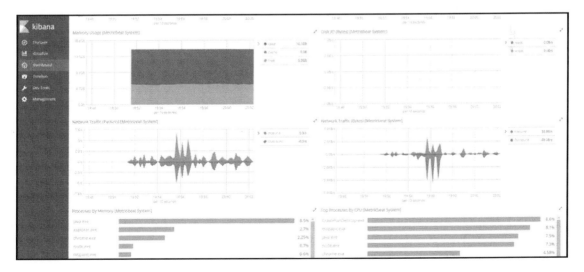

To see the dashboard refresh in real time, in the top right corner, select the time and choose the appropriate **Refresh Interval**:

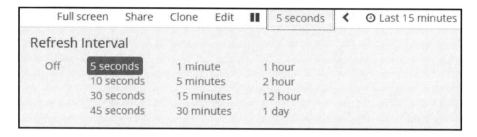

 To view the dashboard in full screen mode, click the **Full screen** button on the top navigation bar. This hides the browser and the top navigation bar. To exit full screen mode, hover over and click the Kibana button on the lower left side of the page, or simply press the *ESC* key.

 Refer to `Chapter 7`, *Visualizing Data with Kibana* to learn how to effectively use Kibana and the different sections of Kibana for gaining insight into your data.

Deploymezs architecture

The following diagram depicts commonly used Elastic Stack deployment architecture:

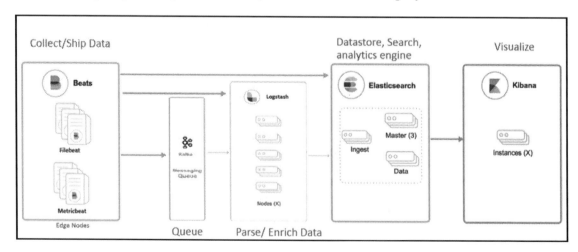

The diagram depicts three possible architectures:

- **Ship the operation metrics directly to Elasticsearch**: As seen in the preceding diagram, one will install various types of **Beats** such as **Metricbeat, Filebeat, Packetbeat**, and so on, on the edge servers from which they would like to ship the operation metrics/logs. If no further processing of events is required, then the generated events can be shipped directly to the Elasticsearch cluster. Once the data is present in Elasticsearch, it can then be visualized/analyzed using Kibana. In this architecture, the flow of events would be **Beats → Elasticsearch → Kibana**.

- **Ship the operation metrics to Logstash**: The operation metrics/logs captured by the Beats and installed on edge servers is sent to Logstash for further processing such as, for instance, parsing the logs or enriching log events. Then the parsed/enriched events are pushed to Elasticsearch. To increase the processing capacity, one can scale up Logstash instances, such as, for example, configuring a set of Beats to send data to Logstash instance 1 and configuring another set of Beats to send data to Logstash instance 2, and so on. In this architecture, the flow of events would be **Beats → Logstash → Elasticsearch → Kibana**.

- **Ship the operation metrics to a resilient queue**: If the generated events are at a very high rate and if Logstash is unable to cope up with the load or to prevent loss of data/events when Logstash is down, one can go for resilient queues such as Apache Kafka, so that the events are queued. Then Logstash can process it at its own speed, thus avoiding the loss of operation metrics/logs captured by Beats. In this architecture, the flow of events would be **Beats → Kafka → Logstash → Elasticsearch → Kibana**.

In Logstash 5.x, one can make use of the persistent queue settings of Logstash and make use of it as queue, too. However, it doesn't offer a high degree of resilience like Kafka.

In the previously mentioned architectures, one can easily scale up/scale down instances of Elasticsearch, Logstash, and Kibana based on the use case.

Summary

In this chapter, we have covered in detail another Beat library called **Metricbeat**. We covered how to install and configure Metricbeat so that it can send operational metrics to Elasticsearch. We also covered the various deployment architectures for building real-time monitoring solutions using Elastic Stack, in order to monitor servers and applications. This helps IT administrators and application support folks gain insight into the behavior of the applications and servers and allows them to respond in a timely manner in case of infrastructure outage.

Index

Printed in Great Britain
by Amazon